Neopolitics
American Political Ideas in the 1980s

Neopolitics

American Political Ideas in the 1980s

Linda J. Medcalf
Olympia Technical Community College

Kenneth M. Dolbeare
The Evergreen State College

Temple University Press
Philadelphia

First Edition
987654321
Temple University Press,
Philadelphia 19122

Library of Congress Cataloging in Publication Data

Medcalf, Linda.
   Neopolitics: American political ideas in the 1980s.

   Bibliography: p.
   Includes index.
   1. Political science — United States — History —
20th century.   I. Dolbeare, Kenneth M.   II. Title.
JA84.U5M44   1985   320.5'0973   84–16041
ISBN 0–87722–388–2

Manufactured in the United States of America

For Joy and Jake

Preface

This is a book about what is happening to American political ideas, why, and what it all means for American politics. The United States is in the midst of a major transformation — economic, social, and political. Established values and beliefs are fragmenting, reconstituting, and merging with new principles and programs to generate a new political spectrum. If this era is precedented in our history, it is only by the chaotic period from about 1877 to 1920, when the country went through industrialization, social upheavals, centralization and bureaucratization, and simultaneously emerged as a leading world power. Even a massive transformation probably happens faster now, and we have been in this era since at least the mid-1960s. We think it is time to take stock of the changes in American political thinking and their implications.

We have tried to tell this dramatic story as faithfully as possible. For example, we have avoided both complicated analytic schemes and outdated labels. It is past time to accept "American exceptionalism" and make it a premise instead of an apology. This has required us to make some adaptations that should be noted. Because we use American-derived labels, historically developed as in the Introduction, we have felt it necessary to provide a glossary, also historically derived, where definitions of the classic labels may be found, expressed in the language of political theory. We try to avoid intruding upon the reader's analysis any more than is absolutely necessary for clarity. We have sought to avoid excessive historical detail but to connect history with our analysis where it is vital to understanding basic substantive issues. We explain our criteria for selection of political belief systems only in the Epilogue, which essentially seeks to place the burden of making decisions on the reader. We present each emerging set of new ideas in its own terms and through its own spokespersons, with a minimum of commentary or judgment. And we have drawn on our experience with adult learners and community college students to write at a level faithful to the average citizens who developed these new ideas in the first place.

We are very grateful for the helpful reviews of earlier versions of this manuscript by Douglas Amy of Mount Holyoke College, James Farr of the University of Wisconsin, Madison, Steven Thomas Seitz of the University of Illinois, James A. Thompson of Grand Valley State College, and Robert H. Trudeau of Providence College. Once again, our friend and colleague

Jeanne Hahn has provided us with the most penetrating and useful commentary we could have wished. Finally, we want to thank the two people to whom the book is dedicated, without whose help we would quite literally not have been able to complete the book at all — or at least not for another year or two.

Contents

Neopolitics
American Political Ideas in the 1980s

Introduction: Change in American Political Beliefs

Political values and beliefs emphasizing their break with the past have emerged in the United States of the 1980s. Carrying prefixes like "new" and "neo," they confidently promise to shape new directions in politics. But no country can shake off well-established values and beliefs and start entirely afresh. And the United States is certainly no exception in this respect. The political premises, goals, and programs now taking shape may be the equivalent of a whole new generation of ideas, but they build on a base of the old.

Most present-day observers of the American scene emphasize how new and different our currently developing beliefs must be. Some argue that such beliefs need to offer a sharp contrast with the past. The distinguished political scientist Robert Dahl, for example, offers this sweeping characterization:

> the most powerful ideologies of our age all suffer from having acquired their shape and substance in the 18th and 19th centuries, or very much earlier, before the world in which we live had come fully into view. They are like medieval maps of the world, charming but dangerous for navigating unfamiliar seas. . . . Liberalism, conservatism, capitalism, socialism, Marxism, corporatism, anarchism, even democratic ideas, all face a world that in its form and thrust confounds the crucial assumptions, requirements, descriptions, predictions, hopes, or prescriptions they express.[1]

This sense of being at sea in an uncharted and fundamentally new context is widely shared among today's activist thinkers as well. Senator Gary Hart, for example, uses the same metaphor:

> We have entered a new economic world, but we act as though we never left the old. We use outdated maps and points of reference, which steer us the wrong way or not at all. And so we miss the reality of our revolutionary times.[2]

Attempts to understand what is happening to American political values and beliefs, however, immediately run into two problems. One stems from the fact that these authors, and the others who employ such images, are quite correct. We are indeed in a period of profound social, cultural,

3

economic, and political change. Deep-running currents in American culture and society, reacting turbulently to the changing world of the post-Vietnam, postindustrial era, are opening up new channels of political possibility while closing others. But the old is far from erased; in human affairs there are no blank slates on which to write wholly anew. Some of the old beliefs yield, others endure, and a distinctive new-old mix emerges to change the course of American political thought. And it all happens very fast, before we have categories and terms with agreed-upon meanings to use in describing what is going on.

Our task is surely made difficult by the scope and rapidity of change. We seek understanding while still in the midst of a transformation whose eventual outcome cannot be known. Naturally, some will even deny that the United States is going through such a transformation. There is increasing agreement, however, that we have entered upon a fundamental economic transformation toward an economy that is distinctly high-technology and services oriented, as well as much more intimately integrated with the rest of the world. In the context of changes of this magnitude, old labels for political ideas simply lose their meaning. We are left without clear ways to characterize the changes that are occurring or to compare them with the past in terms that all will recognize.

The other problem flows from the fact that there are actually two "languages" regularly used to describe and analyze political values and beliefs in the United States. Each has a distinctive purpose. But both employ the same labels. The first is everyday American usage, in which categories like "liberal" and "conservative" have certain established meanings and the primary focus is on how beliefs mobilize people and/or affect public policies. It is the language of ordinary political life, the operational basis for action by people and governments.

The second language is that of scholarly or other informed analysis, in which the primary goal is not action but theoretical understanding. Here, then, the focus is on how sets of values and beliefs compare with each other and with values and beliefs from the past, what premises they rest on, and how such ways of thinking fit in terms of some classic categories (once again, "liberal" or "conservative") derived from European experience. The difficulties created by the simultaneous existence of two different languages using the same labels but with different purposes are exacerbated by the rapidity with which changes are occurring.

In this book, we shall follow everyday American usage. We shall present American values and beliefs in their own terms, using the labels that Americans have actually used for them. A brief historical account of the rise and meanings of various labels as used in the United States follows. For the more classical definitions of political belief systems or ideologies, cast in the language of political theory but again historically derived, the reader should turn to the Glossary.

From the earliest years of the movement for independence, Americans asserted their uniqueness and rejected Old World practices. The language of the Declaration of Independence reflects their sense of the need to explain

American actions to puzzled Europeans. Following the ratification of the Constitution, the simultaneous feelings of uniqueness, rejection of Europe, and need to explain fused into something like a sense of a special mission among nations. America was to serve as a republican model. She would teach the rest of the world a lesson in the nature, simple virtues, and practical workings of (American) republican political institutions.

The label *republicanism* sufficed for the first fifty years after independence. "Republicanism" rested on the self-evident principles of individualism, freedom, and equality (to be more fully discussed in Chapter 1). It meant representative government with constitutional limitations on majorities on behalf of minority rights—to property, that is, and to protection of other personal liberties. It was gradually replaced by a new label, *democracy*, which came to mean essentially the same thing. This was a generally procedural version of democracy, of course, which fit comfortably enough with the developing privately owned, profit-oriented industrial economy. By the time of the Civil War, this economic system was celebrated as *capitalism*. That term included private ownership, profit orientation, the free economic market where sellers' supply would be equated with buyers' demand in a self-regulating manner, and the governing principle of laissez faire ("hands off" by government except for the maintenance of order and the enforcement of contracts).

Despite a large number of slogans, epithets, and colorful third-party names, "democracy," "capitalism," and "republicanism" were the only categories in wide usage that expressed general *sets* of ideas, or belief *systems*. They encompassed the economic and political order in the United States, except as equality and substantive democracy arose in the abolitionist and feminist movements, until late in the nineteenth century. For the most part, definitions of such key terms lay simply in the practice of American institutions at the state and national levels. Labels needed no elaborate definition when their referents were in plain view for all to see.

This situation began to change almost immediately after the Civil War ended, but surely by the threshold year of 1877. The Civil War marked a turning point in the American experience. First, a long-festering anomaly in the American self-image was removed. The commitment to equality no longer coexisted uncomfortably with its total refutation in the legality and practice of slavery. The Declaration of Independence was validated anew. Second, the war confirmed the country's evolution as a single continental power, united federally, rather than as a league of states. Finally, the war gave great impetus to the already burgeoning process of industrialization.

Two momentous events in 1877 mark the beginning of a new era, the one period in our history comparable in scope and character of change to our own. One of these events was the disputed Hayes–Tilden presidential election. The dispute was resolved only days before the scheduled inauguration in a political party bargain that also effectively ended the Reconstruction. The other event is the great railroad strike that occurred a few months later. The most far-reaching and destructive strike in American history, it loudly proclaimed the arrival of a new set of issues on the agenda of an industrializing society. Before the era ended, the national government would be fundamentally reconstructed, a new kind of politics put in place, and changed values and beliefs would dominate.

In a brief forty years, the United States moved from a predominantly rural, agricultural society to an urban, industrial one; from a laissez-faire system to an active, purposeful national government; and from an insular nation to an imperial world power with far-flung colonies and other interests. Simultaneously, separate farmers' and workers' movements engaged in the most protracted and bitter period of protests, strikes, and general social unrest that the United States has known. Unable to join together electorally, these movements were repulsed in the election of 1896.

But a new and more middle-class movement, drawing support from some of their remnants, arose to press for substantial changes in government policies. New coalitions of "progressive" businessmen, bankers, lawyers, and the larger corporations sought similar ends. They used the threat posed by more aggressive reformers to gain approval for apparently moderate but potentially dramatic changes in the role of government. Thus, from this turbulence emerged a national government with wholly new powers and administrative capabilities. As we will see in the Hamilton–Jefferson theme of Chapter 2, the product was characterized as a Hamiltonian government for Jeffersonian ends. It was a government capable of rationalizing and controlling the competitive excesses of the new national economy, of rendering it more stable, predictable, and efficient. Finally, U.S. entry into World War I provided an opportunity to put these new mobilizing capabilities into practice.

The year 1920 marks the end of the era. World War I was over; womens' right to vote was finally established; and a president was elected with the slogan "back to normalcy." The contrast between the United States in 1877 and 1920 was so stark that none could ignore it. But 1920 seemed to begin a time when the pace and purposefulness of change slackened. The full implications of the changes of the preceding era awaited the New Deal, World War II, and the mid-century aftermath. For despite the gap in time, it is clear that the governing principles and beliefs of the mid-twentieth century were shaped in fundamental ways by the transformations of this Populist–Progressive Era.

As indicated, the era gave rise to a number of new political beliefs and labels. First, the process of industrialization in the 1870s and 1880s was accompanied by frequent panics and depressions and sustained hardships for farmers, particularly those struggling under the crop-lien system of the South and Southwest. Both workers and farmers began to cast about for explanations and remedies. Their search led them to deeper and deeper levels of analysis, until in many cases they identified the system of private ownership and profit taking by a few as the real culprit. Soon the term *radical*, meaning "going to the roots" in analysis and search for solutions, came into widespread usage.

Also, the waves of immigrants that followed industrialization brought with them new categories and beliefs derived from the longer European experience in factories and labor movements. Many of them thought in terms of class conflict and the need for the working classes to organize against the capitalists. They too were promptly labeled "radical." Thus, that term now acquired a second meaning: "foreign." In this second sense, "radical" meant quite specifically beliefs that denied the rightness of private ownership of the major means of production and transportation, such as steel mills and railroads. It applied also to any who sought to implement such beliefs. And, indeed, many American radicals, both native born and immigrant, did advocate various forms of public ownership and/or control over the major units of the economy — particularly the railroads, banks, and steel plants.

The category of radical soon developed subcategories such as *socialist* and *anarchist*. To many Americans, these terms meant "foreign" at least as much as they did anything substantive. Gradually, however, the sustained arguments of (and disagreements between) socialists and anarchists won each some separate identity as proposed alternatives to the dominant American version of capitalist democracy.

Socialists were seen to advocate an organized political movement grounded in the working class and seeking social ownership and a planned economy. Particularly visible in the labor movement, socialists sought to establish industrial unions (organizations of all workers in a given industry, rather than of individual strategic and relatively well-paid crafts or skill groups) and to bring these unions into politics. Anarchists were never really understood. They continued to be viewed as rigid, bitter, and often violent individuals opposed to all forms of organized society. Slogans such as "property is theft" and "propaganda of the deed" (a euphemism for bombings and attempted assassinations) helped to build a quite misleading impression of anarchism.

The easy equation of radical with foreign was always belied by totally indigenous movements of workers and farmers and by native-born socialism. All such groups could quite legitimately claim American origins in the pre independence period. Moreover, what these various reform movements generated in the late nineteenth century was a major surge of substantive democracy, fully in the American tradition. In particular, the Populist Party's goals of public ownership of railroads and a new public banking system were both profoundly radical and utterly native. In part, the "foreign" image was a measure of the success of opponents in painting those who sought substantial change in non-American colors. In part it was also accurate. Many immigrants brought with them visions of alternative ways of organizing society that would not have occurred to most Americans, and such immigrants did consistently support radical goals.

In this context of multiple demands for egalitarian change, Americans who defended the status quo came to be known as *conservatives*. While used more precisely by some Americans, to most the term meant simply preservation of existing institutions and practices from the apparently growing threat

of violent radicals of various kinds. Not least of the principles that conservatives feared would be violated was that of freedom for corporations to use
their property as they wished without government controls or restraints. Social reform legislation, such as minimum wage and maximum hour laws or
health and safety regulations, was opposed with special vigor. Conservatism
was intent on preserving as much as it could of the status quo, even as that
status quo drifted toward more and more government "intervention" in the
free market economy.

Conservatives shared two important characteristics. One was a growing
concern for defending the rights of property against what seemed like danger
from all sides. Related to this was a deepening anxiety about the governing
capacity of the majority of people. With so many new immigrants, it was
felt, general popular participation in politics might become even less stable
and constructive. From such a perspective, almost anybody who advocated
changes seemed to pose a threat to property and the American way. Conservatives developed a theme that drew on many of the older versions of the
basic values to celebrate wealth and impugn poverty as evidence of lack of
character and effort. Their argument came to be called "Social Darwinism"
because of its analogies to Darwin's point about the survival of the fittest in
the natural world. Regardless of the aptness of the analogy, conservatives'
insistence on protection of property and denial of social responsibility
reached a shrill peak in the early 1890s.

The vigor of the conservative reaction to the essentially substantive democracy claims of workers, farmers, and socialists opened a wide gap
between the two camps. Many Americans began to locate themselves in the
expanding middle ground between the two. The traditional claim to equality seemed in their eyes to deserve some recognition. Circumstances *were* desperate for many of the unemployed. In the cities, the physical conditions
under which many were forced to live were visibly a scandal. It seemed
necessary to do *something* to reduce the human suffering generated by the
economy. Many began to feel that corporations should be prevented from
pushing freedom to the point where government could put no limits at all on
the use of property.

But they were unwilling to go as far as the farmers and others urged.
They strongly respected the principle of private property and believed in the
sanctity of contracts. They were united in the conviction that reasonable
people could work together to improve the condition of all people. Poverty
and disease could be eliminated through rational use of government and
through modern technologies. Great progress had already been made in material terms. Further progress in raising standards of living and the quality of
life was entirely possible through the (open) channels of (procedural) democracy.

This balanced combination of traditional American values, humane
concern for the disadvantaged, and faith in progress soon became known as
liberalism. At a minimum, liberals argued for the use of government to prevent the economy from imposing major hardships on individuals unable to

help themselves. In its larger vision, liberalism stood for the use of government to actively promote social reforms which would contribute to social progress. The Progressive Era of 1900–1920 was an early high point of this type of middle-class liberal reform. Many of the Progressive reforms were opposed by conservatives. But, enacted nevertheless, they often had the conserving effect of undercutting the substantive democratic demands and reducing the pressure for greater changes.

Liberalism is thus a centrist position. It appeals to middle-class people, particularly professionals, because it seems to apply some of their knowledge and skills to the solution of social problems. But it also attracts forward-looking ("socially responsible") business people and the larger corporations which can afford the taxes to support government social services. With a bit of patching here and there in response to the worst side effects of a growing industrial economy, progress can be assured, stability maintained, and all major claims responded to in some fashion. Generally, this liberal balancing act has been successful, at least as long as the economy did in fact grow steadily so that the have-nots could be satisfied without taking current possessions away from the haves.

But liberals require time and space to work out the necessary accommodations between multiple and conflicting claims. The mechanisms of procedural democracy, when they are operating smoothly, provide this opportunity. Danger looms, however, when the economy contracts, profits and wages drop, and the conflicting claims can no longer be readily accommodated. The extremes increasingly appear to be on the verge of taking rights or property from the other. Under such circumstances, liberalism's middle ground is increasingly squeezed. The procedural mechanisms become paralyzed as the extremes close in to engage each other directly. For these reasons, liberalism has made preserving the procedural mechanisms a special cause in itself. Over time, liberalism has become almost synonymous with maintenance of the regular procedures of the political system, including both property rights and other civil rights.

Finally, first the Russian Revolution of 1917 and then its exportation by the Soviet army after World War II provided new content for the labels *socialism, communism,* and *Marxism.* These events gave specific meanings to what had been abstract philosophies with vague utopian connotations. To Americans, these labels now stood for the political-economic systems of the Soviet Union and the Eastern European countries. They became interchangeable terms for austerity, militarism, and a one-party state denying democracy, property rights, and other liberties. In a way, Americans returned to equating the umbrella term "radical" with the foreign and un-American nature of these subcategories.

American usage of the various political labels simply does not conform systematically to the deeper and more complex (and consistent) meanings that are given them in scholarly discourse, as the Glossary makes clear. But it is the way we have come to understand each others' political values and beliefs. And it is reflected in the way that newspapers and magazines write about what is happening to our political ideas. Given an understanding of American usage of these labels, all that remains is to show how such sets of beliefs may best be understood, how they relate to each other today, and where they may take us tomorrow — which is what this book is about.

CHAPTER 1

American Political Beliefs: The Basic Values

By the phrase "political belief system" we mean the connected values, assumptions, perceptions of problems and possibilities, and political goals and programs that people actually have in their minds. Values and assumptions are the fundamental building blocks — the principles of what is good and what is given — on which every political belief system rests. Often particular values and assumptions are accompanied by distinctive concepts, or ways of looking at the political world. Together, then, values, assumptions, and concepts make up the *basic* elements of a political belief system.

As people look at conditions, events, and political activity in the world about them, they use these basic premises to organize, understand, and interpret or evaluate what is happening. The basic elements may be used consciously or unconsciously, fully or partially, accurately or inaccurately. What matters at this *applied* level is that people are seeing problems and possibilities in the day-to-day working of the economy, government, and society *in terms of their basic values*, assumptions, and concepts.

These various components of the basic and applied levels fit together. They make up a more or less coherent whole, a political belief *system* of mutually supportive ideas. We shall use these components and levels to build our framework for analysis of contemporary American political belief systems. But in this chapter we look exclusively at the basic values that have dominated American political thinking throughout our history. The most important point to be gained from the analysis here is that what may appear on the surface to be broad agreement on basic values is actually ongoing disagreement over the specific meanings of these values.

A readily identifiable set of values and assumptions has characterized American political thinking since prerevolutionary days. They have been and are widely shared, but chiefly in a general and abstract sense. Vigorous disagreements about their proper meanings and quite different priorities among them have been enduring features of American political dialogue. There is no "true" American belief system. Despite the appearance of agreement stemming from the use of a common set of terms, distinct mainstream traditions have always competed with one another. And at the margins of

11

these shared rhetorical symbols, lesser-known alternatives maintain a certain appeal, alternately growing and shrinking in popular strength.

We shall examine each of the six major building blocks of American political thinking — individualism, property, contract, freedom, equality, and democracy — in this chapter. By now, these elements are thoroughly fused, and it will be neither possible nor necessary to draw sharp boundaries between them. Each is highly valued; locked in a mutually supportive system, they powerfully appeal to all of us. We shall try to point out both the core of agreed meaning and the range of different definitions that have arisen as these basic values and assumptions have evolved over time.

INDIVIDUALISM

Probably no country in the world has as deep a cultural commitment to individualism as the United States. Our individualism is widely celebrated ("I did it my way," "The Lone Ranger," "a nation of Robinson Crusoes," etc.) and seems utterly natural to us. We all carry images of splendid isolation, of the fulfillment to be found in not having to depend on anyone for anything.

In the United States, the individual serves as the self-evident starting point for thinking about the nature and purposes of social life. We have no image of society as an independent organism with a life of its own and the right to ask certain behavior from the individuals who happen to make it up at any given time. We do not even have a historical memory of such an image; it is truly "foreign" to our thinking. Instead, we start with the notion of the necessity and propriety of each person seeking individual survival and satisfactions. All other individuals naturally do the same; the inherent nature of all human beings is to seek to serve their own self-interest first and foremost.

To prevent this self-seeking from becoming mutually destructive, however, individuals are said to have certain rights and a government is instituted to preserve such rights. Both society and government are the creations of individuals and are subordinate to the rights of those individuals. They merely maintain the context in which individuals pursue their important private goals.

The availability of all these private opportunities also carries the expectation that individuals will make good use of them. People should advance themselves in the terms that they and others value — chiefly money, land, and jobs with status and security. If they do, they will be satisfied and receive the respect and envy of their fellows. If they do not, they will be judged wanting — even failures — as individuals. Moreover, because they share the same criteria as other individuals, they will judge *themselves* as failures.

These dimensions of American individualism have profound and double-edged implications. On one hand, all individuals are expected to work hard to achieve their goals. They should not rely on anyone else. Self-reliance is a mark of character, an indication that one is truly an individual. Everybody carries personal responsibility for his or her standing on the social ladder. One's position in terms of prestige and property reflects personal effort, character, and achievement. When realized, social mobility marks the individual achiever as a worthy and successful person.

On the other hand, many individuals do not achieve their goals. They do not gain money, land, or high-status and secure jobs. They do not rise on the social ladder. In this case, the American assumption is that they have only themselves to blame. Responsibility for the individual's eventual place in the world lands squarely on his or her own shoulders. In this way, the work ethic and the belief in self-reliance and personal responsibility can combine irretrievably to burden the individual. Failure to achieve material success and social mobility readily translates into a character flaw and/or a lack of personal effort.

Such attitudes have powerful stabilizing effects in American society. Those at the top of the social pyramid often credit their personal character and effort for their success. They may claim special status for that reason, including, for example, the right to make decisions for less favored members of the society. And many people may accept their claim, granting them deference and respect and perhaps even the power to govern. Moreover, strong belief in rugged individualism may cause those at the bottom of the social pyramid to proudly reject needed assistance and/or to denigrate themselves for failure to succeed.

But not everyone reacts this way. With respect to those at the bottom, in particular, shared assumptions begin to diverge and become disagreements. For some people, the responsibility for an individual's inability to fulfill his or her wants and needs does not rest entirely with that individual. Some part of the explanation is seen as lying outside of the individual's control. It is related, instead, to aspects of the larger social and economic system, such as discrimination or lack of educational opportunity. How much of the responsibility is attributable to individual versus systemic factors thus becomes the subject of heated debate—and the basis for subscribing to different belief systems.

Moreover, our individualism is much stronger in rhetoric than in our lived reality. Only a few Americans actually live isolated, purely self-seeking, rugged individualist lives. Parents routinely sacrifice their own interests for their children. People share many scarce resources with each other, particularly in times of crisis, disaster, war, or economic hardship. People give generously of money, time, and energy to community causes and organizations, often at genuine cost to their selfish interests. Our individualism fills our abstract social and political judgments while it contradicts our day-to-day world. Some people recognize this and explicitly call for more in the way of sharing and collective action; others hold firmly to the purer form of individualism. And thus individualism is both a shared value and a continuing subject of disagreement.

PROPERTY

While the concept of property has always been highly valued in the United States, its meaning has changed considerably over time. In seventeenth-century England, the source of many of the basic elements in our thinking, "property" meant primarily land but also included people's capacity to improve or cultivate that land. Soon added was money derived from the sale of crops and livestock, then goods made for sale or trade. It was not long before "property" also included various certificates of investment or indebtedness convertible to money at some future time. Whatever its form, property was taken to be a vital goal of any individual. The rights to hold property, be secure in its possession, and be free to use it as one wished came to be considered as natural rights of individuals, fully equivalent to the paramount rights of life and liberty.

From the colonial period well into the nineteenth century, free or very inexpensive land lured settlers to the American continent and to its expanding west. Land meant the prospect of growing food and of being able to support one's family. In some cases, the production of enough surplus to generate investment capital meant a rise above one's origins. The concept of ownership carried with it the possibility of economic independence and permitted participation as a citizen in the affairs of government.

Thomas Jefferson linked ownership and citizenship on the level of political principle. He argued that land ownership was the only way of assuring the independence necessary for people to act as free and thoughtful citizens in public affairs. If possessed of such a "stake in the society," citizens would inform themselves and exercise their best judgment in the public interest. A landless population working in urban factories would be subject to too many economic pressures and, in Jefferson's eyes, would lose first their independence and then their capacity for self-government.

Alexander Hamilton, on the other hand, accepted the ownership-citizenship link, but he explicitly supported another form of property ownership. Stocks, bonds, and creative uses of indebtedness, Hamilton believed, would spur trade and eventual industrialization. Such a commercial base was necessary if the United States was to gain power and independent stature among the nations of the world. Hamilton thus argued for creation of a "stake in society" for bondholders, financiers, and other commerical and manufacturing property holders.

From the Washington administration well into the nineteenth century, this conflict between *forms* of property and their associated models of economic development continued. Jefferson and his followers supported rural agricultural development, while Hamilton's camp looked to a powerful modern political economy with manufacturing, commerce, and finance at its base. Similar conflicts reverberate within our property concept today as we try to come to terms with such innovations as instantaneous computer transmission of billions of dollars and multinational corporations and banks, with their far-flung operations. And we continue to seek ways to give propertylike rights to public goods, like clean air and water, in order to protect those aspects of our environment from the rights of certain owners to do as they wish with their pollution-producing property.

The essential idea of property ownership remains very strong, however.

It may be most visible in the symbolic aura that surrounds owning one's own home, and in real terms, home ownership is encouraged by government subsidies and tax concessions. The strength of the belief in property ownership certainly helps explain the fact that most feel threatened by those who advocate social ownership of the means of production. People who are believed to be in favor of "destroying private property" are truly "far out" to most Americans. But property ownership is more to Americans than just a widely sought material achievement. The ownership-citizenship link supports democratic participation in certain enduring ways. And ownership and the taxpaying obligation that accompanies it may in turn benefit from the high value placed by Americans on democracy.

CONTRACTS AND LAW

In American thinking, bolstered by actual colonial practice which culminated in the making of the Constitution, both collective social obligations and governments are created by contracts among people. Not only public life rests on the principle of contract, however; business transactions of every kind are carried on through contracts. This, too, traces back to colonial practice. Reliance on future performance of all such contracts was so utterly necessary for commerce and investment that there soon developed the legal principle of "the sanctity of contracts." The notion of many binding contracts is fundamental to development of the modern commercial and participatory society made up of many individuals, corporations, governments, and so forth.

More specifically, colonial experience had fixed two important principles in American minds. One was the idea that government powers were controlled by some form of contract that could be found somewhere. The second was that the origins of this set of controlling limitations lay somewhere outside of and above the ordinary reach of people in power, whether kings, legislatures, or popular majorities. These limitations were truly superior to the everyday acts of public authorities; they were rooted in the natural rights of individuals, that is, in the law of nature itself.

But this link to natural law is far from the only way in which the notion of contract is interwoven with the value attached to law generally and to the neutral, procedural "rightness" of legal mechanisms in particular. To begin with, the American Constitution of 1787 is in effect a contract. It sets forth the powers of government as well as limitations on that government. These provisions have the force of law but flow from a level superior to that of ordinary lawmakers. The idea of a "higher law" was hardly a new one, but in the Constitution it was for the first time combined with the notion of contract to produce an explicit set of governing powers and limitations.

The new republic thus emerged with a written contract–constitution embodying higher (natural) law. It soon became a symbol of things good, unique, and even God-given about the United States. There developed something akin to a "civil religion," or religiouslike faith and sense of mission about our Constitution and the institutions it had created. Faith in the American future, in contracts and constitutions, in natural law and higher law, and in ourselves as individual citizens all came to be tightly fused together. In this context, it was but a short step for everyday positive law (the statutory enactments of legislatures and the steadily accumulating mass of judges' decisions) to claim some of the same elevated status. What law seemed to offer was a neutral set of rules, appropriately concerned with the protection of property, by which individual striving for private goals could be refereed.

Contracts are, of course, written documents. As such, at least arguably, they require interpretation by people with the appropriate skills and experience, namely lawyers. When contracts make up the basis for a society's daily transactions, the people who assert the capacity and right to be the interpreters become very important. Legal skills lead to vital roles as facilitators and adjudicators. And when, moreover, a society employs a written contract as the embodiment of a higher law to limit public power usage, law and lawyers will pervade all its affairs—public and private.

As lawyers come to predominate, so does their defining institution, the court. In the American case, this means the United States Supreme Court. By now, the Court is the operative symbol of the Constitution. It provides most people's understanding of proper governmental conduct according to the Constitution. Public issues involving profound value choices are systematically shaped and reshaped into legal questions. Thus, they can be taken to court and, if significant enough, eventually controlled by the value preferences of a majority of the nine justices. What results over time is a very special role for law, lawyers, and courts in the government of the society.

This very assertiveness on the part of law and the legal profession leads to the major disagreements surrounding the generally shared values of contracts and law. Though derived from the general commitment to contracts, the emphasis on law and legal means of decision making can impinge on the capacity of citizens to make choices and implement their preferences in a democratic manner. Just how much public decision-making authority should be given over to the law and lawyers has therefore been a source of dispute throughout American history.

Similarly, there have been constant disagreements over the extent to which the law and its workings are in fact neutral. Value choices of profound importance lie in such assertedly neutral or mechanistic acts as the interpretation of words and phrases in the Constitution; far from always being readily accepted, the Supreme Court's decisions have often proved highly controversial. It is easier to insist on the fair and neutral procedures of the law when they are working in one's favor than when they appear to be manipulated by others for their private advantage. American legalism, strong as it is, thus barely conceals vigorous disagreements about the nature and proper role of law and lawyers.

Before leaving these three key values, it might be useful to note how thoroughly individualism, property, and contracts and law support the concept of the free economic market. All individuals are and should be free to make their own arrangements for their private advantage. Property is the focus of individual striving. Contracts both limit government interference with private activity (the "laissez-faire" or "hands-off" principle) and facilitate any number of private transactions. The free market is thus not just an image of how an economy might work for the greatest good, but one that takes on the quality of something "good" in its own right from the way that it fits with these basic values.

FREEDOM AND EQUALITY

We shall take up the values of freedom and equality together, because they are so fully complementary that it becomes difficult to discuss one without discussing the other. Historically, the two values have often stood together, twin pillars in the foundation of American social order. And on examination, the pairing turns out to be much more than mere habit. The definition or implementation of one often, though not necessarily, affects the definition or implementation of the other.

Sometimes freedom and equality appear to be in direct conflict, so that one or the other must be given priority. In other words, the more of one, the less of the other. Having to choose one over the other troubles all and can lead to bitter divisions between people. Many would prefer not to choose. But, given the often unavoidable tension between the usual definitions, that luxury merely transfers the choice to others.

Why is there sometimes a conflict between freedom and equality? The definition of freedom has seemed relatively straightforward. Perhaps that is part of the reason it has usually been granted priority in cases of conflict. Generally, freedom means the absence of restraints on an individual. More specifically, it means freedom from government interference with one's personal liberty or economic activities. Freedom finds its strongest expression in the Bill of Rights of the United States and in state constitutions, both of which amount to long lists of prohibitions against arbitrary acts. Under all circumstances, governments must follow a host of procedural requirements before individual life, liberty, or property can be affected.

Recently, another version of the notion of freedom has arisen. If the dominant definition described above is understood as "negative" freedom, in the sense that freedom means the absence of restraints by government, the newer version can be termed "positive" freedom. This is meant to indicate that it involves affirmative actions on the part of goverment to increase the opportunities for individuals to realize their human potential. "Freedom" has thus begun to mean the chance to accomplish some things that would not be possible without government help, if only in the form of keeping others from preventing such accomplishments. But this is a twentieth century development and one that is still clearly subordinate to the dominant understanding just set forth.

By contrast, the definition of equality has been complicated from the start and grows more so every year. Hardly anybody argues that people are or could be made equal in physical strength, intelligence, personality, or talents. Our notion of equality ("all men are created equal . . . ") concerns entitlements with respect to *social* life. There is, however, little consensus as to what these entitlements should be, and some care is needed even to identify the issues involved.

Two major dimensions or areas of life need to be taken into account when defining equality. One is the social and economic sphere. This involves the social status and economic well-being of people and the general social and economic conditions of their lives. The other is the political and legal arena. People enjoy "equal" rights before the law and as citizens, particularly with respect to participation in public decision-making processes.

Attention usually focuses on the second of these areas. Political and legal rights are more formal, visible, and essential as prerequisites to practically everything else. They have their roots in the basic contracts that create governments. Yet even here conflict and problems abound. Those entitled to certain rights of citizenship in principle, such as the right to vote or appear in court, may have to struggle to convert such formal provisions into practical reality. Those outside the range of citizenship struggle for admission to full political and legal status.

In the early years of the republic, full citizenship extended only to white males who owned property of a certain minimum value. Even some who met those criteria were obliged to document their entitlement and assert their right vigorously amidst a variety of physical and social obstacles. White males without property (particularly former indentured servants), black males, and women all engaged in more or less lengthy struggles simply to obtain the franchise. Other entitlements of full citizenship necessary to achieve equality solely in the political and legal sense were slowly and painfully won.

All this attention to the formal side of equality tends to overshadow the social and economic dimensions of the principle. In the early years of the republic conditions of rough social and economic equality actually obtained among the great bulk of the population. Most people either were or could become economically self-sufficient through small-farm ownership. A lively spirit of social egalitarianism had been furthered by the shared experience of the movement for independence. Social and economic equality seemed to be a fact. It was the exercise of equal legal and participatory rights that required further development.

This situation was specific to those times, however, and actually underscores a crucial point. *Without* social and economic equality, political and legal equality may not mean as much as first appearances suggest. When conditions of social and economic life are highly unequal, for example, some people possess so much wealth that they can influence actions in the political-legal world, ensuring that these actions are favorable to them. If for some reason they are unsuccessful in getting what they want through politics, they can use their wealth to achieve their goals in other ways — even in opposition to public decisions.

But the moment that numbers of people try to use their equal participation rights to prevent that, or to gain greater social and economic equality through the use of government, the conflict between freedom and equality erupts. Those who have the most in the unequal social and economic world validly claim that their freedom is being limited. In fact, their use of their property *is* being limited. The prices they can charge may be limited, some of their profits may be taken away in taxes, and so forth. Social and economic regulations appear necessary to assist less advantaged people who need greater opportunities. Freedom seems to lead to social and economic inequality, particularly in an industrial society. But efforts to reduce that inequality through exercise of equal political-legal rights seem inevitably to reduce freedom. The situation of having to choose between the two important values therefore seems unavoidable. And seen in this way, the choice can be agonizing.

Related to this issue of choice are three different versions of "equality" that have developed, each embodying a distinctive mix of the social-economic and political-legal dimensions just discussed. *Formal equality* is the most basic and narrow version. Essentially equality in the political-legal sense alone, this notion does not address the social and economic dimensions. By now, almost nobody in the United States challenges others' right to vote or to equality before the law. Some oppose making voting easier for people, for example, by scheduling elections on weekends or easing registration or language requirements. And opposition exists to helping some to exercise their legal rights, for example, by providing lawyers to criminal defendants or poor people generally. But the formal principle of political-legal equality seems firmly established as a minimum. The question is whether equality should mean anything *more*.

A version of equality with broader implications is *equality of opportunity*. This version assumes that equality entitles people to equal opportunities to compete with others. Individuals should start equal in the race for the goals, economic or otherwise, that they seek in life. This requires and legitimates a variety of government programs, including educational assistance, vocational training, small-business loans, and affirmative action boards. Such programs compensate for existing inequalities or discrimination. They give everybody an equal start. The idea is that equality can be balanced with freedom, with no real conflict ensuing between the two principles.

The problem with this approach is not only that it often requires substantial limits on the freedom of some people or even that it helps some with financial aid drawn from taxes paid by others. More fundamentally, the problem lies in agreeing on when to stop trying to compensate for accumulated social and economic disadvantages in what has become over time a highly unequal society. Equality of opportunity, taken literally, promises to provide genuine equality at the starting gate of life. But it cannot truly do so. And in the attempt, it often incurs the resentment of those whose freedom has been limited in order to provide opportunity for others. At the same time, those whose disadvantages were not effectively compensated for by government action often cry "fraud."

The version with the greatest scope is *equality of condition*. It frankly and completely includes the social and economic sides of equality. In this version equality takes precedence over freedom. Alternatively, freedom is simply redefined to express the need for all people jointly to have certain levels of both opportunity *and* achievement, something like the "positive" form of freedom noted earlier. Equality of condition means that public (and governmental) concern focuses on the actual conditions people experience in their everyday lives. Government action should provide at least a floor of substantive equality for all. To be sure, this version of equality involves a major alteration of the organization of our social order, including how many Americans think. But equality of condition remains an ideal dimly visible on the horizon.

Each of these three contemporary versions of equality poses a particular conflict with received understandings of freedom. The conflict can be solved by openly granting one or the other principle complete priority. Or one can be redefined to fit with a preferred version of the other. As we shall see, both strategies have been employed throughout American history. Perhaps no final victory for one or another combination is possible. But the evolution of the American political belief system cannot be understood without grasping the conflict between contending versions of these two central principles.

DEMOCRACY

Among highly valued basic elements, none is more highly valued than the principle of democracy. In essence it means that people participate in public affairs and exert at least some degree of control over what governments do. But as is true for any highly valued symbol, the precise meaning of democracy has been elusive and changing.

A fundamental change in the meaning of democracy necessarily occurred in the nation's early years. As late as the framing of the Constitution, not only people of property but ordinary citizens as well looked with disfavor on "democracy." Democracy implied mob rule; that is, rule by the people meant rule by the rabble. Obviously, for democracy to become widely accepted and attain specially valued status as *the* defining characteristic of American government, something had to change.

The framers of the Constitution carefully designed a "republic." As such, there were many bulwarks against popular majorities and against "democracy" as it was then understood. But the claim of ordinary people to participate in government grew in the last decades of the eighteenth century and the opening decades of the nineteenth. Spurred by the egalitarianism of the French Revolution and, indeed, of the American Revolution itself, the appeal of democracy spread. Jefferson rode to power as head of the Democratic-Republican Party in 1800. Contrary to Federalist expectations, he did not dismantle the Constitution or its institutions. Rather, he began the process of attaching the (now good) label of democracy to the (good) Constitution and national government. The years that immediately followed saw a general franchise expansion and democratization of state constitutions, within the original "republican" framework. But both the property-defending nonmajoritarian Constitution and the popular rule notion came to be understood as American "democracy."

Thus we come to one of the enduring features in both the idea and practice of democracy in the United States. At any given time, there are some people who think there is *too little* democracy and some others who think there is *too much*. This continuing debate may simply reflect the conflicting governmental goals of providing popular participation and gaining popular support while simultaneously being able to act firmly and decisively. But a deeper and more fundamental factor is involved in the American version of this argument. Two quite distinct and even opposed categories of meaning have become attached to our idea of democracy. We call these opposed understandings the *procedural* and *substantive* definitions of democracy. Each is linked closely to one or more of the different versions of equality just discussed.

The *procedural* definition focuses on the rights and mechanisms for participation that citizens have, in theory and in practice. If these opportunities are in place and working properly, then all the requisites of democracy have been fulfilled. This definition connects, of course, to the political-legal side of equality, in which formal rights such as the right to vote and equality before the law fulfill the principle of equality.

Procedural democracy promises nothing about results. Instead, the essence of democracy lies in the process by which public decisions are made. When opportunities for participation are open and a fair set of rules for goal-seeking is enforced, the results — whatever they are — can be taken as the expression of popular will. This is true whether or not most people actually do participate in voting or other political activity. Those who do not participate can be safely assumed to be either satisfied or too apathetic to matter.

The *substantive* definition acknowledges the great social achievement of procedural democracy. Fair and open processes can enable people to gain many important goals, when they are thoroughly mobilized to do so. But substantive democracy insists that "democracy" should also include concern both for the social and economic conditions of people's lives and for the results of the policy-making process. Thus this definition of democracy is linked to the versions of equality that include social and economic dimensions. Advocates of the substantive definition argue that gross inequality in social standing and economic possessions make fair and open procedures in the political-legal arena more appearance than reality.

The bottom line of this argument is that a social system cannot have genuine political equality together with great social and economic inequalities. The latter condition effectively dominates and therefore denies the former. Wealth, status, and social power will overawe less advantaged people and cause them to support whatever the "better people" offer them or to accept quietly what they do not want. The weight of dominant opinion, shaped in

Values	Definitions		
Property	Jeffersonian		Hamiltonian
Democracy	Substantive (includes social and economic conditions)		Procedural (refers only to legal and political rights
Freedom	Positive freedom: freedom *to* or *for*		Negative freedom: freedom *from*
Equality	Equality of condition	Equality of opportunity	Formal equality

FIGURE 1.1   Tensions and Contrasts Within Basic American Values

the image of those who hold wealth, status, and social power, will almost inevitably cause others to fall in line and often even to participate in discouraging opposition or punishing dissidents.

Advocates of substantive democracy insist that the sense of fairness and social justice basic to the democratic idea ought not to be compartmentalized in the political-legal sphere. It should apply as well to the social and economic conditions under which people live. In other words, democracy should mean some minimum standard of living for everybody. To understand democracy solely in terms of the right of the people to participate in the decision-making process stops short, missing the point of the whole enterprise of democracy. The underlying reason for all this political activity is the desire of people to produce a particular *result*. People participate in order to achieve a goal, for example, to change something about their circumstances that is bothering them. They become involved in politics for a *purpose*, not just for the exercise.

This debate over what democracy "really" means often parallels those other conflicts between versions of freedom and equality. When freedom as freedom from government limits on the use of property meets equality as entitlement to certain social and economic goods through the use of government, conflict results. But it is not only a conflict between negative freedom and equality of opportunity or condition; it is likely also to become an issue between procedural and substantive democracy. The negative freedom side would understand democracy chiefly in procedural terms, while those seeking greater social and economic equality would probably hold a substantive definition of democracy. Each side would sincerely argue its case in terms of the basic elements of freedom, equality, and democracy.

What seems at first to be a solid foundation of basic elements of American political beliefs thus turns out to be shifting sands of contending versions and definitions. Figure 1.1 summarizes the major differences within these key values. These differences are the fundamental ingredients of political dialogue and conflict in the United States. Our apparent agreement on basic principles, however, provides an important stabilizing factor in our society. Hardly anybody denies that any of these basic elements is good and appropriate for us. We argue with each other within that framework of agreement, often without realizing that we are arguing about the *applied* meanings of these basic elements. This permits practical changes to occur without formal recognition, at least for a time. It also results in vigorous arguments that rest on assumptions or meanings long outmoded by changing circumstances.

ADDITIONAL READINGS

Boorstin, Daniel. *The Genius of American Politics.* Chicago: University of Chicago Press, 1953.

Commager, Henry S. *The American Mind.* New Haven: Yale University Press, 1950.

Dolbeare, Kenneth M. *American Political Thought.* Chatham, N.J.: Chatham House Publishers, 1984.

Ekirch, Arthur A. *The Decline of American Liberalism.* New York: Longmans Green, 1955.

Gabriel, Ralph. *The Course of American Political Thought.* New York: Ronald Press, 1940.

Girvetz, Harry K. *The Evolution of Liberalism.* New York: Collier Books, 1963.

Grimes, Alan P. *American Political Thought.* New York: Holt, Rinehart and Winston, 1960.

Hofstadter, Richard. *The American Political Tradition.* New York: Knopf, 1948.

Mason, Alpheus T. *Free Government in the Making.* Englewood Cliffs, N.J.: Prentice-Hall, 1965.

Roelofs, Mark. *Ideology and Myth in American Politics.* Boston: Little, Brown, 1976.

CHAPTER 2

Analyzing American Political Beliefs

Historically most Americans have shared at least abstract versions of the six basic values and assumptions just examined. They also shared some important and equally enduring attitudes about science, progress, and religion. Science was highly respected as the means of discovering laws about natural relationships. And on the heels of scientific discoveries, it was felt, new inventions and other applications of technology would follow. Then, with apparent inevitability, would come progress in controlling nature and thus improvement in the general standard of living. Lawyers tapped into this broad acceptance of science, claiming to be the means of applying a scientific approach to managing social relationships and public affairs. Religion was an ever present force, adding faith and moral fervor to the prospect of fulfilling America's destiny.

As we have seen, within the context of these widely shared abstract values and assumptions, Americans differed substantially over specific meanings and priorities. These differences have usually been patterned and consistent, rather than random, so that continuing strands of disagreement can be followed through the two centuries of our history. In other words, particular versions of the basic values seem to fit together into coherent sets or packages, which have held together across time.

In this chapter, we shall expand our analytical approach. First we introduce two major themes or tensions that run through the two centuries of evolution of American political values and assumptions. Both were foreshadowed in the previous chapter and here will serve to organize and give meaning to the continuing disagreement between sets of definitions that marks our history. Next, we discuss the notion of the political spectrum, which we will use to organize our thinking about the relationships between political belief systems, as well as between sets of definitions of the basic values.

Then we shall develop our own four-part analytical framework, based on what we have seen in the historical evolution of the basic American political values. This framework is designed to serve as a means of quickly gaining understanding of today's emerging political belief systems. Finally, we shall give a brief sketch of the implications of the decline (or "collapse") of liberalism, a decline that was in part caused by and in part gave rise to these new political belief systems. By means of a comprehensive figure we will summarize our analysis and preview the relationships between the belief systems analyzed in the substantive chapters of the book.

TWO CENTRAL THEMES IN THE EVOLUTION OF AMERICAN POLITICAL BELIEFS

There are many candidates for the title of "major themes" in the evolution of American political values and beliefs. We do not argue that the following are the only possibilities. But surely two continuing themes incorporating many of the conflicts between specific definitions of our abstract values are (a) the Hamiltonian versus Jeffersonian models of political-economic development and (b) procedural versus substantive democracy. Together, these two major themes help to explain and make sense out of much of the basic political controversy of the two centuries that brought us to our present point.

Contrasting Models of Political-Economic Development

As we noted in Chapter 1, Alexander Hamilton advocated the development of a manufacturing-based commercial economy that would make the United States an independent and respected nation of the world. Central to his program was active national government support for a new financial system with adequate power to pay debts, stabilize the value of money, promote manufacturing, and provide for a transportation network that would allow commerce on a national scale.

Hamilton's plans rested on a frank preference for people with money and hence the capacity to invest, develop, and otherwise contribute to the new economy. He designed government policies to maximize their opportunities, often at the expense of ordinary citizens. He had little confidence in "the people's" capacity for enlightened self-government. For this reason, he argued for a special role for courts and the law to put an additional stabilizing check on popular majorities.

On the other hand, in Thomas Jefferson's view, a sound economy was based neither on diversification nor on high productivity, but rather on agriculture and particularly on the small farmer. The independence small farmers gained from producing for self-sufficiency would enable them to be truly public-spirited citizens. And what counted was the production of real goods — the food and basic clothing that people needed. Jefferson particularly mistrusted schemes that appeared to provide profits while resting entirely on speculative buying and selling of stocks, bonds, and other "paper titles." He was convinced that corruption would ensue, as the thirst for profits led to various forms of manipulation of such paper certificates. More importantly, those who produced tangible items with real value would ultimately pay the price for the bankruptcies, inflation, depression, and other scandals generated by such "stockjobbers and speculators."

Jefferson also envisioned corruption in politics stemming from detaching people from the land and bringing them to cities to earn their living by working in factories. He was sure that such people would be strongly influenced either by their employers or by demagogues among urban crowds. They would lose their capacity for judgment as independent citizens. Jefferson had more confidence than Hamilton in the capacity of ordinary people, particularly when they had access to education and information. He therefore sought to keep as much governing power as possible in those governments closest to the people. For the same reason, he did not trust any self-nominated elite and resisted expansion of national government powers. For example, he argued for a relatively greater role for popular majorities in interpreting the Constitution, leaving a more modest role for lawyers and the United States Supreme Court.

From the time of Hamilton's first proposals as secretary of the Treasury in the Washington administration, Jefferson led the opposition — but to little avail. Much of Hamilton's program was enacted. And interestingly, Jefferson did little to change things after he became president. He was even obliged to watch while Chief Justice John Marshall steadily carved out a decisive role for the Supreme Court in defining the national government's powers. Further, the Court then supported the implementation of the Hamilton model of a strong and active national government.

However, Hamilton had accomplished only the beginning of his design before leaving office. In practical terms, Jefferson, his followers, and their belief in a limited role for the national government dominated the nation through the first decade of the twentieth century. For most of this period, the U.S. government consisted mainly of post office clerks and customs collectors. Much of the public land not given away to the railroads was sold so that the U.S. government consistently ran a budgetary surplus. Most people did live on farms, and the principle of laissez-faire ruled unchallenged (except for those who sought and obtained special favors from the government).

With a developing commercial economy, however, unbridled laissez-faire resulted in an assumption of power by the private corporations which used the national government to promote their own ends. In about 1890, a major reversal set in. Legislative majorities in the states and to some extent in the U.S. Congress began to enact restraints on railroads' and other corporations' behavior. Congress even passed an income tax in which rich people were obliged to pay more than poor people. Legislative majorities seemed to be acting on behalf of farmers and workers, along Jeffersonian lines. But the Supreme Court's actions at this point were fully in accordance with the Hamilton–Marshall design. The court asserted its power, in the name of the law and the Constitution, to "save" property rights from the popular majorities of the moment. More boldly than it ever had before — or has since — it declared a wide range of state and national legislative acts unconstitutional and therefore void.

A few years after the peak of this controversy, greater cooperation began to develop between the larger corporations and banks and the executive branch of the national government, then led by Theodore Roosevelt. Spurred in part by reformers in Congress and concerned also about popular pressures for even greater reforms, the Roosevelt administration asserted that it was essential that there be a strong and active national government to serve popular needs. Gone was the Jeffersonian principle of laissez-faire or limited government. In its place emerged the Hamiltonian idea of a far-reaching and purposeful national government. Further, the Roosevelt administration felt that public needs were best met in the context of a healthy business climate, and the new agenda included promoting the growth of a complex and powerful economy. This meant a major role for large corporations and financial institutions.

Herbert Croly, one of Theodore Roosevelt's closest advisers and a leading political thinker of the period, summed up the change by characterizing the new arrangement as essentially a Hamiltonian government for Jeffersonian purposes.[1] In other words, to serve the people's needs as Jefferson had desired now required a kind of government that was exactly opposite from what he had envisioned. The increased size of American society required an active, economy-managing government as in the Hamiltonian model.

This new Hamiltonian version of the scope of national powers received some confirmation from the practice of the succeeding Wilson administration and World War I. But it was in the period of Franklin Roosevelt's New Deal and World War II that the Hamiltonian model became fully operational and accepted as the proper way for government to be conducted. The Jeffersonian ideals of limited government, agrarian life, and supremacy of the states were still honored in rhetoric but largely ignored in practice. In these respects two centuries of conflict had ended in a nearly complete Hamiltonian triumph. But the Jeffersonian notion that the ordinary citizen's needs should take precedence in a good society remains. And Jefferson's faith in the ordinary citizen's capacity for self-government also continues to appeal to most Americans.

Procedural Versus Substantive Democracy

The tensions between procedural and substantive democracy have run through our history in complex ways, appearing in somewhat different forms at different times. We noted in Chapter 1 that roughly equal conditions prevailed in the first years of the republic. Many small farmers, artisans, and mechanics enjoyed equal status, wealth, and the ability to control their own livelihoods. In this context, the focus for most people was on the procedural means necessary to realize democracy. Various groups fought for and acquired the right to vote. Many more began to actually exercise the right. The decades after Jefferson's election helped to legitimate the ideal of democracy, and voting turnout surged greatly with Jackson's first election. President Jackson explicitly sought to portray his administration as that of "the common man." Democracy and equality had become powerful national rhetorical symbols.

But changes in the character of the economy were steadily undermining the conditions of rough equality and substantive democracy that had given rise to the focus on expansion of procedural democracy. Industrialization began first in New England and the mid-Atlantic states, then spread slowly west and more slowly south. Railroads, mills, and factories drew workers from their independent workbenches and farms and from other countries. Those with the money and foresight to invest in the new means of producing and transporting goods reaped frequent profits, and with their profits grew their prestige and power. Many small producers and artisans who sold hand-crafted products could now no longer compete. Having no other source of income, laborers in the new economy were forced to work at minimal wages and under the close direction of their employers.

Thus a society of rough equality of condition was starting to move toward social and economic inequality. The capacity of ordinary people to control their lives diminished as the capacity of owners to control the working conditions and opportunities of laboring people increased. Procedural democracy seemed to be in place, and more frequently was stressed as the *only* definition of democracy that was appropriate to American practice. The social and economic world was set to one side, separate from the political-legal world, and (procedural) democracy applied only to the latter.

But this very process of growing inequality occasioned new claims for substantive versions of equality and democracy. Some of these new claims were primarily reactions to industrialization. The so-called utopian socialists sought broad public ownership of the new railroads and factories. Alternatively, they built cooperative communities entirely apart from the industrial economy. Other movements sought to continue expansion of the meaning of equality. They moved from the purely procedural realm to a combined procedural-substantive form. Black people, supported by a vanguard of vocal whites, clamored for abolition of slavery and then for genuine procedural democracy. Women formed another major movement, seeking full political — and social and economic — equality.

The history of the black and feminist movements interweaves almost from the start. Black leaders, feminists, and white abolitionists (often overlapping categories) regularly met together for mutual support and strategic planning. With occasional lapses they jointly sought, for more than a century, to expand the idea of equality. Their movements demonstrate, however, the way in which substantive democracy claims can become converted into procedural democracy changes. What they sought were the social and economic conditions of full citizenship. They claimed not only legal rights, but also status, dignity, and respect. What they obtained, after decades of struggle, was formal change in legal status.

In 1867, the Thirteenth Amendment to the Constitution released blacks from the status of property. Black males received the right to vote, at least in theory, in 1870 with the passage of the Fifteenth Amendment. The Nineteenth Amendment, in 1920, granted women the right to vote. But most of the black and feminist claims for equality and democracy in the economic and social conditions of their lives remained unfulfilled. In the civil rights and feminist movements of the 1960s, the broader demands were revived. Again, primarily procedural gains were achieved, but perhaps with more substantive long-range effects.

The claim for substantive democracy has also been raised by farmers and workers. In this case, claims for some kind of social and economic equality combined with a demand for greater control over their individual life situations. Vigorous protest movements, unsatisfied in the procedural arena of elections and lawmaking, pressed their claims by other means, such as cooperatives, boycotts, and strikes. Eventually, portions of the farmers' and workers' demands were grudgingly granted in the form of rural assistance, workmen's compensation, social security, and rights to organize and bargain collectively. But meanwhile an equally vigorous campaign had purged these movements of all "foreign" and "radical" elements and reasserted the necessity of following the established procedures.

Nothing in our recent experience suggests that this conflict between procedural and substantive democracy has been resolved. If anything, issues involving claims for expanding versions of equality and democracy appear to be more prominent than ever — as are reactions against such claims. Some reflections on the lessons of history may therefore be useful as both summary and forecast.

In a variety of ways, procedural and substantive democracy form a complex whole with continuing tensions. In one period, procedural democracy expanded as substantive democracy declined. In another, substantive democracy claims were met with procedural change and little substantive response. Other times the procedural changes came only after forceful revalidation of the procedural mechanisms. Overall, the situation has been one in which repeated substantive democracy claims have expanded the scope of citizen participation and rights in the procedural arena.

But the procedural definition of democracy has so far held on to its position as the primary accepted version of this key value. And for the most part, procedural expansions have functioned to defuse substantive democracy movements. On occasion, however, the failure to achieve substantive goals can lead to added frustration and resentments against the procedural system itself. We shall see this in connection with the 1960s.

Finally, we should note some continuing implications of the procedural-substantive tension. Today in particular, the root of the tension, and the underlying reason for two quite different versions of the definition of democracy in the United States, is to be found in the great social and economic inequality in our country and in the major cause of this inequality. By its very nature, an industrialized capitalist economy consists of great aggregations of wealth that are owned and managed by a relatively few people in order to produce private profit. The great majority of people are dependent on them for work and income. Inevitably, this results in a highly unequal society.

But as we know, this system also strongly endorses the principles of equality and democracy. The key to being able to have *both* inequality *and* the conviction that equality and democracy are in full effect lies in making a sharp distinction between the social-economic world and the political-legal world. Somehow, the concept of a wall of separation between the two worlds must be developed and sustained. This is necessary so that it remains believable that democracy and equality can be fully served in the political-legal world alone, while the basic structure of the social-economic world is left essentially untouched by government action.

The procedural version of democracy insists that freedom from interference with property rights is paramount. Further, the distinction between the political-legal world and the social-economic world is right and proper. "Equality" and "democracy" can have only those definitions that are consistent with these first principles.

The substantive definition of democracy starts from broader notions of, and higher priority for, the principle of equality. It simply denies the separability of the political-legal world from all other areas of social life. The conflict between procedural and substantive definitions remains unresolved, regularly recurs, and is likely to go on well into the future.

The continuing nature of this conflict shows how vital it is for people who believe in the procedural definition to find ways to maintain its predominance. If they don't maintain the fiction of separation between the two worlds, they will have to defend existing social and economic inequalities, and the political power disparities that go with them, on their own merits. This task would be difficult and possibly a prelude to open conflict. By and large, the procedural definition *has* been maintained. Some people even find it difficult to understand how any other version of "democracy" could be imagined. In other words, what *is* in the United States is the right, only, and universal definition of "democracy." But the notion persists that democracy could or should mean more. And so the conflict endures, sometimes unrecognized and in a variety of forms.

The way in which these two themes have developed and affected the evolution of American ideas has in turn been shaped by one major economic process: industrialization. As the nature of production changed, the way that people earned their living changed with it. So did the nature of social organization and in crucial ways the underlying political belief system. Many other factors contributed to these ongoing changes; few results can be attributed exclusively to industrialization. But if we had to identify one major source of the dynamics of change in political beliefs, industrialization would be our candidate. That is why the current shifts in the nature of the American economy, coming in the context of the social and cultural upheavals of the 1960s and 1970s, seem to us to presage profound changes in American political beliefs today. In the next three sections, we begin to identify the tools that will help us to understand these changes.

THE NOTION OF A POLITICAL SPECTRUM

The word "spectrum" suggests a predictable pattern of colors, which always follow the same order from one end to the other and which fade into one another without sharp demarcations. This is a serviceable, if somewhat crude, image for the relationships among different definitions of basic values and even among various political belief systems. Americans usually visualize a horizontal continuum with conservatism located at the right-hand extremity, radicalism at the left-hand extremity, and liberalism in the middle. We shall add three further thoughts to make this notion of a spectrum a more useful analytic tool.

First, we should try to be more specific about what is being measured along this spectrum, or continuum. Beliefs about the distribution of wealth, status, and power are the obvious candidates, but beliefs about the distribution of any socially valued right or privilege might be involved. Those people who favor the narrowest distribution of the valued resource — where only a few would possess the most — are situated at the right-hand end of the continuum. The status quo (today's distribution pattern) is located to the right but well short of the end of the possible range of the imagined continuum. Some people, further "right," may yearn for an even tighter concentration of wealth and power. But probably many more people would be located at various points along the continuum to the left of the actual status quo. Thus, the continuum is effectively anchored by the status quo and the defenders of present distribution patterns.

More or wider distribution is sought the further one moves to the left. Thus radicals seek the relatively widest distribution to the most people, while liberals seek more modest departures from the status quo. Radicalism is understood to some extent as merely calling for *more* of whatever is at stake than liberals do. Radicalism is also viewed as entailing a desire for greater or more rapid change and/or a critique of fundamental values and social-economic structures. In this last-mentioned sense, derived from its original meaning of going deeper or to the roots in search of explanations and solutions, radicalism also has applications on the right-hand side of the continuum (as in "Radical Right"). But it is used primarily to describe people on the left whose ideas imply too much change to be "practical" or acceptable to the majority, and we shall try to note explicitly whenever we employ it otherwise.

Second, the continuum is a *relative* one. It is set by today's circumstances and the relative satisfactions of different people with present conditions. Further, the whole continuum can move over time. For most of the twentieth century, it has moved slowly to the left or more egalitarian side. Yesterday's radical has often ended up as today's liberal, without much change in his or her personal position. Formerly unimaginable or "utopian" claims have made their way from the left pole toward the center. By the same token, yesterday's conservative has often seemed to slip off the continuum to the right.

But what if the experience of the past no longer holds true and the continuum ceases to move inexorably to the left — or even begins to drift to the right? And what if economic conditions are such that growth is neither great nor steady, and wider distribution to some is possible only at the cost of narrower distribution to those who have now? The continuum itself might have to be reconstructed. At the least, it might have to be reunderstood. As we have suggested earlier, something like this may be exactly what is happening now.

Third, other important assumptions and goals are associated with the continuum at *any* point in time. One example is the definition of democracy held by different belief systems along the continuum. Substantive democracy, as we have seen, includes the most comprehensive definition of equality. It clearly fits best with radical beliefs. Procedural democracy just as clearly is an integral component of liberalism, although it is also compatible with conservatism. Still more limited versions of democracy are conceivable, such as plebiscitary democracy (in which majorities essentially endorse what their rulers have done), but most American conservatives would stop short of advocating such methods.

Perhaps more revealing is the fact that assumptions about human nature and capabilities also seem to differ along the continuum. Most radicals believe that people are or can be cooperative and community oriented (to be sure, some do not always *act* that way). People can therefore be trusted with full power to govern in almost all matters, in a kind of ongoing participatory democracy. Liberals believe that people are by nature reasonable enough but also competitive and self-interested. Therefore, elaborate rules and channels for participation in politics are necessary to prevent them from doing bad things. With such procedures, however, people can rationally design improvements and expect to achieve progress for the society. Many conservatives believe that people are irrational, dominated by short-term and self-interested considerations, and not really capable of understanding their own true public interest. Therefore, they need to be guided by those few who are knowledgeable and successful.

In both these examples, important distinctions range along a continuum paralleling that of the belief systems. In other words, once we imagine a left–right relationship among political beliefs, we can see a whole network of relationships — of connected definitions and assumptions that link up with and help support the basic political values and beliefs. Figure 2.1 sketches some of these relationships. It is very general and suggestive rather than definitive. Each of the three major categories — radical, liberal, and conservative — has a number of variants. Such variants slide to the right or left, and shade into each other, just as colors on a spectrum. Only pure or ideal types are reflected in the labels. Reality is, as usual, much less clear and consistent. But the figure serves to indicate that articulable political beliefs are often only the tip of the iceberg, connecting, as they do, with many other assumptions about the world.

Our continuum is strictly American, moreover. Other countries' political spectrums extend much further right or left, and often both. Scholars often describe the American spectrum as lacking both a far right and a far left. And over time Americans have, if anything, tended to shorten their spectrum rather than widen it. Sometimes American political debate, at

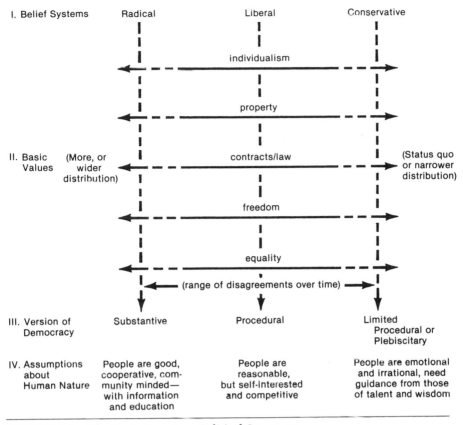

FIGURE 2.1   The Basic American Political Spectrum

least as reported by the news media, seems to be entirely between liberals and conservatives. Moreover, the call to rally against "extremists" from either side strongly appeals to Americans. This is undoubtedly another factor that has made for stability in our system. But the shortened continuum may be caused in part by the fact of its steady leftward movement for most of the twentieth century. If that movement no longer continues, the continuum might very well widen instead. Or, again, it might move to the right, or be entirely reconstructed or reinterpreted in any number of ways. That is part of what is at stake in the era of transformation in which we live.

A FRAMEWORK FOR ANALYZING AMERICAN POLITICAL BELIEFS IN THE 1980s

Let us try to distill all we have seen so far into a way of looking at American values and beliefs that will enable us to see as much as we can in an efficient manner. Clearly, the approach must be sensitive to history, focus on values and value definitions, but be oriented to what people actually see and seek in the present and what that may mean for the future. We think it is possible to develop a four-part framework that will be responsive to each of these needs and yet be manageable when applied. We propose, then, to analyze each of the new political belief systems in terms of these four parts, and each chapter is divided into sections accordingly.

Links to the Past

The historical origins and evolution of a political belief system carry crucial significance for two important reasons. One is that the past has powerfully shaped the language, logic, and habits of mind of everybody's political thinking. For tools of thinking and communicating, we all rely chiefly on what we have been given. It is very difficult to create entirely new words or to give new meanings to familiar words or concepts. Such acts often involve long and only partially conscious social struggles. Similarly, a belief system is powerfully shaped by the sources that led to its original coalescence and by the particular evolution that led to its present form.

Second, many contemporary belief systems define themselves in some way in terms of the past. Each set of beliefs seems to reach back for pieces of what it perceives to have once been important. Identifying with some part of an enduring tradition is a means of legitimating today's positions. Some sets of beliefs claim to be the only current valid versions of particular past principles. Others involve an explicit rejection of some specific past beliefs or events as deviant or undesirable. In any case, the perceptions and judgments of our past associated with a political belief system reveal much about its present character.

Thus, the past not only shapes the present but also influences our capacity to think about the future. It continuously affects what people understand as the range of the possible. The past does not control the future, but past values and ways of thinking play an important part in how a belief system understands the present and addresses the future. We shall try to trace the origin and view of the past of each belief system we examine, not only to see where it came from but also to begin to understand how it thinks about both past and present.

Basic Values and Assumptions

By "values," we mean beliefs about what is good or bad. For example, it is good to be a hard-working, self-reliant individual who succeeds in acquiring property and rising on the social ladder. By "assumptions," we mean things that are taken to be true without the necessity or perhaps possibility of proof. For example, human nature is universally self-seeking and competitive.

Identification of the basic values and assumptions of each belief system will help us to see into the essence of that system, as well as to compare various belief systems — new and old — at this basic level. Some belief systems may rest on consistent basic elements, while in others there may be tensions among these elements. Some values and assumptions will be relatively constant, while others are in the process of adaptation and change. Most belief systems will be characterizable primarily through analysis at this level.

Problems and Possibilities

Each belief system sees something different when it looks at the everyday world that makes up its present environment. In part, it sees things in ways affected by its basic values and assumptions. Conditions in the world sometimes seem to be in conformity with them but at other times seem to be in opposition. In part also, a belief system may look at the world through particular concepts that "fit" with its values and assumptions. A "concept" is a mental construct that helps people to identify and organize relevant "facts" and understand their meaning. For example, the concept of a "free market," unimaginable before the seventeenth century, has dominated our thinking ever since the American Revolution. Values and assumptions infuse concepts and the resulting combination helps people to see and judge the world, all in one instant.

Problems and possibilities, too, are understood differently depending on the perspective of the belief system. Problems are identified and defined, and their causes and importance estimated, in totally different ways. We shall try to reconstruct what each body of beliefs sees in the way of problems, and what each thinks the causes, priorities, and solutions are. From this we shall move to their respective understandings of what, under current circumstances, can and should be achieved in the way of programs and goals. In other words, according to each belief system, what are the *bad* possibilities if things continue as they are? And, according to each belief system, what are the *good* possibilities that can be brought to fruition if its adherents come to power?

Implications and Prospects

In the final section of each chapter, we shall analyze the obstacles and opportunities that the respective belief system faces today. We shall explore its linkages with enduring themes in American political thought and try to assess what the results would be if its adherents were successful in mobilizing people and/or influencing public policy in their preferred ways. This is the point at which our own criteria and judgments become applicable, and some indication of our purposes may be helpful.

Our goal in analyzing the new political belief systems now competing for acceptance in the United States is not primarily either intellectual or academic. These are entirely valid purposes, of course. It would be very satisfying to understand what is happening for its own sake. But our purposes extend further. We want to help people see where we are going as a nation, particularly when, as now, we are in the midst of profound changes. People must be able to act in politics before it is too late to affect the outcome. In other words, we want to help empower people not only to see the forms of the future as they first emerge in ideas but also to play a full role as citizens in the shaping and choosing of new beliefs and programs. What we need first is a brief overview of what is happening today and how these events should shape the organization of our inquiry.

PREVIEW: THE "COLLAPSE" OF LIBERALISM AND THE RISE OF THE NEOS

One major fact of the 1980s has been that the liberalism so dominant for decades essentially dissolved, in ways and for reasons that we shall examine in the next chapter. As we shall see, the liberal center was under attack from both sides and even from within its own ranks. Polarization was clearly evident, and the first side to crystallize effectively was an alliance of conservatives. But the problems and conditions of the 1980s are not likely to be amenable to any ready-made remedies. Much more likely is a continuing period of uncertainty, change, and testing of reconstituted versions of the basic American values and beliefs.

Figure 2.2 situates the major bodies of belief that are competing for support today, indicating both their locations on the American continuum and their links to liberalism. The numbers in the figure refer to chapters in this book, each addressed to a particular system of beliefs.

Liberalism proved to be a belief system with almost as many exits as it had thinkers. When disaster struck, groups donned new labels and abandoned the sinking ship with sometimes unseemly alacrity. Neoconservatism was the first to go, moving sharply toward the growing conservative movement that had its roots well back in American history. In turn, that conservative movement saw some portion of its support move even further to the right with the rise of the New Right, a new kind of "conservatism" that sought to build a broad popular base for returning to the "old values" and restoring American military capability.

The second belief system to abandon liberalism was neoliberalism, which moved moderately to the right as it made the new needs of capitalism its dominant frame of reference. Next were the various programmatic movements (racial equality, sexual equality, environmental and antinuclear, and antiwar), which followed, with even greater rigidity than before, their inclinations to concentrate exclusively on reform in the specific areas that concerned them.

Some of the more left-leaning liberals joined with elements of the long-established American substantive democracy tradition, particularly old populists and radical labor leaders, to build a movement that called itself economic democracy. The far left on the new spectrum, however, is the democratic socialist home of the more radical side of that same substantive democracy tradition, as well as of some holdovers from the New Left of the 1960s and a scattering of American neo-Marxists.

As liberalism fragmented, its various defining characteristics found new

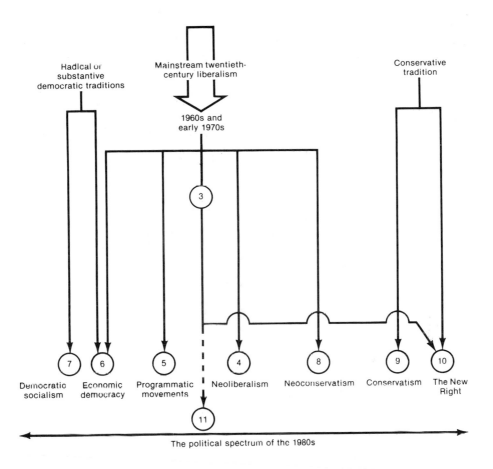

FIGURE 2.2   The Evolving American Political Spectrum

homes in disproportionate ways. Its anticommunism, for example, flowed distinctively to neoconservatism. Its managerial-technocratic inclination, and much of its social engineering propensity, went to neoliberalism. Its genuine reform spirit, however, was inherited by the programmatic movements; the strongest cutting edge of reform went all the way to economic democracy. As indicated in the figure, this pattern meant that neoconservatism and neoliberalism were thoroughly committed to procedural democracy. The programmatic movements were procedural in orientation as well, although in some cases potentially open to substantive democracy principles. Only economic democracy is really within the substantive democracy range, and then despite its inheritances from liberalism.

These are the categories of old, new, and reconstituting values and beliefs to which the decline of liberalism and the ongoing changes in the circumstances of American life have given unparalleled opportunity. In some form, some combination of these new-old values and beliefs will shape the future political system of the United States. If they self-destruct or default, liberalism may arise again to pick up the pieces, once again the familiar lesser evil of the middle ground. But worse results are also possible. We turn now to the analysis of what these new sets of beliefs offer to Americans, in hopes that a better future lies somewhere among them.

ADDITIONAL READINGS

Allen, Robert. *Reluctant Reformers: Racism and Social Reform Movements in the United States*. New York: Anchor Books, 1975.

Beard, Charles. *The Economic Origins of Jeffersonian Democracy*. New York: Free Press, 1935.

Bowers, Claude G. *Jefferson and Hamilton: The Struggle for Democracy in America*. New York: Scholarly Reprints, 1972.

Bruce, Robert. *1877: Year of Violence*. New York: Franklin Watts, 1959.

Croly, Herbert. *The Promise of American Life*. New York: Dutton, 1963.

Destler, Chester. *American Radicalism, 1865–1901*. Chicago: Quadrangle, 1966.

Goodwyn, Lawrence. *The Populist Moment*. New York: Oxford University Press, 1979.

Hays, Samuel. *The Response to Industrialism, 1885–1914*. Chicago: University of Chicago Press, 1957.

Hofstadter, Richard. *Social Darwinism in America*. Boston: Beacon Press, 1944.

Kolko, Gabriel. *The Triumph of Conservatism, 1900–1916*. New York: Free Press, 1963.

Lasch, Christopher. *The New Radicalism in America*. New York: Random House, 1967.

Paul, Arnold. *Conservative Crisis and the Rule of Law, 1887–1895*. New York: Harper & Row, 1967.

Potter, David. *People of Plenty: Economic Abundance and the American Character*. Chicago: University of Chicago Press, 1955.

Weinstein, James. *The Corporate Ideal in the Liberal State, 1900–1918*. Boston: Beacon Press, 1968.

Wiebe, Robert. *The Search for Order, 1877–1920*. New York: Hill and Wang, 1967.

Williams, William A. *America Confronts a Revolutionary World*. New York: Norton, 1976.

Wiltse, Charles M. *The Jeffersonian Tradition in American Democracy*. Chapel Hill: University of North Carolina Press, 1935.

CHAPTER 3

Liberalism: The "Collapse" of an Ever-Resilient Center

Liberalism emerged from World War II at the peak of its strength. It dominated both major political parties, all the institutions of the national government, and all but a handful of intellectuals and their journals. Its body of beliefs was so widely shared that the theme of a leading scholar's history of liberalism was regret that no credible alternative existed to force Americans to better understand the principles they so uncritically accepted.[1] Throughout the 1950s and into the early 1960s, liberal values and beliefs in action seemed to produce an "affluent society." Social conflict was effectively smothered by the material achievements generated by economic growth.

Not two decades later, liberalism is widely perceived to be in total collapse, bereft of creative ideas and leaders, and unlikely to ever again mobilize popular support. Almost no thoughtful political leader or socially engaged intellectual accepts the characterization of "liberal" without some exculpatory prefix or an extended qualifying explanation. What happened to this once dominant body of beliefs to bring it so quickly from the heights of success to the depths of contempt and abandonment?

Undoubtedly, hindsight will show that liberalism was never either so unchallenged in the 1950s or so weak and helpless in the 1980s. To adapt a phrase, the news of liberalism's death may be something of an exaggeration. Liberalism is both long-lived and resilient. No one with respect for history should write off the prospect of liberalism's resurgence — particularly if the extremes polarize, leaving a wide gap in the center as a nostalgic haven for conflict-weary people.

But there *has* been a dramatic turnabout in liberalism's role in the country. That change cannot be explained solely by one or two or even several "causes." Yet it must be understood if we are to assess the changes in American political thinking in the 1980s. New bodies of belief define themselves in terms of their differences from liberalism. Established values and beliefs are reconstituted in new combinations, and sometimes given new definitions, on the basis of judgments about what went wrong with liberalism. And old antagonists of liberalism, fresh and bold in their success, confidently offer answers that liberalism would never have considered. In short, the "collapse" of liberalism has given rise to the present spectrum of political beliefs. All of our new belief systems owe something to liberalism in much the same way that an exploding star is thought to have created our solar system.

In this chapter, we shall explore liberalism's rise and fall through the four-part framework, set forth in the last chapter, that we shall apply to each of the major political belief systems now competing for acceptance in the United States. In almost every case, the nature of a given belief system will require some adaptation of that framework; liberalism is no exception. Here we shall be somewhat more historical, as befits the progenitor of so many nascent offspring and the antagonist against which so many others have struggled for so long. The essential link between past and present is the post–World War II period, the crucible of modern liberalism and the source of its current antagonists. Finally, the well-established character of liberal values and beliefs allows synthesis and summary. We need not turn to advocates for statements of particular positions as we do in later chapters.

POSTWAR AFFLUENCE ENCOUNTERS THE 1960s AND 1970s

The Postwar Years

It would be difficult to exaggerate the effect that the massive international conflict of World War II had on Americans. An entire generation was deeply marked by the unforgettable experience of massive mobilization and collective national effort. And following the war, individuals' energies were poured into achieving success in civilian life to make up for the wartime loss of opportunities. One not insignificant result was a massive "baby boom."

The early postwar years were dominated by concern that the Depression of the 1930s might recur as soon as the transition to a civilian economy was complete. This led the national government to employ in an even more vigorous manner the structures and policies that seemed to have worked in the 1930s. The Employment Act of 1946 was a major milestone in American history. It both confirmed a new role for government in the economy and established the institutions needed to carry out this role. Government now possessed in legal theory the responsibility for managing the economy that it had begun to acquire in practice in the first decades of the century. Indeed, World War II and its aftermath extended to their furthest reach the new forms and practices of the national government that had first been constructed in the Progressive Era.

Another distinctive mark of this period was the sustained prosperity that soon took hold. Not only did the feared depression not recur, but the nation began to enjoy unprecedented affluence. The United States had emerged from the war as the world's leading military and economic power. It was able to profit substantially from this stature. The governmental policy of encouraging business enterprise while assuring at least minimum individual security seemed to be a highly successful formula. Economic growth and rising real personal income were steady and seemed assured. Whether the dominant belief system and government practice was termed "welfare liberalism" or "corporate liberalism," it seemed to work and had few serious opponents. If it did not work for all, it did for most of the politically significant population.

But the distinguishing feature of this period was surely the rise of the cold war between the United States and the Soviet Union. The United States believed the Soviet Union was determined to expand even beyond its newly extended borders. It moved to contain that expansion through military preparedness, including threats to use the American nuclear arsenal. The United States deployed troops and exerted its influence around the world in an effort to prevent the spread of communism in any form. An atmosphere of hostility and danger prevailed between the "free world" and the socialist nations. To Americans, it was a "battle for men's minds." And the battle did rage all over the world by a variety of means short of all-out war.

The domestic impact of the cold war was a vigorous and sustained campaign against some real and much imagined internal subversion and "un-American" activities. Many people suspected of present or past cooperation with Communists, and many ordinary American radicals, came under heavy attack. Conservatives who feared threats to property rights had mounted similar campaigns before, particularly during the "Red Scare" period of the early twentieth century. But this one served also as a symbolic rallying call with broad appeal to a wide range of Americans. Reaffirmation of such traditional values as property and religion fused with expressions of loyalty and nationalism, as well as with resentment against some of the recent changes in social practices and government role wrought by the New Deal period.

The anticommunist crusades of those years not only gave vent to energies long felt yet contained, but also established lasting criteria of belief and practice for all Americans. Politicians and citizens alike, all across the political spectrum, accepted the necessity of both foreign and domestic anticommunism. Any connection with principles associated however distantly with socialism or communism could destroy credibility and prevent serious consideration for one's ideas. The entire left side of the traditional political spectrum lay under a cloud of suspicion, and radicals literally went underground.

In effect, a new theme in American political thought was created out of this combined revival and expansion of efforts to discredit all those who challenged property rights. Internal anticommunism was a synthesis of reaffirmed traditional values and practices with expressions of resentment against changes of various kinds. When invoked effectively, many nonconservatives responded to and continue to respond to its appeal. Though always potentially powerful, anticommunism is an appeal that draws much of its strength from real or imagined past virtues and achievements. It is most likely when reaction is playing a major role for other reasons. Thus, we have every reason to expect that this theme will be seen and heard in any period of transformation.

The 1960s and 1970s

This period began with strident reminders of the immediate past. John F. Kennedy ran for president on a characteristic cold war platform. He promised to close a missile gap later found to be nonexistent and to generally put us ahead of the Russians — on the moon as well as elsewhere. He defeated Richard Nixon, then chiefly known as one of the leaders of the anticommunist crusades of the 1950s. The Kennedy style, and the reawakening of national pride and sense of omnicompetence that it promised, occasioned much media attention. But it was not long before the power of the civil rights movement, the rise of the New Left and militant feminism, and the chaos generated by the Vietnam War took over and defined the period. Sweeping cultural changes occurred, soon followed by a national trauma over the ending of the Vietnam War and the Watergate scandal.

On top of this came the worsening economic conditions of the post-1973 years. The status of the United States as the world's paramount economic power began to crack as early as 1968. At that point, the modernized European and Japanese economies became truly competitive and the Vietnam War undermined the dollar as the standard of value in the world's monetary system. Trade deficits, inflation, and pressure on the dollar forced severe protectionist action in 1971. In 1973, the oil price increases began. The resulting drain of billions of dollars from the U.S. economy helped to spur the spiraling inflation of the decade. Contrary to all prior experience, high inflation and high unemployment began to occur together, sending shock waves of doubt and resentment through the society.

But, from about the mid-1970s, even these developments were overshadowed by a massive new social phenomenon. Profound changes in cultural values, lifestyles, and social practices had occurred with great media visibility in the 1960s and early 1970s. One of their greatest impacts, however, was the reaction of millions of other Americans who neither desired nor accepted the changes wrought. Many of them blamed these changes on the liberal belief system and its predominance in the national government. A diverse but militant alliance of conservatives soon mobilized to defend the status quo and reassert "traditional" values. They took aim as much at liberal permissiveness as at radical presumptuousness. Particular targets were liberal social engineering and the arrogance of bureaucrats, planners, academics, social workers, etc., who seemed intent on imposing their values on others.

The last two points, though necessary for a full perspective on liberalism's dilemma in the 1980s, have taken us somewhat ahead of our story. We now turn to analysis of just what those newly challenged liberal values, beliefs, perspectives, and goals actually were. We then return to exploration of the causes of liberalism's downfall in greater detail.

LIBERALISM: THE BASIC VALUES

The liberal belief system rests solidly on centrist versions of the six basic values set forth in Chapter 1. Indeed, that particular itemization of American political values could just as properly have been entitled "American liberalism." Each of those values is a key defining component of liberalism. Together they constitute a complete statement of liberalism's fundamental meaning. The fact that these values are so deeply embedded in American history and experience is one of the reasons for suspecting that liberalism may rise again, at least in some modestly reconstituted form.

Obviously there is a range of disagreement in each of the six major values. However, it is the particular mix of specific definitions distinguishing contemporary liberalism that concerns us here. Liberalism, as a matter of principle, seeks the centrist, "moderate" versions that mark the middle ground. It avoids extremes in any direction, delicately balancing competing interests within the parameters that result from adopting moderate versions of *each* of the major values. The issue inadvertently raised by this commitment is whether these centrist versions *can* be harmonized under present social, economic, and political conditions. We shall return to this question after taking note of the specific definitions with which liberalism seeks to work.

For liberals, the individual and his or her satisfactions are the major focus. The purpose of government is to provide the conditions whereby individuals may pursue their own rational self-interest. People are entitled to certain kinds of assistance to equalize opportunities, but personal effort remains vital to achieving one's ends. There is a point after which government aid is unjustifiable. Private property rights are highly valued as necessary to individual well-being and protection. However, the public interest may require reasonable regulations. Law and legal mechanisms are of paramount importance, especially in the protection of individual and minority rights. Given their objective and rational character, courts, almost in and of themselves, embody the proper solutions to problems.

Similarly, equality of opportunity is strongly supported, and to the extent practical, liberals endorse a version that will compensate for past disadvantage. Freedom includes the right to use one's property as one wishes; however, it is subject to the limits that public health and welfare and equality of opportunity make appropriate. Civil liberties stand on higher ground as absolute areas of freedom, but here too courts (only) may impose limits based on the need for public stability. Liberalism's balanced version of freedom is summed up in the phrase, "My freedom to swing my arm ends at your nose."

Finally, democracy is understood in procedural terms and the process is celebrated as capable of satisfying all legitimate needs. Once something has been enacted through the regular channels of procedural democracy, it is presumed to be the best possible approximation of the public interest — and one that all should accept. No other criteria exist by which to judge whether or not the output of the American political system is morally just, in the public interest, or otherwise appropriate. If there is a question as to constitutionality, the Supreme Court will decide the matter. Questions of moral validity or of the adequacy with which the public interest has been served are not answerable or even appropriate within the liberal system.

Looking over these six specific versions of the major values, one may come to feel that they are not so specific after all. Indeed, they are sufficiently ambiguous that they can hardly be said to chart anything like a clear course. Words like "reasonable," "appropriate," "realistic," and "practical" fill the crucial junctures in liberal principles, substituting studied ambiguity for definite standards of judgment.

This ambiguity is neither coincidence nor deliberate caricature on our part, but rather the hallmark of mid-century liberalism. Intent on filling the middle ground and maintaining the flexibility to respond to steadily rising demands, liberalism made virtue out of not being locked into any specific substantive position. Only its procedures were fixed, and even these could be adjusted under heavy pressure. This combination of flexibility and lack of definite standards led to what is termed "interest group liberalism" or "special interest liberalism." Both terms refer to the same thing: a system with no definite standards of its own that seeks to respond to whomever and whatever applies the most pressure. Not surprisingly, when demands grew in number and began to fundamentally conflict with each other, liberalism was in danger of simply becoming overloaded.

This is the feature of liberalism that most triggered the impatience and then contempt of radicals and conservatives alike. From both sides, liberalism was assailed for failing to take principled stands. Once people begin to feel the rightness of a polar position, the "wishy-washy middle" draws their fire even more than their most hated opponents, who are at least principled like themselves. It is much more difficult to be passionate in defense of moderation and reasonableness, and liberals were in many respects unable to respond effectively. Both radicals and conservatives have clear polar definitions of the basic values, as well as distinct priority rankings among them. They are not particularly interested in balancing or moderating them, as liberals would do.

Radicals argued that liberalism was interested only in cosmetic changes that would not threaten the stability of the capitalist economic system. They saw liberalism as either a captive of or otherwise so enmeshed in capitalism that it could function only within the range of what capitalism deemed acceptable. But what radicals most resented was liberalism's sanctimonious rhetorical commitment to equality and democracy. What they missed was the fact that those terms had always meant something quite different to liberals than to radicals.

The dominant commitment of many radicals was the expansion of equality toward something like equality of condition. Certainly radicals were clear that equality of opportunity was a never-to-be-realized illusion, continued invocation of which at some point amounted either to willful ignorance or deliberate hypocrisy. But most liberals still thought equality of opportunity was a realizable and worthy goal and that to expand it too much would be a truly unjustifiable infringement on the freedom of others. The gap between the radical commitment to substantive democracy and the liberal inability to see beyond procedural democracy needs no further explication. Nevertheless, these differences in definition of the commonly used terms seemed to imply bad faith and hypocrisy to people on both sides.

Like the radicals, conservatives adhered to a specific and internally consistent set of definitions of the basic values — and they were just as impatient with liberalism's failure to take a clear stand. They argued, for example, that the appropriate definitions of individualism, freedom, and property were the traditional ones — without any qualifications. Constant efforts to expand equality, in their eyes, were not only unworkable but also actively destructive of individual incentives and ultimately character. Conservatives insisted that liberalism must give up its rhetorical endorsement of expanded equality of opportunity in the name of freedom. Furthermore, liberals were creating unfulfillable expectations on the part of the lower classes.

But the conservatives' heaviest resentment focused on two major failings of liberalism: (a) its toleration of licentious behavior on the part of so many people; and (b) its inability to assert a definite public interest that, if necessary, should be followed regardless of popular preferences. These twin defects made liberalism unfit to govern. It was as if liberalism had no way to assert and defend any principles at all and now was merely a helpless spectator as the American social and economic system crumbled around it.

The question remains whether it would have been *possible* to harmonize moderate versions of all six values at one and the same time. The empirical answer seems to be that liberalism did not find a way to do so and for this reason it drew attacks from both right and left. Ironically, many liberals feel most comfortable when they are being attacked from both sides. That assures them that they truly must be located in the middle. There is, however, a crucial issue. Is liberalism being attacked for having taken a principled stand on the merits of an issue or for failing to take any stand but one that says certain regular procedures must be followed? It is a critical difference.

Liberalism's difficulty seems to go even deeper. If one holds moderate versions of each major value and accords equal weight to each, then as issues arise one will always face the need to "trade off" a little from first one value and then another. Harmonizing centrist versions of six emotionally charged and historically complex values of equal priority is itself a process of accommodation in which no rigid benchmarks are possible. But once a given value has been shaved or "traded off" in one case, it will be difficult not to do so in other cases. And thus all values become malleable in every case, and liberalism leaves itself vulnerable to the charge of being deliberately unprincipled.

PROBLEMS AND POSSIBILITIES

Liberalism's perceptions of the problems it should address are, naturally enough, linked to its versions of the basic values and to its past experiences.

The depression of the 1930s, World War II, the cold war, and the postwar imperative of continued economic growth — all of which liberalism credits itself with having handled effectively — loom large in liberalism's memory. What appeared to work as solutions then make up the storehouse from which to draw solutions today. It is difficult for a belief system to ease away from the problem definitions and proven remedies of the past, particularly when it remains in power. Intellectuals, political leaders, and continuing institutions like the Congress or a political party see some merit and certainly less risk in following previously broken paths. Established policies often have a self-reproducing character, such that they become the equivalent of the old patent medicines — remedies for any problem that is troubling.

Many of the problems that liberalism saw and sought to solve were real enough, but the more problems it addressed, the more seemed to blossom. Part of liberalism's difficulties was that it acknowledged a large number of problems as compelling. In attempting to respond, it applied temporary remedies to a great many of them without locating the fundamental causes. We shall take up only four important issues, but they illustrate the range of problems perceived and the kinds (and consequences) of the solutions applied.

One of liberalism's basic assumptions is that the private economy, in this case modern capitalism, provides a set of givens that serve as the background for all public decisions. Some liberals regularly complain that this makes for private affluence, leaving public needs poorly attended. But such complaints have by no means ruptured the basic complementarity of capitalism and liberalism. The concept of the free economic market is also a powerful element in liberal thinking, shaping approaches to understanding and ability to act. It is within this sort of context that liberals seek to solve the problems they see.

Four Leading Problems

One of liberalism's greatest concerns is to moderate the excesses and hardships of the free market's operation. It was just such goals that brought the current version of liberalism into being in the first place. In the early twentieth century, the national government, at the urging of the corporate and banking communities, accepted responsibility for stabilizing the economy, regulating competition, maintaining some sort of floor of security under individual workers, and setting standards of health and safety for consumer products and workers alike. National government regulation of business practices, particularly after certain scandals and excesses were exposed during the Depression, had become a thoroughly accepted principle. When consumer advocates and environmentalists urged greater protections, therefore, it was no basic change of direction for liberals to seek to achieve such ends through vastly expanded regulation.

For liberals, very close in importance to this first concern is the need for sustained economic growth. The ability to respond to new demands for expanded versions of equality and basic social services depended on expanding revenues. In turn, such revenues depended on the ability of corporations and the wealthy to pay increased sums in taxes, or, in other words, on steadily growing profits and incomes. The expansion of social services and retirement benefits is clearly redistribution from the rich to the poor. In the liberals' world, this redistribution is really practical only when the total economic "pie" is expanding. As long as the pie is growing, increments can be drawn off to serve new demands without incurring prohibitive resistance from the rich and/or current beneficiaries.

Thus, liberal success became intimately tied to sustained economic growth. For many liberals, the imperatives of growth threatened to dominate all policy considerations. Other liberals, however, began to lose sight of this imperative in their concern to respond to growing demands through increased regulations. As in other areas, liberal problem definitions and solutions began to conflict with each other.

Liberals also find the potential expansion of the Soviet Union, or of communism generally, to be a major problem. From the earliest days of the cold war, liberals have viewed most socialist, nationalist, or progressive movements in Third World countries as "communist inspired." And if communist, they are potentially dangerous to the United States. In part, this liberal emphasis was an attempt to counter the conservative claim that every change of government around the world amounted to a "loss" of that country to communism and it was the liberals' fault. But it also reflected a genuine anticommunism and concern for the containment of Soviet influence as well as a positive responsiveness to denials of civil liberties and procedural democracy.

The last key issue for liberals is the commitment to maintaining regular procedures and full civil liberties at all levels within the United States. Liberals must be able to believe that the established political processes are open and working. Otherwise, their confidence in the whole procedural mechanism for managing problems and fulfilling individual rights will be undermined. As a result, there is a continuing concern among liberals for the protection of freedom of speech, the separation of church and state, and the rights of all individuals to the economic and political opportunities provided by law.

A crucial part of the process is the possibility of vindicating legal rights in the courts. Social progress can almost be understood as the steady march of authoritative specification and expansion of individuals' legal rights. Thus, where people are not financially able to obtain the services of attorneys in order to pursue their legal rights, liberalism calls for government-provided lawyers. In this way, open conflict will be reduced and social change accommodated more readily.

The Liberal Solutions

The solutions that liberalism offers for these four problems are often mutually contradictory, always require an expanded state bureaucracy and technocratic expertise for implementation, and in other ways contain the seeds of their own ultimate failure. This may seem a harsh indictment, but it is one that liberals themselves began to make in the 1980s.

The concern for ameliorating the harshness of the free market economy, for example, led to extensive regulations and the administrative oversight capability to make them effective. Protection of the environment, the health and safety of workers, or the interests of consumers in safe and lasting products — all are better achieved by monitoring activities at the work place than by multiplying legal remedies to be pursued later in courts. But this means either massive new reporting requirements for businesses or an extensive network of personnel for regular inspections and enforcement — or both.

At some point, such expansion in administrative oversight becomes counterproductive. Business costs rise and growth is slowed, regulations conflict with each other, the technical expertise and required equipment places a heavy financial burden on the government, and/or political reaction is provoked. The prospect of effective resistance seems to grow as more efforts are made to really bring about the goals that initiated the regulatory effort.

A similar dilemma arises in efforts to "fine tune" the economy to accomplish steady growth. A vast body of data is needed, the collection and interpretation of which, while the ostensible province of experts, is nevertheless open to vigorous debate. The tool kit traditionally employed by liberals, at least since the Depression, is known as Keynesianism, after the English economist John Maynard Keynes. The basic principle is that government should manage the business cycle, eliminating both too rapid upturns (inflation) and excessive downturns (recession) through its fiscal policies. When the economy seems headed up too fast, government should put on the brakes by reducing its spending and increasing revenues. When the economy is declining or not growing fast enough, government should stimulate it by running a deficit, that is, by spending more than it takes in through taxes.

There are several problems with Keynesian theory, as the 1970s made clear. One is that it is not designed for periods when inflation and unemployment occur together. Its remedies cure one by causing the other. Thus, when the two occur together, any action taken will worsen the other. Nor does it work when inflation is caused by factors other than too much demand (or money) in search of consumer products. For example, fiscal policies cannot compensate for oil price increases or corporate pricing in monopoly situations.

Another problem is that it is politically easier to increase government spending than it is to cut spending or increase taxes. Keynesian deficits worked well to stimulate the economy in times of low inflation and high unemployment, as occurred in World War II and again in 1983. They are so effective that nearly all presidents and Congresses tend to stimulate the economy in these ways prior to elections. But Keynesianism has never been purposefully invoked to prevent excessive expansion, and liberals were politically unable and/or unwilling to attempt it while inflation was at its peak in the 1970s. Thus the liberal tool kit was ultimately unequal to the new conditions of that decade. Both Keynesianism and liberalism suffered accordingly.

Liberal efforts to cope with the other two problems illustrate the same tendencies. Liberal policies to contain communism, for example, reached their inevitable nadir in Vietnam. Despite mobilization of vast material and human resources, application of all the latest expertise and technology, and expenditure of hundreds of billions of dollars, the war was effectively lost. Measured liberal methods did not work. The United States appeared to be too involved to get out and yet unwilling to get involved enough to win. And so for the first time in history, the United States lost a war — and to a modest albeit determined Third World power. The repercussions in domestic politics and with regard to American influence around the world are still mounting ten years after the war's conclusion.

The liberal fixation on legal methods, particularly in the expansion of individual rights, also had unfortunate consequences. The volume of litigation leaped beyond all prior levels; overloaded courts fell further and further behind despite hundreds of new judicial appointments. A veritable "rights explosion" occurred. The best and brightest of a generation of college graduates were drawn into law schools and legal careers, while our leading economic competitors produced scientists, engineers, and managers. And yet it appears that little real progress was made by the courts in solving the various problems committed to the legal mechanisms.

In short, liberalism's perception of problems and choice of solutions succeeded only in binding liberalism ever more tightly in bonds of its own making. None of the solutions to which it was inclined seemed to work, at least for very long. Liberalism clearly faced increasing difficulties. It also faced new economic conditions — conditions that it probably could not cope with unless it departed in some basic way from the specific definitions and mix of values that it held. Such a departure would require repudiation of some part of that mix — that is, a shift away from liberalism itself. Liberalism was trapped. Meanwhile, the reaction began to build.

IMPLICATIONS AND PROSPECTS: THE NEW AMERICAN SPECTRUM

From the hindsight perspective of the 1980s, one might wonder if the real question shouldn't be not why liberalism seemed to collapse, but why it was so successful for so long. But to adopt this as the basic question would be to fail to understand liberalism's enduring strength as mainstream American political thought. Worse, it would tend to discount its future. Liberalism's longevity is owed to its flexibility and adaptability, which in turn are grounded in its emphasis on procedure rather than substance.

Liberalism is so closely linked to modern capitalism that in practice it functions as the latter's political-legal arm. Liberalism prospers when capitalism prospers. While growth was easily achieved, and before conflicting demands became problematic, liberalism effectively provided humane social services and various political opportunities for Americans of all classes and origins. It was the belief system and practical mechanism that sought to implement the American dream of material success, social mobility, and individual fulfillment. In many instances, it enabled individuals to realize those aspirations. In many others, it offered enough of a glimpse to be reassuring. And for most people, liberalism became synonymous with American democracy, in sharp contrast to other political systems in existence. Liberalism simply meant opportunity with security — economic, social, and political. It solved the problems of its day and earned broad acceptance.

And so we return to the original question. Why did this eminently practical and opportunistic governing belief system suddenly lose its support? What does this tell us about changing conditions and beliefs and about the future directions of American political thought? We suggested earlier that part of the reason for liberalism's collapse lay in its particular values, beliefs, and practices, part in the new economic and world conditions, and part in the massive reaction that the 1960s and early 1970s generated in the United States. We shall summarize the first of these briefly, and then take up the other two.

The Causes of Liberalism's "Collapse"

The first two decades after World War II should be recognized as a period of unprecedented affluence, widely if not fully distributed. New Deal–Great Society liberal principles seemed able to deliver, as well as promise, many things to many people — and all at once. The national government sustained military expenditures and social insurance programs of various kinds. It fine tuned the economy for continued domestic growth and promoted new investments and markets abroad. It contained communism and began to extend capitalist democracy to the Third World. And it furthered individual and civil rights at home. In this very success, however, lay the seeds of liberalism's collapse.

Inherent Characteristics of Liberal Values.   As we have seen, much of liberalism's success depended on the United States' postwar dominance and the opportunity thus provided for sustained economic growth. Competitive advantages and the availability of resources and markets enabled the biggest American corporations and banks to expand rapidly. Their earnings, shared with workers in the form of increased wages and the taxes supporting new social services, were the essential pillars of affluence. This practical "trickle down" distribution might not have occurred, of course, without continuing political pressure (through the liberal system) from ordinary people. Thus, some basis exists for the view that part of liberalism's problem today lies in "excessive" popular expectations.

But it was not only the apparent success of the New Deal–Great Society that led to its downfall. Its basic dual principle — protecting the individual while promoting business profitability — only postponed an inherent and inevitable conflict. Once the economic pie stops growing, conflict over its distribution, and redistribution, is bound to develop — particularly when some already believe that existing inequalities are unjust and should be changed. The image of a zero-sum society is now familiar; one person's gain seems possible only at the cost of another's loss.

The zero-sum principle seemed also to obtain in noneconomic fields such as social status. If an issue had to do with the respect and dignity accorded women or minorities, anything additional accorded to lower-status people seemed to be subtracted from those of higher status. Status seemed, in other words, to depend on there being somebody lower on the social ladder. Lower-middle-class white males were probably especially affected. The New Deal–Great Society government took responsibility for implementing civil rights that carried powerful status implications. Thereby it incurred risks that could only be postponed by the general economic affluence. Inevitably, when that affluence diminished, much of the resentment felt by those who saw others advancing on their hard-earned social status would focus on the liberal government that was the apparent agent of all this change.

Thus, by the early 1970s, when inflation overtook growth and real incomes began to drop, all of these potential conflicts were waiting to explode. Only renewed growth, with reduced unemployment and permanent control of inflation, could effectively defer such an explosion. But the nature of the American and world economies was changing rapidly, and growth was suddenly problematic. These changes raised compelling new questions for all political belief systems about both economic policy and the proper world role for the United States. Liberalism probably could not have extricated itself from the inertia of past problem definitions and remembered solutions even if it had had the appropriate new understanding and remedies in hand. In any event it did not.

Changes in World and National Economic Conditions. As always in hard times, economic analysis and proposals started to dominate political thinking. Hard times raise questions in many minds about how well the whole social-economic system is working and for whom. They pose potentially powerful threats to social stability and cause policymakers to cast about for new solutions with the promise of success. A deep recession — a politically costly cure for inflation — was the remedy eventually applied in 1981–1982. What remained unclear was what should be done about the more fundamental changes occurring in the American and world economies and how such policies might be incorporated in new or modified political belief systems.

The transformation underway has at least two dimensions. First, both *what* is produced in the world and *where* and *how* it is produced and sold are undergoing something like a revolution, a change comparable to that from agricultural to industrial economies in the nineteenth century. Instead of basic metals, heavy machinery, and labor-intensive durable goods, production is shifting toward lighter, high-technology, and energy-efficient items. Computers and other information-managing systems are increasingly employed to control production processes, keep records, and manage distribution. Their capabilities are leading to a "knowledge society." Jobs in the services sectors are rising steadily while jobs in heavy manufacturing are dropping even more sharply. The prospect of unemployability for many blue-collar workers in the older industries is high, and the prospect of widespread social dislocations is even higher.

The other dimension of the transformation stems from the rapid growth of integration and interdependence in the world economy. It is not only that most major corporations have become multinational in the scope of their operations. Components of various products move quickly from lowest-production-cost areas of the world to final-assembly locations and, as finished goods, to markets around the globe. Exports of American agricultural and manufactured goods, and increasingly services as well, make up a vital share of all gross profit and generate more than 20 percent of all jobs. The ability of the United States to export its goods and services depends on the economic prosperity of other countries, their trade policies and success in finding markets for their own exports, world currency values and stability, and so forth. The same is true for all the countries that are our trading partners. Nations of the world have never been as mutually dependent.

Economic success in this new world economy, however, depends on being able to compete effectively in the markets of the world. In this vital area, the United States suddenly found itself trailing other countries. Partly as a result of flows of American investment and the sale of technology abroad, foreign companies were able to exceed the productivity of American producers. For example, Americans learned in the late 1970s (with some shock) that the Japanese could produce cars that were better and priced lower than comparable-sized American models. And while Americans were losing ground in various areas, American per capita income dropped to tenth among the industrialized nations of the world. The country that had led the world in economic achievements during the postwar period appeared on the verge of being left behind.

Part of the reason for foreign companies' productive and competitive edge seemed to lie in their development of new forms of business-government cooperation. Investment, financing, and trade policies in Germany and Japan, for example, were closely coordinated by government agencies. Thus, new industries could be developed and markets captured in a quick and purposeful manner. In view of the vigorous governmental role in these successes, a major debate soon arose in the United States over whether the adoption of similar policies could return American companies to their former competitive position. The traditional American reluctance to accept deep government intervention in the economy stood in the way of such solutions, but the problem of declining competitiveness was widely acknowledged.

These profound world and national economic changes occurred simultaneously with a sharp reduction in the American capacity to influence events around the world. The failure of the massive U.S. military investment in Vietnam had many consequences. It revealed the limits to military power in distant parts of the world, particularly when U.S. power was offset by that of nations like the Soviet Union or China. It encouraged smaller countries to be bolder in seeking to serve their own interests, as in the cases of the oil price increases of the 1970s and the Iranian seizure of American hostages in 1979. And events like these in turn had repercussions. The oil price increases, for example, led to indebtedness on the part of non-oil-producing Third World nations that was of such magnitude as to threaten the stability of the world monetary system.

The United States is thus obliged to seek its goals in world affairs from a position of less relative strength and in the context of more potential dangers than at any other time in the post–World War II period. In both economic and military terms, the United States is at best first among equals and no longer the dominant voice. There are, of course, many ways of exercising power and influence still open to the American government, and in what many countries would consider ample supply. But the available tools and the nature of the problems are both very different from what they were before. All American political belief systems, and especially liberalism, must resolve issues concerning the proper American world role under these changed circumstances.

Americans' Reactions to Changes in the United States and the World. From the late 1960s on, many Americans began to display deeply negative reactions toward the changes that had occurred under liberal beliefs and government practices. Some of the negativity was directed toward the gains made by the various social movements of the liberal years. In the 1980s, some of these movements (such as womens' organizations and environmentalists) continue to actively press for their goals. Others (such as consumer and some minority groups) have lost some support and been forced to go on the defensive. But enough achievements and ongoing pressure exist to provoke anxiety and resentment even today.

The changes that have provoked reactions are not limited to the substantial tangible gains of organized groups and movements. They include changes in the most basic cultural values that underlie the social order and give it meaning. For example, many people feel that our highly valued *concept* of the family is threatened by the availability of divorce and abortions, freer sexual relations, and franker acknowledgment and acceptance of homosexuality. One result has been a recent focus on social issues, with various groups seeking legislation to reverse many of these changes. Religious movements in particular have engaged in political activity to restore former standards. Equally strong and widespread is the feeling that somehow Americans today no longer appreciate the importance of work and/or have lost their sense of purpose and self-confidence under liberal government.

We must add to this catalogue of reactions the effects on the country of the Vietnam War. The war caused deep social divisions and marked many people for life. For the tens of thousands of men and women directly involved, the war and its aftermath at home were a profoundly wrenching period. Despite their many sacrifices and troubling experiences in Vietnam, they not only were not appreciated when they returned home but were often ignored or even denigrated.

Equally troubling, the nation appeared to have lost a war for the first time in its history. This fact affected many millions more Americans, in a variety of ways that may not yet be fully visible. Some self-confidence was lost, and some greater pugnacity developed, as a result. The vigor of the opposition to the Panama Canal Treaty in the mid-1970s stemmed in part from resentments over a diminished American role in the world. National humiliation and frustration over the inability to rescue American hostages in Iran played a major role in President Jimmy Carter's defeat in 1980. The Reagan administration's effort to restore American military superiority and presence in the world is also part of the still-incomplete set of reactions to the Vietnam experience.

The combination of all of these conditions, problems, and reactions had led by the early 1980s to profound doubts among Americans about how well their government and their whole social order was working. Surveys showed confidence in national institutions and leaders to be at their lowest levels since such studies began in the 1960s. Beset by doubts and skepticism, many people sought new and more satisfying beliefs. At least for the moment, liberalism had lost both its popular appeal and its major thinkers. Its older stalwarts often moved to the right as neoconservatives; its rising younger leaders turned to technocratic, managerial, and cost-benefit criteria of action, assuming the label of neoliberalism. Both groups embraced capitalism's need for economic growth with an exclusivity and enthusiasm that would have embarrassed their liberal predecessors.

ADDITIONAL READINGS

Allen, Robert L. *Black Awakening in Capitalist America.* New York: Doubleday, 1969.

Blumberg, Paul. *Inequality in an Age of Decline.* New York: Oxford University Press, 1980.

Clecak, Peter. *Crooked Paths: Reflections on Socialism, Conservatism, and the Welfare State.* New York: Harper & Row, 1978.

Friedan, Betty. *The Feminine Mystique.* New York: Doubleday, 1965.

Galbraith, John Kenneth. *Economics and the Public Purpose.* Boston: Houghton Mifflin, 1973.

Hacker, Andrew. *The End of the American Era.* New York: Atheneum, 1971.

Hart, Jeffrey. *The American Dissent: A Decade of Modern Conservatism.* New York: Doubleday, 1966.

Hartz, Louis, *The Liberal Tradition in America.* New York: Harcourt, Brace, & World, 1955.

Kaufman, Arnold. *The Radical Liberal.* New York: Atherton, 1968.

Lowi, Theodore J. *The End of Liberalism.* New York: Norton, 1979.

Mitchell, Juliet. *Woman's Estate*. New York: Vintage Books, 1973.

Newfield, Jack. *A Prophetic Minority*. New York: Signet, 1966.

Rendon, Armando. *Chicano Manifesto*. New York: Macmillan, 1971.

Roszak, Theodore. *The Making of a Counter Culture*. New York: Anchor Books, 1969.

Smith, Duane, and Gerberding, William, eds. *The Radical Left: The Abuse of Discontent*. Boston: Houghton Mifflin, 1970.

Teodori, Massimo, ed. *The New Left: A Documentary History*.Indianapolis, Ind.: Bobbs-Merrill, 1969.

CHAPTER 4

Neoliberalism: Pragmatic Idealism and Industrial Policy

Neoliberalism presents itself as a modernized, adapted version of all that was good in John F. Kennedy style liberalism and as the appropriate successor for the 1980s and beyond. On the one hand, it is a quite new body of beliefs dating from the economic troubles of the late 1970s and the widespread rejection of the Carter administration. Under those conditions, many liberals began to distance themselves from the "old liberalism" that seemed to be collapsing. On the other hand, as we shall see, neoliberalism has deep roots in American thought and practice, drawing from Alexander Hamilton's ideas about using government to direct and support the private economy.

The defining characteristic of neoliberalism is, in terms that neoliberals often use, "pragmatic idealism," a "tough-minded" and "nonideological" approach that recognizes fiscal and other limits while still seeking to promote social justice and equity. Sometimes defined as "compassionate realism," neoliberalism purports to readily help those in real need without attempting to be all things to all people.

Most important, neoliberalism recognizes the absolute necessity of economic growth. Since growth depends primarily on the expansion and profitability of the private sector, American entrepreneurs and "risk takers" are enthusiastically encouraged. In view of the rapidly changing world economy, however, government policies are crucial to private success. Thus, major new policies and even institutional changes become necessary to enable the U.S. economy to recover its leading role.

Neoliberals also believe that the Soviet Union remains a hostile and expansionist nation which has now built up its military power to a truly dangerous level. As a result, the United States must make a major effort (but not the wastefully massive crash program of the Reagan administration) to restore both its nuclear deterrent and conventional capabilities. These steps are necessary in order to fulfill our limited but decisive role as leader of the free world, and so that we can proceed with the urgently needed arms limitation agreements from a position of parity.

Within the context set by these three primary principles, neoliberalism remains true to the commitment to a humane society. For example, minorities and women should be afforded full citizenship rights and enjoy genuine equality of opportunity. Scarce public funds will have to be conserved for the most needy. But a well-conceived government policy can itself go a long way toward assuring equity and social justice while maintaining progress toward a better society for all.

Neoliberals deny that they are merely liberals who have yielded to the supposed rightward movement of American political thinking. They vigorously insist that their program embodies new ideas synthesized with the humanitarian essence of liberalism. The result, they claim, is a realistic idealism that will be capable of inspiring and satisfying Americans to the end of the century and beyond. Restoration of American faith and hope is a central neoliberal goal. Indeed, it is seen as a necessity if the economic and social challenges of the day are to be successfully met.

THE ORIGINS AND EVOLUTION OF NEOLIBERALISM

We have suggested that neoliberalism fell heir to the technocratic, managerial component of liberalism when the latter fragmented. While neoconservatism got most of liberalism's strong anticommunism and the programmatic movements much of its reform impulse, neoliberalism inherited liberalism's pragmatic determination to make government work efficiently and effectively. Neoliberalism has real faith in the continued development of scientific, technological, and administrative capabilities. It is anxious to apply such expertise to the task of making government work better. Working better, moreover, means more than mere efficiency in fulfilling assigned tasks, which is important enough. It also means meeting the challenge of new conditions by furthering the cause of economic development in previously untried ways.

This is a significant and enduring strand in American thinking that links neoliberalism with the Kennedy and Franklin Roosevelt administrations, then reaches back to the Progressive Era and through it to the first patron of modern capitalism, Alexander Hamilton. Leading neoliberals like Senators Gary Hart and Paul Tsongas cite John Kennedy as the model for much of their political orientation. They also view the New Deal's celebrated nonideological pragmatism as the appropriate way to solve today's problems. For example, Tsongas says, "I view my approach as compassionate realism . . . non-ideological, clear-eyed realism. My interest is in what works, not what should work, and then within the boundaries of what works my interest is in the application of liberal democratic values."[1]

One model for efficient rationalization of a changing economy through the vehicle of the national government was provided in considerable detail by Herbert Croly's *Promise of American Life* in 1909. Croly was a close adviser to Theodore Roosevelt and later editor of *The New Republic*. He advocated "a Hamiltonian government for Jeffersonian ends," stressing the need for cooperation between big business and government. The model that shaped Croly's views and really underlies neoliberalism is Alexander Hamilton's creative approach to helping the private economy:

Capital is wayward and timid in lending itself to new undertakings, and the
State ought to excite the confidence of capitalists, who are ever cautious and
sagacious, by aiding them to overcome the obstacles that lie in the way of all ex-
periments. . . .

It is well known . . . that certain nations . . . enable their own workmen
to undersell and supplant all competitors in the countries to which those com-
modities are sent. Hence the undertakers of a new manufacture have to contend, not only with the natural disadvantages of a new undertaking, but with
the gratuities and remunerations which other governments bestow. To be able
to contend with success, it is evident that the interference and aid of their own
governments are indispensable.[2]

Practically every departure proposed by neoliberalism has its precedent in
one or another of Hamilton's innovations. The dominant principle of each
system is the bold use of government to promote economic growth, as much
self-sufficiency as possible, and independent strength in the world economy.

Two particular problems seem to have triggered the emergence of
neoliberalism. One was the apparent helplessness of the U.S. government
during the oil crisis of the mid and late 1970s. National security in both
economic and military terms seemed to be at stake. The crisis should have
created drastic and comprehensive long-range policies on the part of the national government. Instead, the "business as usual" approach of consumers
and businesses prevailed. The other problem was the obvious decline in productivity and competitiveness of the U.S. economy. This seemed to require a
major shift of government policies to encourage what was originally termed
"reindustrialization." Essentially, this meant "belt tightening" on the part of
the beneficiaries of government social programs, workers, and consumers so
that new incentives and assistance for business investment could be given
first priority. Again, the necessary policies were not adopted.

In both cases, the short-sightedness and selfishness of individuals and
special interests alike stood in the way. Everyone sought to serve their own
interests without regard for the whole, or national, interest. Neoliberalism
began to build on a felt need to use government coherently for the benefit of
the society considered as a whole. Government could no longer afford to act
as a trough from which all claimants could take whatever they demanded.
Experts began to talk of a need for sacrifice, even austerity, on the part of the
general populace in order that more investment could be made in new productive facilities and technological development.

White House adviser Amitai Etzioni gave voice to this kind of reindustrialization need in 1979, as did a special issue of *Business Week* in June
1980.[3] At the same time, Senator Paul Tsongas—long a highly rated
liberal—startled the annual convention of Americans for Democratic Action
by launching a critique of many long-standing liberal principles.[4] In particular, he called for revitalizing American industry through encouraging
private enterprise and ending a variety of supports for organized labor.

But it was after the election of 1980 that neoliberalism really came of
age. The Democratic party generally was on the defensive, apparently lacking any new ideas or alternatives to the free market and "supply side" pro-

grams of the Reagan administration. Into the breach came several economists with a variety of proposals for a new "industrial policy." These were essentially proposals for the creation of new private enterprise opportunities through a variety of government inducements, subsidies, and protections. They are spelled out in works including Lester Thurow's *The Zero-Sum Society*, Robert Reich and Ira Magazine's *Minding America's Business* and Reich's *The Next American Frontier*, and several articles by the New York financier Felix Rohatyn.[5]

A number of other well-credentialed liberals like Charles Peters of the *Washington Monthly* as well as Hart and Tsongas expanded neoliberalism from its core of economic renewal policy into other dimensions of traditional political and social liberalism.[6] Journals like *The New Republic* and many members of Congress soon joined the neoliberal ranks. Liberalism's collapse was almost celebrated in the rush to articulate a new body of beliefs (and hopefully, after Reagan, government practices) to take its place.

NEOLIBERALISM'S BASIC VALUES

Neoliberalism has made some significant adaptations of the mainstream American values. Particularly noticeable is the way that, unique for a centrist belief system, it has rather comfortably come to terms with the use of the national government. Neoliberalism proposes to transcend conflict between individuals and special interest groups, disdains adversarial processes generally, and seeks to rise above "politics as usual" in order to define and act on a shared public interest. While asserting respect for risk takers and the free economic market, neoliberals nevertheless propose a more legitimate allocative role for government than it has ever had. Generally, the government would act on behalf of agreements made by business, labor, and government. Small wonder that, at least in its early stages, neoliberalism was far more popular among former liberals and Democrats than among business executives. Let us see how modest changes in several basic values add up to neoliberalism.

The first important modification, significantly, occurs with respect to *individualism*. In "A Neoliberal's Manifesto," Charles Peters, after delivering a critique of liberalism, declares in opposition "the primary concerns of neoliberalism: community, democracy, and prosperity." Although most of his argument addresses ways of accomplishing prosperity, he is very clear on the importance of community. There is no mention of individualism as such. Rather, he deplores a divided nation and, specifically, "the politics of selfishness that has divided this country for more than a decade." In Peters' eyes, "the adversary approach to problems has come to dominate our national life, at a disastrous cost to all of us."[7]

The sense of a compelling need to find, articulate, and then implement the national interest is relatively new in American politics. And the idea of a national interest as a whole, larger than the sum of the interests of its parts, is certainly new to the center of the spectrum. Both conservatives and radicals are confident that they can identify a "national interest." But liberals have traditionally either denied that there was any such thing or viewed it solely as the net product of individual interests. Neoliberals are backing away from such views. They argue that it left liberalism paralyzed, unable to act coherently in behalf of long-range social and economic needs that did not have a powerful current advocate.

How great a departure is involved in this assertion of primacy for the notion of national interest over self-serving individualism? The rejection of self-interest as a basis for action is a theme that runs through many neoliberals' writings. Lester Thurow, for example, derides "rugged individualism" and calls for "company loyalty" instead. Gary Hart talks about "the many," "all," and "justice" in direct opposition to "the few" and "personal greed." And Peters describes our pressing need for "a rebirth of patriotism, a rebirth of devotion to the interests of the national community, of the conviction that we're all in this together and that therefore fair play and justice for everyone is the vital concern for us all."[8] Some of this emphasis on national interest may be attributable to the context of economic crisis in which much of this work was written. Moreover, as we shall see, it is tempered somewhat by other neoliberal emphases: the emphasis on merit-based standards and the celebration of individual entrepreneurial efforts as a necessary part of economic growth. But depite such qualifications, this aspect of neoliberalism remains a significant departure from mainstream individualism of the past.

A second major adaptation in values concerns the notions of *freedom and property*. Economic growth is so vital to every other goal that entrepreneurs must be freed to use their property in more creative ways than has been the case. In short, there must be more freedom for property to produce wealth. But changing world conditions make government assistance essential to the success of business. Thus the needs of business begin to define the priorities of government. This ultimately leads to new mechanisms for achieving agreement between business, labor, and government, so that government may have a blueprint to carry out. But we are getting ahead of our story.

Neoliberals want to encourage growth by setting free the risk takers, the old-fashioned American entrepreneurs. As Peters says, immediately after listing the three principles of neoliberalism quoted above:

> Economic growth is most important now. It is essential to almost everything else we want to achieve. Our hero is the risk-taking entrepreneur who creates new and better products. . . . We want to encourage the entrepreneur not with Reaganite policies that simply make the rich richer, but with laws specifically and precisely designed to help attract investors and customers. . . . We also favor freeing the entrepreneur from economic regulation that discourages desirable competition.[9]

Only economic growth will succeed in defusing the conflict that is captured in Thurow's metaphor of the "zero-sum society," in which every gain by some is an equivalent loss to others. Tsongas makes this point quite explicitly:

> Liberalism, the vehicle that carries generosity and compassion into the public arena, needs a healthy economy. A stagnant economy is, by definition, illiberal. If the economy is expanding, we can open our hearts to the aspirations of others, since the growth can accommodate their demands. If the economy stagnates, or declines, those aspirations can be met only at the expense of other segments of society. All of us end up fighting for the same share of the pie.[10]

But these endorsements of growth suggest that neoliberalism has reversed the priorities assigned by liberalism to equality and freedom/property rights. Under liberalism, equality seemed to be expanding in meaning, challenging freedom for first place; here it is clearly relegated to a subordinate position. Freedom to produce new wealth is the highest priority, and all others follow. But, as all neoliberals would hasten to add, the freedom they endorse is not Reaganite unlimited freedom for the rich to do whatever they want. Rather, it is freedom channeled by broad public needs and goals, as expressed by the triumvirate of business, labor, and government.

And what of *equality* or *justice* in the neoliberal rank order of values? It seems quite clear that equality is being returned, more or less, to the older definition of equality of opportunity. Social justice, too, is being equated with equality of opportunity. And together they receive reduced priority because they have to be adapted to a rank order shaped by the expansion of freedom and property mandated by the overwhelming need for growth. So redefined, equality and justice are genuine neoliberal goals. Gary Hart offers a typical statement:

> The litmus test of justice in a democratic society is equality— both equality of rights and equality of opportunity. We have more to do on both counts before true justice is realized. Our nation still must fulfill its promise of equal rights for all. Our Constitution still does not afford equal rights for women as well as for men. . . . Minorities still are discouraged from exercising their basic right to vote. Our society has yet to offer all its citizens equality of opportunity — a fair chance for both economic advancement and the "pursuit of happiness" promised by our Declaration of Independence."[11]

This is about as strong a statement on behalf of equality and justice that one can find among neoliberals. More often endorsement of these values is qualified carefully by concern for economic growth, as in the following lines from Tsongas:

> Although in some sense it is "justice" that can claim moral superiority for our society, it is actually the nurturing of incentive that is the essential condition for achieving justice. The reason is that if we maximize "justice" we destroy the conditions for economic growth. In more speific terms, if you maximize all your "just" social programs, the costs would be so burdensome as to cripple the economy, leading to sharply reduced governmental revenues, and the collapse of those very programs as a result. . . . Americans have a deep-seated desire for

a better future, one with the promise of more "justice" for their children. The only hope for this brighter future, however, lies in restoring the goose to health — this is essential for a fair distribution of golden eggs to our children.[12]

Neoliberalism is particularly committed to educational opportunity because education serves the needs not only of individual citizens but also of greater competitiveness and increased economic growth. A characteristic statement by Charles Peters reveals this emphasis:

Our concern about the public school system illustrates a central element of neoliberalism: It is at once pragmatic and idealistic. Our practical concern is that public schools have to be made better, much better, if we are to compete economically with other technologically advanced countries. . . . Our idealistic concern is that we have to make these schools better if the American dream is to be realized.[13]

Neoliberalism at first seems to offer less change in regard to the value of *democracy* than in regard to the other values discussed. Peters ranked democracy as one of neoliberalism's three "primary concerns," but the notion is undefined and its requirements unexamined. There are similar endorsements from almost every other neoliberal as well as an equivalent lack of analysis of what democracy means or what (if any) obligations it entails. The conclusion seems warranted that by "democracy" they intend traditional procedural democracy.

However, when we reach the neoliberal program for political revitalization, we shall see that one implication of the new arrangements for mobilizing cooperation behind decisive government action is a reduction in democratic participation. Thus it may be that neoliberalism actually involves a contraction in the public decision-making role from that traditionally offered by procedural democracy. This is a controversial issue which must be deferred until we take up the neoliberal proposals for change in political structures and practices.

With respect to the concept of human nature, neoliberals clearly draw back from the more reformist liberals' sense that people are or could be cooperative, good, and rational. Images of excessive selfishness requiring change or control abound in neoliberal writings. Speaking with specific reference to rivalry with the Soviet Union, but clearly intending his point to have general application, Tsongas expresses a characteristic neoliberal assumption:

Man's instinct for survival is paramount. In many respects it is the ultimate reality. . . . Man views man as aggressive, and that aggressiveness is in evidence in every walk of life. Sports are the most obvious example, but our entire free enterprise system is based on aggressiveness. . . . To a degree we all inherit a basic aggressiveness, and political philosophy must take this into account.[14]

Individually, these refinements in the basic values are relatively modest. However, when taken together, and when applied in neoliberal proposals for solving today's problems, they begin to add up to a substantial new role for government in serving the needs of the private economy. It is this latter feature that gives neoliberalism its distinctive character as a body of beliefs and establishes it as a potentially important transitional category.

PROBLEMS AND POSSIBILITIES: THE NEOLIBERAL ANALYSIS AND PROGRAM

What went wrong—with liberalism, with the United States—to bring about the economic decline and political changes that were evident in 1980? Neoliberals believe we failed to keep up with changing conditions and continued to think and act in accordance with an outmoded ideology. What is needed now is a strong dose of *realism*, followed by the (by now familiar) *pragmatic idealism*. Neoliberals may overstate a bit their sense of changed conditions in order to distinguish their views from old liberalism. But it is clear that assessments of these new conditions are a major factor in shaping their principles. Gary Hart, for example, first complains about our leaders' penchant for "forcing today's problems into the framework of yesterday's world" and debating only "false choices which ensure wrong answers." He then goes on to declare:

> These outmoded debates are being rendered increasingly irrelevant by a new set of realities emerging in the 1980s and 1990s. They include international economic competition and the resulting domestic industrial dislocation; instability in the international financial community resulting from huge governmental debts; the emergence of an information and service economy; the proliferation of nuclear materials, technologies, and capabilities; increased toxicity in our environment; biogenetic research breakthroughs; global water and land shortages; third-world nationalism; energy supply and price manipulation; and a communications revolution, among others.[15]

Similarly, Tsongas sees current policies as "taking America on a collision course with reality." He focuses on eight key realities—"finite energy resources, Soviet aggressiveness, economic productivity, resource allocation, Third World nationalism, international trade competition, environmental overload, and inflation."[16] We shall explore within three general categories some of the problems that neoliberals see today and attribute to failures to properly address these new "realities."

Problems

U.S. Economic Problems. Neoliberals are very well provided with statistics showing the decline of the American economy in comparison with both its own past performance and the performance of other industrial economies. One of the most comprehensive of these comparisons is given by Robert Reich and Ira Magaziner in their *Minding America's Business.* Reich and Magaziner include a devastating indictment of both business management and government policy. Much of the neoliberal analysis can be summed up in the concept of competitiveness. American products are no longer competitive in world economic markets. They are more costly, not as well made, and not as aggressively marketed as products of other countries such as Japan or Germany. Therefore they do not sell in the volume needed to make the American economy prosperous. The fault readily can be allocated among government, management, and labor.

Reich introduced the term "industrial policy" into the American vocabulary, using it to refer to all the economy-related policies of a government. The chief neoliberal complaint, of course, is that government has been used incoherently, in response to special interests, rather than with a comprehensive overall design. In their book, Reich and Magaziner claim that "the United States has an irrational and uncoordinated industrial policy. . . . It is an industrial policy by default, in which government and business are inextricably intertwined but in which the goal of international competitiveness has not figured."[17] The U.S. government talks free trade, that is, of keeping borders open for the free exchange of goods and services. But it acts in irrational and selfish ways to protect politically powerful American producers (and thereby risks foreign retaliation), rather than following coherent plans to help either exporters or importers. Tax laws encourage nonproductive investments, overseas investments, and other uses of capital that do not result in improved ability to produce efficiently in the United States.

Management failures include short-term profit orientations, in which immediate results are sought at the expense of long-term development of plants and other facilities. Reich coined the term "paper entrepreneurialism" to refer to the creation of the appearance of profits from such nonproductive activities as mergers, takeovers, and tax-minimizing behavior. Both he and other neoliberals have expressed regret about American society's production of many lawyers but relatively few scientists, engineers, and managers, a pattern in total contrast to that of Japan or Germany.

But it is organized labor that draws neoliberalism's greatest criticism. High wages and extensive benefits are often blamed for raising the production costs and reducing the competitiveness of major American industries. Reduced productivity (i.e., fewer units produced per labor hour invested) is blamed on increased safety regulations and other work rules in American industry or on simple lack of effort on the part of workers. Few neoliberals charge corporations or investors with seeking higher-profit investments elsewhere or deliberately failing to invest their capital in modernization of American plants and facilities. Instead, they blame workers for their refusal to link wage increases to productivity increases and to give up seniority, benefits, or the work rules gains of the last decades. Peters succinctly states this position:

> In both the public and private sector, unions were seeking and getting wage increases that had the effect of reducing or eliminating employment opportunities for people who were trying to get a foot on the first rung of the ladder. . . . Our

support for workers . . . does not mean support for unions that demand wage increases without regard to productivity increases. That such wage increases have been a substantial factor in this country's economic decline is beyond reasonable doubt.[18]

Other neoliberals have explicitly called for widespread wage and working condition concessions by labor. These would be followed by greater flexibility on the part of management and even some exploration of worker ownership incentives. The title of a 1982 article in *The Washington Monthly* suggests neoliberalism's message—"Industrial America's Suicide Pact"—but the real call is for wage and benefit concessions by labor. Similarly, Tsongas chides labor for its poor public image and loss of membership. He says:

> The only way it [unionism] can reverse its current decline is to present a new face to America: tougher, leaner, more flexible, more innovative, concerned about efficiency and productivity, and intolerant of featherbedding. . . . Steel mills, automobile assembly plants, electronic component facilities, all should have workers who think constantly about their Japanese, West German, and Swiss counterparts. These are the "enemy" in the long run. The mission, then, is a kind of partnership necessary to hold off the enemy, not only for today but also for the future.[19]

Neoliberals are also concerned about the scope of social dislocations sure to follow in the wake of what they see as the major economic transformation underway. The decline of heavy industries and the rise of new technologies, which will bring with them the new knowledge society and services occupations, mean widespread changes in who will be employed, where, and in what sorts of jobs. Many American jobs have been exported to low-wage Third World countries. Many others are moving to the South and West. Some are simply disappearing, to be replaced by fewer jobs for much more highly skilled people. These emerging problems make urgent the need for thoughtful, long-term use of government to shape the society's adaptation to its inevitable future. All of this, of course, means that the current performance of government must be reversed.

The Failures of Government. There are many policy failures of government, some of them already suggested above. Particularly important to neoliberals are failures with respect to energy, export-import trade, and inflation. Energy consumption should have been reduced and conservation fostered, transitional fuels brought to the point of readiness against the time when they will be needed, and research and development spurred for long-term fuel sources such as nuclear fusion and solar photovoltaics. Exports should be promoted more aggressively, with financing assistance if needed. And imports should be temporarily reduced or prohibited as necessary to help weak producers modernize or shift capital into other areas. Inflation should be addressed much more vigorously, through budget controls, fiscal policies, and tighter governmental controls over the economy.

But policy errors are always likely and can usually be corrected in time. What concerns neoliberals even more are two factors that relate to the question of the government's *capacity* to accomplish whatever ends it is assigned. One is the matter of overload. Neoliberals believe that government has been asked to do too many things on behalf of too many people and interests. In part, this is another dimension of neoliberalism's attack on self-seeking individual and special interest behavior in a zero-sum situation where the major loser is the national interest as a whole. A favorite neoliberal line is, "If you want the government off your back, take your hand out of its pocket." But it is also a critique of government's own reaching out to endlessly multiply rules and regulations, with the result that fewer and fewer of them can be intelligently administered.

The second factor addresses the character and attitude of government bureaucracies themselves. Peters, from his Washington location, is particularly critical of the lack of performance standards in government, the emphasis on credentials, and the unwillingness to insist upon excellence. He says:

> We aren't against government, period, as — with the exception of the national security apparatus — many conservatives appear to be. But we are against a fat, sloppy, and smug bureaucracy. We want a government that can fire people who can't or won't do the job. . . . Neoliberals share this concern with actual performance because they want to encourage productivity and discourage the bureaucratization that credentialism fosters and that has become one of the most severe problems in our government and in our large corporations. The search for credentials is also undermining our economic prosperity.[20]

Neoliberals share the neoconservatives' expressed distaste for the "new class" of intellectuals, who appear to disdain patriotic, religious, and family values. They see a thinly veiled contempt for ordinary people on the part of bureaucratic liberal "social engineers" and believe this may indicate lack of faith in democracy.

The Soviet Threat and the Imperatives It Poses

Neoliberalism is convinced that the Soviet military buildup mandates substantial expansion of U.S. military capabilities. The nature of the American military buildup to be undertaken, moreover, amounts to a brief summary of neoliberal principles. It is heavy on new technological developments, enhanced managerial capabilities, and frugality. The goal is not superiority ("madness," according to Tsongas), but an enduring parity that provides the basis for mutually advantageous arms limitations agreements. Nuclear proliferation is so dangerous to the entire world that rational steps to control such weapons must be taken soon, before it is too late.

At the same time, major efforts must be made to help Third World countries toward economic stability and independence. Neoliberals recognize that the Soviet Union stands to gain from instability but refuse to see Soviet agitation behind most nationalist or economic justice movements in Third

World countries. As disciples of JFK, they believe in economic assistance and support of indigenous nationalist movements. Once again, they oppose the hawkish Reagan policies but see themselves as much more determined and "realistic" than liberals of the last decade.

Programs

As neoliberalism moves from analysis of problems toward programs to solve them, the world seems to be characterized by a general drift and decline that clearly calls for new kinds of government action. Neoliberals are almost as probusiness as the Reagan administration, but from an entirely different perspective. They deny that the Reagan combination of laissez-faire reliance on the free market and favoritism for the rich few will succeed in benefiting the many whose interests depend on renewed economic growth.

Only a well-designed and comprehensive program of government incentives, assistance, and upgrading of both physical infrastructure and human resources will generate a period of sustained and widespread prosperity. No single business or industry, or even the entire business community, has the perspective or capacity to forgo immediate advantages and act in the long-range interest of the whole economy. Besides, much of what business needs, such as trade agreements, currency valuations, and favorable fiscal policies, can, almost by definition, only be provided by government. The free market is simply inadequate as a device to serve the needs of sustained growth. The sooner that enlightened businesspeople come to terms with this new reality, the better.

In moving from basic values to analysis of problems to proposed solutions, we run the risk of making any set of developing beliefs appear far more rational and coherent than it actually is. Some belief systems are highly concerned with the nature of their values and not much given to specific programs, while others seem to be consumed by policy proposals and little interested in deep reflection on their animating values. This latter is particularly true of neoliberalism, with its special pride in pragmatic and "nonideological" problem solving.

Neoliberals do not first clarify their values and then march systematically to solutions. Perhaps more than the adherents of other belief systems, they find their values in the patterns of solutions they work out for problems and *then* celebrate them. We earlier noted that the full implications of some of the value changes being made by neoliberalism would not be evident until we had examined the details of the neoliberal program. Here we shall survey five major components of that program. We shall then return to the question of neoliberalism's values and its vision for the future.

Industrial Policy.   Neoliberalism is distinguished by the comprehensive approach it takes to economic renewal. In the context of neoliberalism's image of decline and transformation in the U.S. economy, government has multiple policy obligations. First, it must set up a system of incentives and financial assistance to enable the shift of capital from older, declining industries to the areas of future opportunity, principally in high-technology production and applications. This could mean national development banks or loan guarantee programs, retraining and/or relocation assistance for workers, and various forms of aid to communities affected by the massive shifts of capital and jobs.

Next, government should articulate import restrictions with export promotion so that declining industries gain temporary protection and new producers are able to enter potential markets promptly. Declining industries should be helped only for the period it takes to modernize and return to competitiveness or to orderly shift capital and workers to new uses. National government assistance should come with strings attached. Recipient companies may be required to make specific improvements in facilities or practices. Or the government may insist that workers or public representatives be given seats on the board of directors.

A related program would be international financial policies to stabilize currency values, maintain export markets, and promote regular repayment of existing debts. The massive debts piled up by Third World countries soon after the oil price increases of the 1970s represent a serious danger to the international banking system. If debtor countries cannot earn dollars by exporting their products, they cannot repay their debts. U.S. banks are some of the biggest lenders and highly vulnerable (together with the world's monetary system) to any inability or refusal on the part of such countries to repay.

Greater energy independence is another important part of neoliberal industrial policy. This requires a sustained emphasis on conservation and greater efficiency in all energy usage as well as development of alternative sources. Such changes could be accomplished in part through taxation and other incentive policies. Although the greatest emphasis is on developing renewable energy sources to the fullest possible extent, nuclear energy is not ruled out as one of the necessary sources.

Neoliberals also champion a major and sustained program to rebuild the infrastructure of the American economy. It is estimated that U.S. highways, bridges, terminals, water and sewer systems, etc., will require hundreds of billions of dollars in repair and improvements over the next decade. If funds could be made available, this effort would also help to stimulate the economy. Neoliberals would also provide widespread training and retraining of workers as a form of infrastructure development in human capital.

Neoliberals propose a variety of new institutions for negotiating agreements between business, labor, and government and for planning the implementation of these programs. Some, like the New York investment banker Felix Rohatyn (architect of the financial "rescue" of New York City in the mid-1970s), believe that a large new development bank run by leading bankers should do the job. Gary Hart urges a presidentially focused process in which all relevant interests are represented and work out agreements. Others prefer economic advisory councils of various kinds which, in most cases, report to the Congress. The first question is what kind of national economic planning should be undertaken. The second, and equally important, question is whether planning should occur in an open, political process or in a process protected from politics and managed by insiders and experts.

Tax Reform.   Neoliberals consider the present tax system unfair, irrational, and inefficient. Riddled with advantages for special interests, it is a testimonial to political power rather than public purpose. It should be made simpler, fairer, and more effective in promoting the goals of industrial policy. Some neoliberals, like Senator Bill Bradley, have proposed flat-rate, two-level taxes that eliminate most deductions. Gary Hart has made the most comprehensive proposals for linking taxes with price and wage levels, taxing spending in order to encourage savings and investment, and simplifying the entire system.

Education for Excellence and Competitiveness.   Neoliberals focus particularly on education as the means to restore American leadership in various fields. In this emphasis, they are hardly unique. But it serves well as the primary outlet for their commitment to equality of opportunity and fits their sense that merit-based standards need to be revived. Neoliberals see a need for a major federal role, both in funding and in encouraging particular types of research and experimentation. With regard to education, their basic position is again that only a national perspective, in which all our needs are identified and ranked and resources allocated efficiently to meet them, can be adequate to solving the acute problems that exist.

The major goals to be served by this educational renaissance are the restoration of American competitiveness in business and leadership in science and technology. The national interest is the first beneficiary, individuals' opportunities are secondary. In 1983, two prestigious national commissions, though appointed by the Reagan administration, issued reports consonant with these neoliberal goals. Both made a major point of education's relevance to the ability of American producers to compete in the world marketplace.

Expanding U.S. Military Power.   The revitalization of the American economy and the expansion of military power are linked to achieving a single goal: restoring the United States to its world leadership position. No neoliberal sees these as separable. Neoliberals are nearly as concerned with the growing Soviet threat as they are with economic renewal. The U.S. military buildup, however, should be a measured, cost-effective program in which improved management receives as much attention as new weapons. Some neoliberals advocate resumption of the draft in order to have a military that is representative of the population it is intended to serve. Some advocate a wider national obligation in which all young people would serve their country in some capacity for two years soon after high school.

Restoring Political Vitality and Government Capacity.   Neoliberals are committed to finding a way to rise above the individual self-seeking, special interest powers, and adversary process of American politics. They seek a more decisive government with full capacity to act in the general public interest. But they also want a way to link the democratic expression of public preferences with that new governmental capacity. Indeed, neoliberals can sound almost conservative when they talk about the need for decisive government action despite probable opposition from various sides. Lester Thurow offers an example:

> Our society has reached a point where it must start to make explicit equity decisions if it is to advance. . . . We have to be able to decide when society should take actions to raise the income of some group and when it should not take such actions. If we cannot learn to make, impose, and defend equity decisions, we are not going to solve any of our economic problems.[21]

Political pressures constitute a major problem for government's capacity to make reasoned decisions in the public interest. Neoliberals have not resolved the question of whether to try to find ways to achieve agreement in an open, political process or to simply insulate government decision makers against politics and try to legitimate their decisions in some other way. Thurow advocates efforts to restore the participatory opportunities and bargaining, accommodating role of political parties. Peters urges cutting back civil service protections to provide greater appointment powers for newly elected presidents and much expanded public opportunities to hold government jobs. Felix Rohatyn, on the other hand, argues the need for a "government of national unity" that would be above politics. He says:

> The country's problems are so deep-seated, domestically and internationally, economically and socially, that even temporary and partial solutions (and that is probably the best that can be achieved) will, in my view, be beyond any one man, one party, one ideology. They will require an enormous bipartisan effort.[22]

Neoliberalism has not yet found a way to solve the problems it sees and probably could not unless it came into power. Even then, the grip of the free market imagery on American political thinking is so great that neoliberalism's proposed new role for government would probably have difficulty gaining acceptance without the most convincing demonstration.

IMPLICATIONS AND PROSPECTS

Neoliberalism is distinguished by the fact that it proposes to extend the Hamiltonian use of government further than has ever been contemplated. This would amount to a major reversal of the dominant free market principle of American political thinking. No doubt that principle would continue to be honored in rhetoric for some time, but it would nevertheless have been fundamentally changed in meaning.

If neoliberalism were successful in gaining the willing involvement of business, labor, and government — and in constructing mechanisms that would permit agreements to be reached and implemented — it would create a government capability unprecedented in American experience. With this new government role would come a managerialism and technocratic role for experts that would exceed even that of the early New Deal or the most engineering-oriented days of the Great Society. Data gathering and interpretation, technical analyses and policy recommendations, and comprehensive oversight would all be vital to effective central direction of this sort.

But if the neoliberal framework were in place, many people from both left and right would probably be concerned about the emergence of a corporatist system. The term "corporatist" is usually applied to those political-economic systems in which all major interests are brought together in some way so that government can act decisively. This is ostensibly done for the good of the whole, but in practice it has always been for the benefit of the few most powerful individuals or corporations.

Neoliberalism would have to be ready to show how its new system avoided the dangers of rule by a few that corporatism historically poses in the name of efficiency and the national interest. The idea of "national unity" for the purpose of meeting a grave crisis is naturally an attractive one. As long as there is widely shared agreement about the nature of the crisis, and a sense that both sacrifices and benefits are being equally distributed, the idea seems compatible with democracy.

But the need for "a government of national unity" has historically been a rallying call for those who have grown impatient with the inefficiencies or incapacities of democracy. It is a call that could here, as it has elsewhere, mask efforts to detach real decision making from popular control. This may be one of the reasons John Anderson's "National Unity Party" has not experienced much success, even though it is centrist and thoroughly neoliberal in its programs. (Probably a more important reason is the bias of the American electoral system against third parties.)

Discussion of the prospect of corporatism usually calls up images of business leadership, or at least eagerness on the part of business to be first among equals in a newly centralized system. This is certainly not the case in the United States today. Neoliberalism has a major selling job ahead, as its proposed business constituency seems at best tentative and skeptical and often openly opposed. Neoliberalism has had success with the most "progressive" larger corporations and banks, particularly those heavily involved in international markets, trade, and investments. But the basic business response to neoliberal programs has been one of skepticism and clear preference for Reaganite "free market" policies, that is, reductions in taxes and regulations and general withdrawal of government from "intervention" in the economy.

Organized labor, on the other hand, has been a grudging supporter of neoliberal industrial policy — even if it has resented being the target of frequent neoliberal criticism. In the context of current pressures for givebacks and concessions, together with declining membership, labor has been hard put to find a new policy it could be *for*. Given this lack of alternatives and the fact that labor's semiautomatic influence within liberalism is no longer meaningful, industrial policy has apparently seemed the least damaging option.

Neoliberalism could well argue that it is effectively offering to save organized labor as a viable force in American politics by including it in the business-labor-government triumvirate to be given decisive new power. If neoliberalism's perception of a high-technology and services future is correct, for example, organized labor might not be able to look forward to anything but continued decline. Neoliberal support may come at a high price, but one that at least assures continued existence.

Both of the above reflections suggest that neoliberalism today amounts to a still inchoate set of beliefs in search of a solid constituency. It is in effect a transitional category not yet fully formed or located on the evolving American spectrum. The intriguing question is, transitional to what? We have suggested that the essence of neoliberalism may be its perceived need for, and insistent justification of, a much more pervasive role for government in the economy and society. What neoliberalism sees at stake is the adaptation of the society to the fast-changing future. What it is striving for is a decisive vehicle to facilitate that adaptation while preserving the basic framework. In this sense it is truly conservative, in the classic manner. But in the United States it is forced to defend what looks like a radical program.

Neoliberals are increasingly clear in their understanding of what is at stake. They are searching for ways to communicate the urgency of the need for an instrument of adaptation. Lester Thurow, for example, has stressed his belief that very broad changes are needed, even though he immediately adds that he does not expect others necessarily to agree:

> The time has come. . . to admit that the pursuit of equity and equal economic opportunity demands a fundamental restructuring of the economy. Everyone who wants to work should have a chance to work. But there is no way to achieve that situation by tinkering marginally with current economic policies. The only solution is to create a socialized sector of the economy designed to give work opportunities to everyone who wants them but cannot find them elsewhere.[23]

And Robert Reich bluntly states the long-term nature of the neoliberal perspective and program: "We're building new frameworks. Administrations come and go. The frameworks can remain for generations."[24]

What neoliberalism counts on is the capacity of this new program to mobilize support from a large number of people who recognize the need to think freshly about the country's broad range of unprecedented problems. It is not just economic revitalization that they seek, but social and political revitalization as well. As Charles Peters notes, that will require willingness to take risks—the risks that necessarily accompany opportunity:

> Risk is indeed the essence of the movement—the risk of the person who has the different idea in industry or in government. . . . Risk-taking is important not only in career terms but in the way one looks at the world and the possibilities it

presents. If you see only a narrow range of choices, if you are a prisoner of conventional, respectable thinking, you are unlikely to find new ways out of our problems.[25]

Despite its respectable origins, neoliberalism seems at this point to be caught in much the same way that reform liberalism always was. It offers a plausible and in essence not very threatening route to social and economic improvement. However, when it comes down to actual implementation, its program seems too radical for more than a small portion to be carried out. Most difficult of all is mobilizing a constituency around a program designed to save capitalism when the capitalists themselves are demonstrably unenthusiastic. Only prolonged economic crisis, with more drastic solutions being urged from both left and right, can really provide the context for neoliberalism to gain strength enough to be a decisive force. If such developments occurred, however, neoliberalism could succeed to liberalism's center role on the American spectrum.

ADDITIONAL READINGS

"America's Competitive Challenge: The Need for a National Response." Washington, D.C.: Business–Higher Education Forum, April 1983.

"A Nation At Risk: The Imperative for Educational Reform." Washington, D.C.: National Commission on Excellence in Education, April 1983.

Etzioni, Amitai. *An Immodest Agenda: Rebuilding America Before the 21st Century.* New York: McGraw-Hill, 1983.

Hart, Gary. *A New Democracy: A Democratic Vision for the 1980s and Beyond.* New York: Quill, 1983.

Peters, Charles. "A Neoliberal's Manifesto." *Washington Monthly,* May 1983.

Reich, Robert. *The Next American Frontier.* New York: Times Books, 1983.

Reich, Robert, and Magaziner, Ira. *Minding America's Business: The Decline and Rise of the American Economy.* New York: Harcourt Brace Jovanovich, 1982.

Thurow, Lester. *The Zero-Sum Society.* New York: Basic Books, 1980.

Tsongas, Paul. *The Road From Here: Liberalism and Realities in the 1980s.* New York: Knopf, 1981.

CHAPTER 5

The Programmatic Movements: Carriers of the Reform Cause

The major programmatic movements have been forced into a more independent role by the decline of the liberalism which served as their umbrella. They were once the main source of liberalism's reform agenda, its conscience, and its dynamic cutting edge. Today, they each remain a potent expression of American values and beliefs, although the full impact of their ideas awaits one or another possible form of integration among them.

We shall take up four major programmatic movements — those focused on racial equality, sexual equality, preventing war, and preserving the environment (including safe energy sources). Each has developed a significant body of beliefs involving both adaptations of the basic values and a particular view of problems. Together they represent an otherwise missing component of the American political spectrum.

We omit consideration of other movements such as the senior citizens, consumers, and organized labor movements in part for space and efficiency reasons. But we also believe that the leading four are more deeply linked to the wellsprings of change in American values and beliefs. Thus, they carry greater potential for impact on our future.

We call these four movements "programmatic" because they primarily seek change in one broad area of social life. This commitment is the source of all their efforts to effect policy changes in various specific fields. Their concerns go deeper into the realm of basic values and beliefs, and extend more widely into various sectors of life, than would be suggested by the term "single issue." Each has a distinctive constituency, a long and respected tradition, and an established role in promoting programs of action on a wide front in American politics.

What justifies the joint consideration of these four programmatic movements here is that *together* they have unequaled potential for effecting basic changes in the underlying values and beliefs of the American system. Today each stands on the brink of analyzing the causes of problems at a deep new level of explanation. Such an analysis would enable, even force, these separate movements to integrate with each other and construct a new agenda for change in basic values and beliefs. It would move people sharply to the left, perhaps even once again spur the stalled American political spectrum into motion. But it is by no means certain that such deep analysis and integration will occur. Our focus in this chapter is therefore on the mix of obstacles and opportunities that will determine whether this threshold is ever crossed.

ORIGINS AND EVOLUTION OF THE PROGRAMMATIC REFORM MOVEMENTS

Each of the programmatic reform movements has deep roots in the American political tradition and played some part in giving modern liberalism its essential character. Historically, these movements also share a partial eclipse immediately after World War II, followed by a substantial rebirth in the late 1950s and 1960s. By the mid-1970s, each had (at least arguably) achieved the greatest successes in its history—and generated considerable resentment and opposition as well.

Racial Equality

Perhaps the oldest of these movements is that for racial equality. Although much of the early antislavery agitation fell far short of advocating equality of the races, it was grounded in an important moral position. Whites were charged with responsibility for their relationships with other human beings, in this case black people. The same paternal sort of responsibility was involved in white relations with the indigenous population, Native Americans. Despite the racist mythologies that arose to justify treating one group as property and the other as savages, this moral dimension combined with the commitment to equality articulated in the Declaration of Independence to sustain a nagging opposition to the dominant practices of white America.

In the early decades of the nineteenth century, the movement's primary focus was, naturally, slavery. Slave insurrections were the basic manifestation of black resistance until free and escaped blacks took up the abolitionist campaign along with white ministers. The abolitionists provoked Southern reaction, expanded their ranks with Northern white support, and eventually helped trigger the Civil War. Much of this white support melted away soon after the war's close. Reconstruction, and thus federal government support for the welfare of blacks, effectively ended with the political party bargain of 1877 that conceded the presidency to the Republicans in exchange for the withdrawal of troops from the South.

For the next decades, blacks, with a scattering of white allies, were left to their own devices. Their circumstances in both the North and South were such that basic questions of life and survival dominated their concerns, rather than more advanced or subtle concepts of equality with whites. Out of their often desperate day-to-day struggles soon emerged the beginnings of an enduring dichotomy within the movement for racial equality. Some black leaders sought integration into white society as an eventual goal but economic and educational advancement for all blacks as a first priority. They were willing to wait until they had built a base of self-help experience and economic strength before laying claim to full equality. Others insisted that blacks could never become fully equal unless they demanded all their rights as American citizens from the start, even if that meant confrontation. They denied that this meant that only a few especially capable blacks would rise while the others were left behind.

These different tactics reflected a basic disagreement involving both ends and means.[1] The ends ranged from integration into white society as individuals and on essentially white terms to cultural pluralism, separatism, and nationalism — that is, an arms-length relationship between strong, self-sustaining black communities and white America. The means ranged from docile acceptance of white domination while the race acquired education and economic strength to outright conflict if needed to attain acceptance from whites as full citizens. The disagreements between Booker T. Washington and W. E. B. DuBois fit squarely here.

Washington believed that blacks had to improve their own economic and social status, individually and collectively, and needed white support to do so. He was willing to trade away immediate claims for citizenship rights in order to build black strength and believed that on the basis of such strength integration and equality would ultimately be possible. DuBois thought that no black achievements were safe unless they were protected politically by the right to vote and other means of exercising power; blacks therefore had to insist on all their rights immediately. He sought integration on terms of complete equality, or a kind of pluralism in which blacks as a group enjoyed fully equal status. Some black leaders, such as Marcus Garvey believed that their only future lay in abandoning all efforts to enter white American society. They believed blacks needed to seek a national existence apart from the United States.

As Jim Crow laws and segregationist practices reached resurgent heights in the early twentieth century, DuBois, other militant blacks, and a number of white supporters formed the National Association for the Advancement of Colored People (NAACP). In those times, the goal of ending segregation was radical enough to be viewed as subversive. Nevertheless, the NAACP stood at the forefront of reform-oriented liberals in demanding for blacks the realization of the long-established liberal value of equality.

Following World War II, the movement gathered momentum, spurred in part by support from white liberals, the trade union movement, and the example of newly independent Third World countries. The NAACP artfully conducted a legal campaign challenging Jim Crow laws and segregation practices. Slowly segregation in schools and then in all other public places fell before the Supreme Court axe. In an unprecedented display of courage in the face of multiple forms of intimidation, individual blacks soon began to press for the civil rights that had been denied them for centuries.

Thus the civil rights movement of the 1960s was born. Before that movement had run its course, as described earlier, it had profoundly expanded the legal basis of individual rights and reconstructed federal-state relations in the United States. It also provided a new precedent for and model of white-black cooperation and support that could not be effaced by the later black power and separatist stages of the movement. And, finally it inspired other minorities, particularly Native Americans, Hispanics, and Asian-Americans, to new levels of assertiveness. Soon a genuinely new and multicultural vision of a United States composed of many equally respected cultures began to take shape. The process of achieving such a reality, of course, remained painfully difficult. And much else was going on.

Sexual Equality

As we have seen, in the United States the movement for equality between the sexes has always been linked with that for equality between the races. Hence it was not surprising that a new feminist movement burst upon the scene in the 1960s. Feminists had made themselves individually heard in the eighteenth century and been active in the abolitionist movement of the early nineteenth century. But their most visible beginning lay in the Seneca Falls Convention of 1848 and its Declaration of Sentiments drafted by the convention organizers, particularly Elizabeth Cady Stanton. One of the prominent voices on the floor of that convention, and the source of the decisive argument for the declaration's passage, was the black abolitionist Frederick Douglass.

What feminists of that period sought should sound familiar. Their aims included voting equality, which took seven decades to achieve, legal equality, which is still unfulfilled, and genuine cultural-social equality, which lies even beyond that. These dimensions of equality have proved very difficult to wrest from patriarchal American society. Even blacks, long closely associated with feminists in the campaign to make equality a fact in the United States, have on occasion proved inconstant. The Equal Rights Association, established jointly by black abolitionists and white feminists before the Civil War, for example, essentially fell apart after the war over the issue of whether to grant black men the vote before women of all races.[2]

For this reason, along with deep-seated white male resistance and denigration, feminists were forced to go it alone. And so they did, pressing ever more vigorously for acceptance of a notion of equality that would allow women to vote. Suffrage became the exclusive focus of the women's movement for several decades. Ironically, it was achieved only when white male voters felt more threatened by the disruptive prospects of increasing (male) immigrant votes than those of women. Even then, leading anarchist-feminists like Emma Goldman were telling women that true emancipation would require far more than the right to vote and own property.

But it took the multiple stirrings of minority movements for racial equality and white movements for social justice to reawaken the unfulfilled aspirations of women. The new movement, born in the 1960s, had both middle-class and radical origins and continues to have both moderate (though far-reaching) and radical goals. Middle-class women, characteristically, began with a book, Betty Friedan's *The Feminine Mystique*.[3] Friedan articulated the unexpressed sense of frustration and lack of "personhood" that many such women felt in the midst of apparent affluence. A more radical critique was generated by women who were participants in the early civil rights and antiwar movements. Their critique grew in part out of their experiences in these movements. Though running the same risks as men, they were being patronized and/or exploited in intolerable ways by their "comrades."

The more radical women argued, and their older sisters concurred, that men were acting out patriarchal dominance in ways that denied basic human dignity. This was particularly galling when many such men announced they were in the process of building a new and better social order. For the liberal moderates in the 1970s, feminism meant equal pay for equal work, equal responsibility for child rearing and home maintenance, and full equality in career and life opportunities (necessitating, e.g., legal access to divorce, abortion, and child support). Even these were significant demands to impose on the American social structure, as the strength of the soon-generated reaction testifies.

More radical feminists empathetically supported such demands but went further for themselves. Some demanded acceptance of homosexuality — a demand that made them special targets of criticism and hostility. Most were intent on working out a reconstruction of the American social order that would enable men as well as women to be free of the disabling need for patriarchal, racial, or other justifications for the supremacy of one category over another.[4]

Together, the movements for racial and sexual equality account for much of the dynamism and growth in the concept of equality that has occurred in the United States in the last three decades. No other group or movement has generated comparable momentum nor created so many new dimensions to the idea of equality. Equality of opportunity has been expanded, sometimes to the breaking point. Even then, many have found it wanting and promptly moved on to creative new levels of argumentation about what "real" equality would require in the way of social and economic preconditions.

Prevention of War

The physical isolation of the United States, combined with the sense that this nation was intended to be a republican improvement on the quarrelsome, destructive kingdoms of Europe, has given special impetus to antiwar and anti-imperialist movements. George Washington warned against "entangling alliances." Opposition to the War of 1812 was widespread. The antidraft riots in New York were only the surface manifestation of public unwilling-ness to fight the Civil War. More significantly, the Spanish-American War was bitterly opposed by some of the strongest Social Darwinist conservatives of the period.[5]

By the time of World War I, there was a substantial antiwar move-ment, which was only partially anti-imperialist in character. It also in-cluded Quakers and other pacifists, socialists, and people of German origin or descent. Together these groups mounted an opposition that succeeded in electing hundreds of candidates in 1917, only to be crushed by patriotic fer-vor and a massive government campaign. The movement was unable to sur-vive the coordinated deportation of immigrants, prosecution of alleged antidraft activism, and investigation of subversion and syndicalism in the labor movement. At no other period in the nation's history has there been repression equal to that visited upon pacifists and the political left during this "Red Scare" of World War I and immediately thereafter.[6]

But enough pacifists and religious antiwar elements remained to receive a measure of vindication in the "Merchants of Death" Congressional investi-gations of the 1930s. By providing evidence of wartime profiteering, these investigations gave support to new antiwar and "America First" movements. Despite this shift in the 1930s, World War II proved one of the few occasions when public opinion appeared broadly supportive of a war. Even then it took a clear fascist threat together with the fact of being attacked to mobilize all but a small band of religious pacifists in support of the nation's war ef-fort.

The destructive power of American nuclear weapons, demonstrated in the last stages of World War II, helped to restore antiwar sentiment soon af-terward. The Korean War was fought in a context of reluctant and anxious cold war concern for repelling unjustified communist expansion. In view of this concern, most antiwar sentiment was confined to defusing right-wing determination to win the war by escalating it to the nuclear level if neces-sary. In the 1950s organizations with no outside political ties, like the Com-mittee for a Sane Nuclear Policy (SANE), made nuclear destructive capacity itself the focus. They were soon joined by a variety of organizations and millions of unaffiliated people in the massive antiwar movement that mobi-lized (mostly spontaneously) against the Vietnam War.

The United States has never known an antiwar movement of the scope and power of that in the Vietnam years. It is currently fashionable to deni-grate that movement in various ways. However, there is no denying the fact that it had at least vital, if incomplete, responsibility for forcing a change in policy.[7] No other antiwar effort in our history ever approached that level of achievement, and the example has not been forgotten. Both nuclear freeze and disarmament efforts today owe much of their impetus to this precedent. Each new piece of evidence of the proliferation and destructiveness of nuclear weapons calls up not only renewed determination to negotiate reductions in such armaments but also the Vietnam antiwar example of suc-cess in redirecting national military policy.

Protection of the Environment and
Assurance of Safe Energy Sources

Today's environmental protection movement has origins as far back as the traditional New England "commons" and Jefferson's concern for providing ample open land within new towns. But it was during the Progressive Era that conservation became a major national cause. Protection of unspoiled wilderness areas and their animal population, the national park system, and the general notion of conservation of resources gradually grew into a major focus of public attention. These goals later helped to promote support for such New Deal programs as the Civilian Conservation Corps employment project and the massive new public works programs represented by the Tennessee Valley Authority and the Bonneville Power Administration.

Once again a major reform movement reached a peak of support and success in the late 1960s and early 1970s. By this time it was clear that past and present pollution and degradation of the environment, wastage of resources, and thoughtless destruction of fish and animal life threatened the quality of life both immediately and for future generations. The search for remedies was given new urgency. Several new environment-preserving statutes were passed, and new standards for clean air and water established.[8]

In the early 1970s, the apparent destructiveness of large-scale modern technologies combined with energy shortages to spur development of another form of the environmental movement. Opposition to nuclear power generation intensified, for several reasons: (a) on the grounds of both safety and cost; (b) preference for safe and environmentally neutral energy sources such as the sun, wind, and tides; and (c) a general commitment to small-scale alternative technologies as a manifestation of a new and more independent lifestyle. The result was an almost complete halt to nuclear construction programs and vast new conservation that cut the total usage of energy for several years.

To be sure, both achievements were owed in part to massive cost increases. But few movements touched so many people or succeeded in raising so many questions about the nature of the American economic order. Environmentalism, this time of a new kind, was back on the American agenda, enjoyed support that cut across class and political party lines, and seemed quite unlikely to go away again.

THE BASIC VALUES: REFORM-ORIENTED LIBERALISM

The four programmatic movements were often uneasy allies, and occasionally competitors for the leadership role, on the reform side of liberalism. They have been set on their own by that belief system's decline. Indeed, it can be argued that their very aggressiveness is in part to blame for the strains on liberalism and the reaction that led to its fragmentation. In any event, these movements now have no joint home; each is obliged to find its own way.

But at the level of basic values and beliefs, the movements still have much in common. And it is precisely because of what they share and what they are developing in the way of changes in this area that they remain potentially powerful reform vehicles on the American political spectrum. None can achieve more than part of its goals by itself. To fulfill their specific goals and their larger potential, they must reach a fuller integration than ever occurred within the liberal framework. What we shall see in this section is that the *potential* clearly exists for a coherent new package of 1980s-style reform values and beliefs. Realization of such potential, of course, is an entirely different matter.

As might be expected of movements long on the cutting edge of liberal reform, the definitions of the basic values that underlie the programmatic movements tend to the left of the U.S. spectrum. Instead of individualistic solutions, for example, each of the four more or less naturally turns to collective responsibility. The use of government or other collective means to achieve goals comes much more readily to these movements than to most of the other belief systems. This may be inherent in the public nature of the goods they seek, but it is nevertheless distinctive. They also all stress solidarity among the members of their sharply defined constituencies. They have a stronger sense of community and mutual obligations than do most of the belief systems. Their sense of what it means to be an individual does not include as much personal responsibility or isolation. There is more acknowledged interdependence between people.

All four movements grant importance to property rights but rank certain other rights ahead of property. In particular, they give first place to the intangible dimensions of their highest values. These highest values all involve *conditions or qualities* rather than merely tangible elements. Status, dignity, respect, peace, clean air and water, natural beauty, and the reduction of hazardous risks of various kinds to life and health — all these values involve at least some aspects that are unmeasurable, especially in monetary terms. They can only be sensed or felt and are certainly not reducible to cost-benefit calculations.

For reasons that have already in part emerged, all four movements hold a highly ambivalent sense of the value of contracts and law. They are not highly respectful of the role of contracts and law when it comes to protecting property rights at the expense of others or maintaining individual privileges of any kind far into the future. As noted, these movements seek to promote collective goods, often ones heretofore unrecognized by the law or, if recognized, not highly prized in comparison with the right to use one's property as desired.

At the same time, all four of these movements have made many substantial gains through litigation. The legal-procedural mechanisms of the liberal system gave them their first great victories and their chance to mobilize popular support to gain further successes. Creative uses of the law and litigation have been hallmarks of each of these movements. A whole new body of constitutional law and individual and group rights has been developed in the process of their separate struggles.

In contrast to the basic values thus far discussed, there is little deviation from the liberal mainstream when it comes to the principle of democracy. With only the modest exception to be noted, all four of these movements stand squarely with liberalism in accepting the procedural definition. Democracy is highly valued in all cases, but it is a version of democracy that stresses the right to vote and equality before the law. It closely hews to the accepted procedures of the political-legal world. Only the antiwar movement has really gone "outside the law" as a matter of deliberate tactics. Even then, many adherents acknowledge the validity of the law and their arrest, welcoming it as an opportunity to challenge the policy in the legal system on constitutional or other higher law grounds.

Very few people from any of these movements make any connection between the rules of the political-legal arena and the social and economic conditions that lie behind them. They do not see democracy as limited or denied by virtue of inequalities of wealth or power in the private world. They trust that their goals are all available through the political world alone. In other words, in this respect these movements are truly *liberal* belief systems.

The programmatic movements are making their most original contributions with respect to the values of equality and freedom. Here they are pressing forcefully toward new definitions with far-reaching implications.

We noted earlier that the movements for racial and sexual equality have given the principle of equality its dynamism in the last three decades. They began by accepting liberalism's "equality of opportunity" at face value. They merely sought to make that notion of equality real by obtaining full citizenship rights for minorities and women, mainly through litigation. For a while, obtaining the right to vote and equal access to jobs were wholly engaging tasks. The movements met with and had to overcome layers of resistance built from centuries of unconcern and semiconscious unwillingness to yield white male prerogatives.

But the attempt to make equality of opportunity real soon raised new questions. Clearly, advocates of racial and sexual equality could not be satisfied with merely formal definitions of the principle. They would have had to close their eyes to the social and economic facts. As a group, minorities and women were less well educated or trained for the jobs that carried the higher salaries, security, and status. But it was not just a lack of skills that stood in the way. In many cases, long-established practices had perpetuated patterns based on past experience (or discrimination). Seniority rules, for example, favored those who already possessed particular skills or qualifications. And apprenticeship opportunities often were allocated to the sons of craftsmen who had long been established in a given trade. More generally, national patterns of assigning certain jobs almost exclusively to one race or sex were rooted deep in American cultural traditions and proved very hard to alter by purely legal means. Indeed, they were hard to alter by any means. People, including the very minorities and women whose interests were at stake, had to come to *think* differently than before. But this is precisely what put these movements at the cutting edge of change in the general understanding of equality.

In short, the liberal principle of equality of opportunity simply was not adequate to the kinds of changes these movements sought. The supplementary notion of "affirmative action" was tried for a while. It meant that special efforts had to be made to recruit minorities and women for particular jobs. Where equally capable people were found, minorities or women should be given precedence in hiring or admission. Affirmative action was seen as a means of compensating for past patterns of discrimination. It didn't work, however, for two basic reasons. The first was that there were far too few minorities and women in the appropriate educational and skill categories to fill the jobs that did open up. The social, cultural, and economic facts of life in the United States were so entrenched that the society simply could not quickly produce a whole new mix of people with the requisite backgrounds and aspirations. The second reason was an equally powerful one. Most white males, as well as some minorities and women, resisted affirmative action either openly or subtly. The notion seemed to deny individual merit and personal achievement as the basis for advancement, running counter to long-established values. Many argued it would lower the quality of performance overall. And it was resisted as another instance of government-promulgated social engineering. But even with the supplementary effects of affirmative action, equality of opportunity as a basic principle would require decades to generate real equality in jobs alone. And jobs were only one of several important parts of the notion of equality that these movements sought.

What racial and sexual equality required, and what these movements had to press for, consciously or not, was something that would reach the deepest social, economic, and particularly cultural levels where the roots of inequality lay. The movements were forced, in other words, beyond equality of opportunity and toward something like equality of condition. In the American context, however, the latter was much too drastic a step to take all at once. Understandably, the movement was reluctant and tentative. In the 1980s, it is still far from complete or even conscious. Many adherents to these movements' beliefs would probably deny any such aspirations. But there is no other place for them to go. Either they confront the underlying reasons for inequality or they content themselves with a very long timetable for achieving the equality they genuinely seek.

An analogous process seems to be underway with regard to the understanding of freedom, this time with the peace and environmental movements in the forefront. They are not advocates of freedom in the traditional liberal sense of freedom from government restraints on the use of property. Rather, they identify other threats to the individual — threats that would destroy the life and/or quality of life of that individual as well as succeeding generations. They seek a freedom *from* fear and destruction; they seek a freedom to hope, to look forward to continued human life on the planet. There is more than a touch of genuine conservatism in this changed definition: for almost the first time, explicit consideration is being given to the needs and conditions of life for generations yet unborn. And sacrifices are to be made by people today in order that future needs may be better served.

This sort of freedom can be thought of as a vast expansion of the idea of individual rights. It makes them collective and adds new dimensions to "life, liberty, and pursuit of happiness." It relocates the major threats to individual development and fulfillment opportunities. The danger to freedom now comes from rigid and technocratic corporate-and-government policies that endanger the earth, land, and sky—and people.

This new definition of freedom also involves fundamental change at the cultural level. It would require Americans to think differently about basic personal priorities and social purposes. Individually, people may have to restructure their personal values. Affluence may need to give way to survival, perhaps including vast new transfer programs to other nations. As a society, the United States would have to become less technological, much less profit oriented, and less anticommunist. Merely to state such imperatives may make the prospect of change seem highly unlikely. It is. But this is the *direction* in which the peace and environmental movements' beliefs and goals lead.

Underlying such changes is a more optimistic view of human nature. People can be more collectively oriented, willing to sacrifice their immediate wants for the sake of their children and future benefits that they might not realize themselves. But this kind of change is something like what the movements for racial and sexual equality are also asking of Americans. All four movements think about the character of society in longer-range terms than has been usual in the American experience. This change in orientation is quite fundamental and not easily accomplished. And yet, all four of these programmatic movements seem to point in this same general direction.

PROBLEMS AND POSSIBILITIES: THE QUESTION OF INTEGRATION

Each of the four programmatic movements carries with it the basic dilemma of reform liberalism. On the one hand, they see their respective problem area as *the* problem that the nation must somehow resolve in order to make good on its basic values and goals. And in their early stages they tend to hold to the view that all that is really required to solve the problem is for people of good will to reach adequate understanding, add to their numbers, and work together to bring the matter to the attention of both the public and policymakers. Then the currently wrong or mistaken policies can be replaced by more appropriate versions. Many advocates never go beyond this sort of analysis.

As movements progress, however, some people recognize that in fact a number of policymakers are not just mistaken about the correct policy. Some officials are strongly committed, with the support of many constituents, to carrying out the wrong policies. This perception generally leads to an attempt to work hard to replace such policymakers at the next election. Less often, these people see that the wrong policies endure or recur despite changes in officials. This can lead to efforts to reform particular government institutions.

On the other hand, a sense of frustration pervades all four movements. Despite clearly visible policy changes, the problems remain. Race and sex discrimination continue. In some cases — for example, the gap between white and black income levels — the problem seems to have increased rather than diminished. The world seems headed implacably toward higher and higher risks of nuclear destruction. The more governments talk about disarmament, the more they build and deploy sophisticated new weaponry. Worse, they sell their newest weapons to client states all over the globe, thereby multiplying the dangers. With what seems like daily regularity, new threats to the environment and health are discovered, at the same time that those in power justify old threats as necessary or tolerable and further delay the implementation of long-established safeguards.

Each movement has worked hard and achieved significant results. Yet the problems they set out to solve seem barely dented. At the same time, each set of beliefs has begun to inch further left on the American spectrum. Even this slight movement has left them feeling just a bit exposed and perhaps vulnerable to the uncomfortable charge of being "extremist." This is particularly true with respect to the values of equality and freedom, where change is greatest and increasingly difficult to conceal. Each movement is caught in the same powerful bind: inadequate results but excessive reputation.

The dilemma posed is essentially that of the conflict between a *liberal* analysis and preferred approach to solution and a *radical* goal that can only be achieved through a more radical analysis and solution. Each movement would prefer to see its problem as isolated, separate, and compartmentalized *and* as capable of being solved without fundamental challenge to or change in basic American values, economic structures, or social and cultural traditions and practices.

The perception of a major problem, however important and personally consuming, as part of a more general set of problems facing the social order — and at the same time requiring change in the basic values, structures, and cultural patterns of the society — is a truly staggering one. Those who arrive at this perception are in danger of simply becoming paralyzed by it. The easiest and most natural response they can make, therefore, is to deny their own insight, go on about their business, and keep on trying to resolve things without threatening any important societal underpinnings.

But problems do not seem to get solved this way. And so the pressure to move toward deeper analysis and more fundamental solutions continues to build. All the time, of course, new generations of recruits to any given movement insist on giving the established reform methods a full try. They resist "extremism" until all other remedies have been proved clearly insufficient. The movement is caught between being mainstream enough to draw new supporters and convincing even its long-term adherents that mainstream remedies really will not work. And each policy change actually accomplished provides ammunition to those who want to give the established liberal procedures every possible opportunity to deliver before they will even consider more drastic alternatives.

What if all these problems *are* really connected, perhaps all products of the same basic causes? The deeper analysis from the radical left argues that what "really" prevents these movements from achieving their ends are some intimately interconnected factors that lie at the most basic level of American values and economic and social structures. In short, the problem is a capitalist economy, complicated by racism, patriarchy, and other supporting values.

Radicals thus offer a single, integrated answer to all four of the programmatic movements. Private ownership, moved by the goal of private profit and a continuing need to support a patriarchic, racist, and otherwise unequal society, creates a complex web of relationships and imperatives which requires constant tending. There is thus a comprehensive system of mutually supporting props. None of the components of the system can yield anything important to the goals that are sought by the programmatic movements, and all are threatened by any serious efforts to achieve such goals.

More specifically, this system is built on the need to keep people divided in order that wages may be minimized, social control facilitated, and continued profits assured. Racism and sexism are functional in these respects and, though originally independently caused, are now historically inseparable from modern capitalism. War and the threat of war are good for profits and also necessary means of controlling threats to continued control over resources and markets. The resources of the nation are needed to promote profitability. The environmental side effects of efficient production are tolerable costs, which must be borne so that business may prosper and an adequate standard of living be maintained.

The radical description of the capitalist system sounds terribly crude, particularly to reform liberals and many members of the programmatic movements. They have heard it many times before, and each time have resisted the conclusions that the radical arguments urge upon them. If they had not, they would no longer be reform liberal advocates of programmatic movement goals. Reform liberals are in constant dialogue with radicals to their left and mainstream liberals to their right. Theirs is a middle position that *they* have come to treasure just as liberals do in relation to the larger spectrum. It has the merit of being (usually) safe and yet more satisfying than the liberal avoidance of commitment.

A major factor distinguishing between reform liberals and radicals and serving to preserve the formers' position despite its frustrating dilemma is the boundary betwen procedural and substantive democracy. We have stressed that liberals, and all the programmatic movements with them, are totally committed to the procedural version. This means that they look almost exclusively at the political-legal arena when they think about democratic rights or the enforceable scope of equality. They accept the notion of a wall of separation between the political world, where equality is a properly enforceable right, and the social-economic world, where inequality reigns without consequences for democracy. It does not matter that this amounts to a logical contradiction; what does matter is that it is a basic tenet of liberal faith and endures as such.

This acceptance of the wall of separation as right and proper is a major bulwark sustaining reform liberalism. As long as it stands, faith in the capacity of the liberal-procedural system is a necessary ingredient — or else the programmatic movements have no basis for hope that they will someday succeed. The alternative, of course, is to breach the wall and begin to see social, economic, and cultural factors as coherently integrated with the (no longer separate) political world and as controlling outcomes within it. Once this happens, new explanations for the lack of success of any of the programmatic movements become possible. All of a sudden, there are no more mysteries about why those movements are constantly frustrated.

IMPLICATIONS AND PROSPECTS

What are the chances that any one or more of these movements will escape its dilemma, cross this threshold, and reach a deeper explanation and prescription? The potential that they may is what gives them their significance as possible transitional categories of political values and beliefs and entitles them to comprehensive consideration. But their real prospects of doing so seem slim. Too many obstacles exist and reform liberalism still has too strong a grip on Americans to make this more than an outside possibility.

The most likely prospect is that each will continue on its independent way for the foreseeable future, surviving on new waves of faith in reform methods and occasional victories. Failure discourages only those who tried repeatedly or who were aware of the effort to achieve something more. Of these, only a small portion look further for explanations or alternatives; most go on about their other business, newly "realistic" about politics. The much larger number of previously uninvolved people (and/or later generations) remain fixed in their faith, providing a nearly endless pool of new recruits for continued efforts.

From time to time, legal or even legislative victories are achieved and the forward march of the movement is celebrated enthusiastically. By concentrating energies in specific problem areas, it is argued, effectiveness can be increased. Avoid all but short-term tactical alliances, be ready to punish enemies and reward friends, employ intensive lobbying tactics that accept all other conditions except the one you want to change, and your chances will be improved. These and other articles of reform liberal faith operate powerfully to contain efforts toward change within an acceptable range.

The next most likely outcome is an electoral alliance between two or more of these programmatic movements. Such an alliance, prefigured by the term "rainbow coalition" in use in the early 1980s, would be a horizontal linkage of movements for essentially tactical purposes. It would enable each to increase its chances of electing responsive candidates and perhaps even to achieve policy successes. This kind of alliance might even serve as the core for a reconstituted liberalism, a rebirth of mainstream principles and practices on the basis of moderately leftward moving values and a firm commitment to procedural democracy.

The least likely prospect is genuine integration among these movements at a deep theoretical level. This would be a vertical integration in which the same explanation, cast at the level of basic values, social and economic structures, and cultural traditions, would make the previous failures of all movements understandable. Naturally, such an explanation would also point the way to a probably much more drastic solution for all the problems at one and the same time.

That explanation, of course, would be essentially the profit focus of modern capitalism, entwined with racism, sexism, and capitalism's additional panoply of needs. Capitalism demands new resources, labor, and markets in order to assure growth and maximize profits. It thereby sets in motion the combined private and public forces that lead to the problems that the four movements seek to solve. The values on which capitalism rests are essential pillars of the problems and operate to preclude solutions. Clearly, to reach this analytic point would require breaching the wall of separation between politics and economics, seeing all factors as one unified whole, and (by implication) crossing the threshold to openly embrace substantive democracy.

As already suggested, such an explanation and the remedies it would suggest might prove paralyzing — more paralyzing, perhaps, than the reform liberal dilemma was frustrating. Many Americans shrink from an explanation that implies the necessity or desirability of decisive action to effect change. To commit oneself as fully as is required to accomplish such decisive action can threaten one's career, social relations, and eventually one's personal identity and entire life adjustment. This is more than most people bargain for when they set out to help solve what they believe to be a minor problem troubling their otherwise satisfactory social order.

Some elements in each of the four programmatic movements have already crossed this threshold, however, and others seem to be approaching it. Black thinkers such as Robert Allen, Manning Marable, and James Boggs, and feminists such as Zillah Eisenstein and Batya Weinbaum have merged their search for equality with the goals of democratic socialism.[9] Leading thinkers in the environmental and antiwar movements have begun to do the same. William Ophuls, for example, declares that:

> merely reformist policies of ecological management [are] all but useless. At best, reforms can postpone the inevitable for a few decades at the probable cost of increasing the severity of the eventual day of reckoning. . . . liberal democracy as we know it is doomed by ecological scarcity; we need a completely new political philosophy and set of political institutions.[10]

Similarly, in his moving polemic on the nuclear threat, Jonathan Schell says:

> The task we face is to find a means of political action that will permit human beings to pursue any end for the rest of time. We are asked to replace the mech-

anism by which political decisions, whatever they may be, are reached. In sum, the task is nothing less than to reinvent politics: to reinvent the world.[11]

Ironically, if many people *do* reach this point, they would probably abandon their now limited commitment to any particular programmatic movement. The logical place for them to go would be either to economic democracy or democratic socialism, both of which rest on much the same explanation and offer many of the same remedies, or to some other new set of beliefs such as those we shall consider briefly in the last chapter. This is another reason why the programmatic movements are likely to remain within the reform liberal framework. And it is a further reason why they are likely to serve at most as transitional categories in the evolution of American political beliefs.

This is not to say that the programmatic movements are insignificant factors in shaping particular outcomes or patterns of outcomes in American politics. That would be far from the truth. Despite their many inconsistencies and their basic dilemma, the programmatic movements remain the primary source of reform pressures and, more generally, a major dynamic among American belief systems. Any prospective rebirth of liberalism will be dependent on some kind of alliance among at least some of them. The only comparable force thus far in the 1980s is that represented by the New Right.

ADDITIONAL READINGS

Arlidge, Robert C. *First Strike! The Pentagon's Strategy for Nuclear War.* Boston: South End Press, 1983.

Bond, Julian. *A Time to Speak, A Time to Act.* New York: Simon and Schuster, 1972.

Deloria, Vine, Jr. *We Talk, You Listen: New Tribes, New Turf.* New York: Macmillan, 1970.

Ehrlich, Paul R. *The End of Affluence: A Blueprint for Your Future.* New York: Ballantine, 1974.

Evans, Sara. *Personal Politics: The Roots of Women's Liberation in the Civil Rights Movement and the New Left.* New York: Knopf, 1979.

Grossman, Richard, and Daneker, Gail. *Energy, Jobs and the Economy.* Boston: Alyson Publications, 1979.

King, Martin Luther, Jr. *Why We Can't Wait.* New York: New American Library, 1964.

Mitchell, Juliet. *Woman's Estate.* New York: Vintage Books, 1973.

Morgan, Robin, ed. *Sisterhood Is Powerful.* New York: Vintage Books, 1970.

Ophuls, William. *Ecology and the Politics of Scarcity.* San Francisco: Freeman, 1977.

Rendon, Armando. *Chicano Manifesto.* New York: Macmillan, 1971.

Schell, Jonathan. *The Fate of the Earth.* New York: Knopf, 1982.

CHAPTER 6

Economic Democracy: Democratic Neopopulism

The term "economic democracy" describes a set of beliefs coming to be shared by fragments of several reform movements. The principal goal is to extend the practices of political democracy to the major institutions of the corporate economy. Economic democrats believe that people need and want to gain control over the decisions that affect their lives. The notion of democracy that economic democrats hold is clearly substantive in fact, not just in potential. And democracy so understood is their highest value.

Economic democrats try to look at the whole range of active participants in the American political-economic system at once. They believe that the reason piecemeal reforms have not worked in the past is that there is a community of interest among the biggest corporations, banks, foundations, political parties, etc. This combination successfully works to blunt and delay reform efforts, while its individual components profit excessively from their advantages.

The solution urged by economic democrats is for all change-seeking groups to join in a grand grass-roots-based coalition that will work to tame and reform the undemocratic powers of these dominant institutions. There is continuing debate about the propriety of seeking power through the Democratic Party or a new third party. But broad conviction exists that any such effort would have to be grounded in many local coalitions, at least some holding city and state offices.

We locate economic democracy in the populist tradition because it is a thoroughly American perspective resistant to great concentrations of power from whatever source. It is more interested in identifying obstacles to democracy and eliminating them than it is in theoretical understanding of all the relationships involved. Economic democrats start by postulating the self-interest of many different groups and people, acknowledging the justice of their respective claims. The only way to serve these just claims is through the collective action of all the interests. With such an alliance, the promise of democracy and equality can be made real in the present United States.

As a comprehensive body of beliefs, economic democracy is readily distinguishable from the programmatic movements to its right on the American spectrum. The latter are much narrower in their focus, seek change only in the one program area, and essentially accept the basic political-economic framework of the American social order. Economic democracy is far broader in its orientation and would democratize a wide range of institutions and functions of the private economy.

Distinguishing economic democracy from democratic socialism, its cousin to the left on the spectrum, is a bit more difficult. In fact, for tactical purposes, some leading leftist thinkers use the term "economic democracy" when they really mean democratic socialism: American audiences tend to raise their mental defenses very quickly when confronted with the word "socialism." However, there are substantive criteria that can be used to clearly distinguish between economic democracy as we have defined it and democratic socialism.

Democratic socialism is the heir to the rich tradition of Marxian political-economic thought. One of its primary goals is to select, refine, and adapt Marxian concepts and approaches to American reality. It is more concerned with the notion of social class or its equivalent, and particularly with finding some central role for the working class and organized labor, than is economic democracy. It is also more tuned to cultural levels, such as the nature of concepts and the meanings of words — or processes of communication generally — by which domination is achieved. It is more deeply theoretical, historical, and comparative than economic democracy. But it is no less democratic or American, which is why it merits analysis in a subsequent chapter.

THE ORIGINS AND SOURCES OF ECONOMIC DEMOCRACY

Economic democracy coalesced as a movement in the mid-1970s. A number of radicals and reformers from the former New Left and various programmatic movements began to search for a more comprehensive analysis of the American social order. Their reform efforts having proved, at best, only marginally successful, they sought to understand something more of the causes of inequality and injustice. The power and autonomy of large corporations seemed to be at the core of the explanation. They concluded that poverty and powerlessness for the many were both obvious and likely to endure unless a broad coalition of local groups with different reform goals could be focused on the task of democratizing the power of the big corporations.

One of the first expressions of the move toward economic analysis and prescription came in the early 1970s. Jack Newfield and Jeff Greenfield published *A Populist Manifesto: The Making of a New Majority*, declaring their purposes in this way:

> This manifesto is. . . an effort to return to American politics the economic passions jettisoned a generation ago. Its fundamental argument is wholly unoriginal: some institutions and people have too much money and power, most

people have too little, and the first priority of politics must be to redress the balance. For the past two decades, most of conservative politics has been based on fear — fear of Communists, fear of blacks, fear of crime. We believe the only antidote to fear, the only thing deeper than fear, is self-interest. Thus, the political appeal of the program we suggest in this manifesto is based not on moralistic or humanitarian grounds, but on pure self-interest.[1]

From the start, this version of populism asserted its concern for the achievement of civil rights and equality for minorities and women. But, it argued, democratizing the economy was a necessary step toward realizing them. The term "economic democracy," however, came into general use with two events of 1976. One was the creation of a "Peoples' Bicentennial Commission." The commission issued several publications and a monthly journal called *Common Sense*, all of which used the term regularly.[2] The other was the California campaign of Tom Hayden for the U.S. Senate. His "Campaign for Economic Democracy" remained in existence as a loose alliance of local organizations devoted to the general cause and not any single candidate.[3]

Hayden was a founding member of the New Left who helped write its famous Port Huron Statement in 1962. His own career illustrates one of the tracks by which people have come to be economic democrats. His 1980 book, *The American Future: New Visions Beyond Old Frontiers*, is one of the major documents of the movement. It sets forth a complete agenda of needed policy changes and a design for democratizing the society. Another somewhat deeper and more programmatic book that helped give the movement its name is Martin Carnoy and Derek Shearer's *Economic Democracy: The Challenge of the 1980s*.[4] The authors are both California based, one an economist and the other an urban planner. Both are deeply involved in local and state politics as economic democrats.

Many other reform movements of the late 1960s and early 1970s served as sources for what became the economic democracy movement. Recruits have come from the environmental, ecology, antinuclear, antimilitary, consumer and public interest, minority, and feminist movements. Many of them had considerable experience in these left-liberal political activities, developing valuable political skills — along with considerable frustration. A few came from movements as diverse as the alternative technology, "steady state," or "human scale" movements that opposed continued economic growth and consumption.

What moved them toward economic democracy was the shared sense that the problems they sought to solve were rooted in the nature of the corporate economy. Whether they focused on sheer size and power of the largest corporations, or the dominant role of money in financing campaigns, or the sense that inequalities of wealth and power are part of the basic nature of the U.S. economic system, the trail led back to the private economy. In any event, they came to believe their original goals could not be achieved unless the existing power of big corporations was curbed. Democratizing changes were required in the private economy. To accomplish that, they needed allies from other like-minded movements; coalition under the economic democracy umbrella made sense.

Economic democrats come also from another major source—the left wing of the labor movement with its commitment to full employment. The goal of providing a job for every person able and willing to work has been part of organized labor's aspirations ever since the New Deal. But it too has proved to be an elusive goal. It is apparently too radical for labor's liberal supporters as it consistently gets traded away when organized labor makes its accommodation with the dominant elements in the Democratic Party.

In the present declining state of the trade union movement, however, most of the established leadership has joined the neoliberal call for a new industrial policy. Within the industrial policy approach, job development is a secondary priority and the notion of *full* employment is totally absent. This has freed the remaining fragment of labor leadership and a number of left-leaning supporters among economists and others to develop a comprehensive new program for full employment.[5] In analysis and purpose, their program fits squarely within the framework of economic democracy. Moreover, as they reach out for new adherents, they meet economic democrats reaching toward them for a base in the labor movement.

The linkage between full employment's adherents among labor and minorities and economic democracy's chiefly middle-class activists is still tentative and awkward, but seems to be steadily solidifying. One of the enduring problems of the American left has been the difficulty of building a coalition across race and class lines. Economic democracy is in a sense reaching even further. It is trying to bring together what it calls a "rainbow coalition" of races, classes, interests, and sexes—historically accomplished only briefly, if ever, in the United States. As we shall see, whether this goal is in fact viable remains *the* question about the future of economic democracy.

THE BASIC VALUES OF ECONOMIC DEMOCRACY

For economic democrats the highest value in social life is democracy. It is the basis from which people can realize their full qualities and potential as human beings. Taking part in politics in a meaningful way allows people to play a real part in shaping the conditions under which they live, to develop their sense of personal worth, and to feel engagement with other people in a community. The overriding importance economic democrats attach to the principle of democracy carries special consequences for its definition and for the way other key values are understood. We shall present economic democrats' basic values in the way that they see them, that is, as linked to their notion of democracy.

Basic Values

Economic democracy's definition insists that the major divisions between people, particularly race and sex barriers, must be broken down before democracy can become real. Such divisions may be deep and difficult to overcome, but no political or economic program can call itself democratic without giving very high priority to achieving full equality in these crucial terms. Many economic democrats would rather fail while seeking such goals than succeed by compromising them. They are of the essence of democracy itself.

A value of such importance deserves to be extended throughout all areas of social life. This extension is essential for two leading reasons. The first is to convert the illusory equality of citizens in the political world into a reality. Until there is greater equality in the economic and social worlds, accumulation in a few hands of wealth, status, and power will continue to shape the outcomes in politics. At the very least, great inequalities of wealth and power deny the goals of democracy. In some cases, they make the great principle of democracy into a mere sham. Discrimination on racial and sexual lines, while having independent sources, is also encouraged by economic factors.

The other reason is that only if democratic practices are extended throughout all areas of social life — the family and the work place, for example — can people really develop the sense of personal worth and solidarity with others that permits a full life as a human being. People need to feel that they are in control of their lives, and not the mere pawns of others. And their capabilities need to be exercised to become real. Moreover, the results of cooperative action to solve problems, such as organizing work to achieve both efficiency and quality of product, lead ultimately to a better life for all.

The basic means of accomplishing this democratization is participatory decentralization. People *must* be able to take part in making the decisions that affect their lives. Translated, this means that important decisions will have to be made where people can actually be present to take part. Both initial choices and continuing implementation must be subject to the preferences of those affected. Particularly crucial to economic democracy are democratization of the work place, employee ownership plans, and, most importantly, social control over capital investment.

Some economic democrats think of this change in terms of the formation of a "new social contract." A social contract is, of course, a fiction. It is an image of an underlying agreement among people with respect to organization of their social order and the distribution of rights and responsibilities. But trying to characterize its nature forces people to pay attention to the first principles, purposes, and priorities of their system. One group of economic democrats expresses the need for a new social contract as follows:

> We believe that a New Social Contract in America must reaffirm and energize the fundamental dynamic of our history: democracy . . . [some people] think that the way out of the current crisis is to leave decisions to a few — the "experts" in our complex industrial economy. But increased expertise and corporate bureaucratization for the sake of higher private profits is precisely what has made post-World War II America head down the road to crisis. . . . America must now find ways . . . through *greater*, not less, democratic participation.[6]

Economic democracy also takes up individualism in the sense of individual rights, extending it from the political-legal world to the economic world. Nearly all economic democrats talk in terms of the right to a job, economic rights in general, or an "Economic Bill of Rights." Many of those who start from a commitment to full employment promptly translate that goal into an individual right to a job. An example is Representative John Conyers' draft legislation entitled "The Recovery and Full Employment Act," the first declared purpose of which is "the establishment of an enforceable right to earn a living."[7]

The economic democrats' idea of rights extends well beyond the right to a job at wages adequate to sustain a moderate standard of living. It includes various dimensions of economic and social security, such as rights to education, housing, health care, environmental quality, and adequate retirement income. In part, this is intended to establish a floor of social and economic guarantees, a kind of minimum level of conditions for all that will make equality of opportunity more genuine. But it is also part of the economic democrats' notion of freedom, which requires assurance of certain levels of social and economic conditions (or security) so that people will be free to develop themselves in directions of their choice.

The manner in which the extension of individual rights to the economy intersects with a version of freedom is well illustrated in excerpts from two quite different sources. The first is the call for a new social contract in which "government does not restrict liberty, it expands it and makes it a reality."[8] The second is from a leading alliance of organizations called the Full Employment Action Council. After asserting the right to a job as part of human freedom, the alliance goes on to describe "the essence of the freedom we desire":

> The national government cannot emphasize certain kinds of freedom and forget others. Free markets reward those who have market power, but they do not improve opportunities for those who have little wealth or income. . . . Freedom is indivisible. We cannot emphasize only those forms of freedom that benefit mainly the powerful.[9]

Economic democrats also modify the traditional view of individualism with their concern for fostering and developing community life and the capacity of communities to control their own futures. A variety of communities is envisioned in which each community has the ability to affect what happens to it. In part, this is also the way that democracy is to be extended:

> Greater democracy means that those with jobs will have much more to say about the way those jobs are organized; those who live in communities will have more to say about what happens to those communities — even whether a plant can simply up and leave after thirty years. . . . and all citizens can decide together whether the human race should be destroyed by nuclear war or survive in a saner world.[10]

Summary

Let us try to summarize briefly what economic democracy is doing with and to traditional American values. It seems clear that even though economic democrats perceive self-interest as an important factor, they have expanded the notion of individualism in significant ways. Self-orientation has been supplanted by notions of community and of shared risks and opportunities. An even greater expansion, though one that might be thought to preserve the isolated-individual focus, is occurring in the extension of individual rights to the economy. At some point in the expansion of rights, a fundamental change in the nature of the society itself will be involved.

At the same time, property rights have just as clearly been downgraded and nonowners given a major voice in deciding how property should be used. Equality has been expanded beyond equality of opportunity into the realm of equality of condition. Similarly, freedom has been redefined to fit with this new version of equality and to mean space and/or security to try to realize basic human aspirations. Contracts and law, and established procedures generally, play a much lesser role than they did for more liberal reform beliefs. Indeed, they are often seen as part of the way that dominant corporations deflect reform efforts. But that does not mean that economic democrats are unwilling to use litigation or initiative and referendum tactics to harass corporations and banks and their political agents.

What is involved here is an expansion of the notions of equality and freedom even beyond those that were being generated by the programmatic movements. This expansion puts an equivalent pressure on the other basic values in a coherent democracy-promoting direction. The version of democracy sought is a fresh new substantive variety. Procedural democracy has been examined and found wanting on two counts: its incomplete nature in the political world (race, sex, and other discrimination) and its complete absence in the economic world. A number of other changes are closely connected, but these take the form of value-linked concepts that are central to economic democracy.

Value-Laden Concepts

Economic democrats think in terms of an integrated political-economic world in which drawing a distinction between the two spheres is not only conceptually unjustifiable but quite possibly deliberately mystifying. In other words, the conscious or unconscious wall of separation between politics and economics so characteristic of liberalism is explicitly attacked by economic democrats. They recognize it as one of the thresholds that people must cross in moving from programmatic reform to economic democracy. This separation is what enables the restriction of the notion of democracy and its implications to the political sphere.

Economic democrats have no higher priority than replacement of the liberal concept of separate compartments with a holistic image of an integrated society. Until people have such an image, democracy cannot become the pervasive ideal and fact in all areas of social life, and this, of course, is the defining goal of economic democracy. There are many barriers to developing a concept of democracy that is genuinely applicable to all areas of social life, but economic democrats do not underestimate the problem.

This leads to another conceptual feature of economic democracy — rejection of the idea of the free market as a model of how an economy should work. That is, economic democrats deny that a free market maximizes efficient use of resources, is self-regulating without government participation, or is appropriate as the basic allocator in a society. Nor do economic democrats accept the market-inspired implication that efforts to promote equity in economic affairs necessarily mean lower levels of efficiency in production and distribution.

Instead, economic democrats believe that *all* areas of social life are dominated and managed by a coherent set of people, beliefs, and practices. No area is independent or subject only to objective, neutral forces that determine outcomes apart from human preference or control. The whole system works together to produce benefits primarily for the few who happen to own the largest amount of land or capital or whatever is required to produce things that people need and want. *Social relationships*, not impersonal machines or markets, determine patterns of distribution and how people live their lives in a society. It is imperative that people see that the basic conditions of their lives, both at work and outside of work, are traceable to the power and preferences of other people who seek to preserve that basic structure of ownership and the pattern of distribution that it accomplishes.

Economic democrats thus consider it imperative that people set aside their images of a separate economic sphere in which efficiency is or can be maximized by neutral laws and competing individuals in a free market situation. Only then can democracy and equality become real alternatives. Carnoy, Shearer, and Rumberger express this argument as follows:

> Adam Smith and his present-day conservative followers can separate economics and government by assuming that the economic system is self-governing. We contend not only that this assumption is palpably false but that an alternative must integrate economics and politics on a new basis — a democratic, participative governance of polity and economy.[11]

The point here is that once the walls separating politics from economics start to come down, many new insights and demands are likely. For example, owners and managers lose much of the rationale for their control over the conditions surrounding actual production. It is neither a technological requirement of the machinery nor the imperative of efficiency that leads to authoritarian control over work. It is merely the convenience of the employer. Different rules and practices better suited to workers' preferences might very well result in more and better quality products, to say nothing of truly democratic social relationships in this important one-third of people's lives.

An integrated view of social life also makes the new economic democracy versions of equality and freedom mutually supportive. As noted earlier, economic democrats see equality as meaning more than merely formal or legal-political equality, and indeed, more than equality of opportunity made real. To them, it means genuine equality of social and economic circumstances, at least in the sense of a floor of security and entitlements that people can count on because they are citizens of a democratic society. The *purpose* of such equality, however, is to make possible the opportunity for people to develop themselves as far as they can or want to—which is itself the definition of freedom in a democratic society. Equality and freedom when so defined are entirely harmonious.

The contrast with established liberal understandings of equality and freedom is sharp, if not stark. Equality, if it is to mean anything beyond legal-political equality, will require the aid of government. Neither equality of opportunity nor any other form of equality can be achieved without government action to reduce existing inequalities. But all such action, if only in the form of taxes required to provide education or training assistance, represents an interference with individual freedom. This will be the case just as long as freedom is understood as freedom from government limits on what one can do—essentially the way that freedom is defined in a liberal society with strong free market convictions.

PROBLEMS AND POSSIBILITIES: ECONOMIC DEMOCRACY'S ANALYSIS AND PROGRAM

Economic democrats see a troubled American economy and in general a society with destructive priorities. They differ sharply in their analysis of what is wrong with the economy and society from those they call "mainstream" economists. And economic democrats have an extensive and highly detailed program for the reconstruction of the American economy. They fully recognize that economic reconstruction also requires the revitalization or reconstruction of American politics. An itemization of what is wrong with the American economy and where it is headed will prepare the way for discussion of the economic democracy program.

U.S. Economic Problems

Economic democrats see domination of the American economy by giant, often multinational corporations as its most salient feature. These corporations represent aggregations of assets so vast, and so global in character, that they operate without effective control by any government. Thus they can transfer their productive facilities anywhere in the world, avoiding higher-wage areas and effectively depressing all wage levels. They can close up still-profitable plants in order to invest in whatever offers the highest returns, regardless of the impact on workers. Or they can pollute, discriminate, and use up scarce resources with impunity.

Of most significance today is the fact that these corporations have violated the tacit contract they have with workers and consumers to share a fair proportion of their earnings in the form of wages and taxes. Instead, the corporations have almost unanimously sought to roll back wages, crush the unions, and slash both social programs and the taxes that support them. For working people, this has meant a steady decline in real wages, joblessness and the threat of joblessness, and sharply reduced government supports, financial and otherwise.

These cutbacks hit hardest at the very people who make up the economic democracy constituency. Minorities and women are the most likely to be affected by reductions in government social assistance programs. Environmentalists are aggrieved by loosened environmental protections, lower air and water pollution standards, and the like. Antiwar and nuclear freeze advocates are shocked by the scope of the military buildup. This last is particularly provocative to all economic democrats.

To economic democrats, one of the most damaging commitments of the American government — and one that enjoys widespread support from American business — is the vast investment it makes in military expenditures. Hundreds of billions of dollars are taken out of the U.S. economy and simply wasted. Many more jobs could be produced, and far more useful facilities built or products developed, if the same sums were invested in other areas or simply left in the hands of consumers to spend as they wished. Economic democrats uniformly contend that military spending is wasteful as well as dangerous in its effects on the global arms race. But some go beyond this to say that American capitalism has come to depend so heavily on this massive injection of public funds that some equivalent prop, such as a vast public works program, will be necessary to accomplish a transition away from heavy military expenditures.

What this military investment really shows, in the eyes of economic democrats, is the complete irrationality of modern capitalism. New weapons of mutual destruction are produced in numbers far exceeding what could ever be used. Not only does this great expansion in military spending occur at a time when most of the world's people, including substantial numbers of Americans, are barely subsisting, but it actually is used as a reason to further reduce social program expenditures that enable poor people to have some chance to improve their life situations. In this way, as well as through the unprecedented national budget deficits resulting from these policies, the costs of the current military buildup are passed to future generations.

The irrationality of modern capitalism only begins with the massive waste of military spending. Many products are so shoddy or dangerous that buyers can be found only through vast advertising campaigns which serve no useful purpose except that of making profit. Meanwhile, real needs go unmet because higher profits can be made elsewhere. Public, social goods such as the air, land, and water are polluted or seized for private profit purposes, destroyed, and then dumped on the public for reclamation. Systematic waste becomes a defining characteristic of modern capitalism.

This warped set of priorities is specially damaging at a time when so many real needs are felt by so many people. Moreover, in order to defend and maintain these priorities, money and influence are widely deployed in the political world, corrupting the media, political campaigns, and the representative process. The result is an increasingly crass and ignoble public

life. Mainstream economists are essentially apologists for those remedies that
are congenial to the owners and managers who created this set of priorities in
the first place. Carnoy and Shearer state the case, suggesting the different
way in which economic democrats would try to solve the problems:

> We believe that economists and other governmental policymakers cannot im-
> prove the situation primarily because . . . they accept a set of ideological as-
> sumptions about the "naturalness" and "perfectibility" of capitalism as an eco-
> nomic order. . . . [but] we think it is crucial to political-economic discussion to
> accept openly the fact that assumptions about ownership and power are part
> and parcel of the economic problem. Rather than discussing the best methods
> for "fine tuning" the economy, we want to shift the debate to strategies for
> changing the structure of the economy so that it better serves the interests and
> needs of all Americans. . . . Neoclassical economics represents a point of view,
> a political position, a set of assumptions about the way the world should be and
> about human behavior. We will present an alternative view based on an alter-
> native set of assumptions.[12]

The Economic Democracy Program

The programs that various economic democrats put forward contain some
widely shared elements and only slight differences in substance or priority. Essentially, the overall program involves implementation of the New Social Contract and/or Economic Bill of Rights noted earlier. Some key legislative changes
and widespread democratization of political and social institutions would, of
course, be necessary. But redistribution of wealth and power, and democratization of both politics and economics, must proceed on a step-by-step basis.

In a first-priority category are restoration of the "social wage," correc-
tion of the worst of the present economic tendencies, and development of a
democratic planning system. By the social wage, economic democrats mean
the various protections instituted since the New Deal against the dangers of
life under capitalism. These include unemployment compensation, social security, health care, education, housing, and all the other forms of assistance
to the poor and minorities that were so sharply cut back in the early years of
the Reagan administration.

The social wage is another way of stating the notion of extending individual rights to include economic and social rights. This idea is absolutely fundamental to economic democracy. Almost every publication contains either a list
of such rights or a reference to a particular Economic Bill of Rights. In the
founding document of the Campaign for Economic Democracy, for example,
the first principle of economic democracy is listed as "an Economic Bill of
Rights which recognizes that every citizen is assured the rights to work,
health, housing, education, personal safety and environmental sanity."[13] The
other principles, in order, were: participation in economic decision making, in
democratic economic planning, and in public enterprises; a sane energy and
agricultural policy; decentralized and community-based social services;
employment policy for meaningful work; real equality of opportunity; progressive tax reform; and a foreign policy that serves human needs.

The United States is an industrialized, highly urbanized nation possessing great wealth and natural resources. All inhabitants of the United States should have the right to a decent life, free from fear of economic insecurity. Citizens of all races, creeds, sexes, and cultural backgrounds should have the opportunity to develop their unique potential as human beings through meaningful work, a decent family life, and fulfilling leisure. It is the duty of government to provide for these opportunities.

Therefore, the Congress of the United States, as representatives of its citizens, shall pass the necessary laws and adequately fund programs to ensure the following economic rights:

1. The right to a decent job for all those willing to work.

2. The right to adequate health care for all regardless of income.

3. The right to a good education.

4. The right to decent, affordable housing.

5. The right to protection from the fears of old age through a secure social security system.

6. The right to nutritious food at a reasonable price.

7. The right to provision of the basic utilities of light, heat, telecommunications, and transportation at a fair price.

8. The right to a clean, healthy urban and rural environment in which to live.

9. The right to a secure and stable community.

10. The right to participate democratically in places of work and the affairs of local and national government.

FIGURE 6.1   Economic Bill of Rights Resolution
Source: Proposed congressional resolution. Reprinted in Martin Carnoy, Derek Shearer, and Russell Rumberger, *A New Social Contract: The Economy and Government After Reagan* (New York: Harper & Row, 1983) p. 230.

The full employment side of economic democracy has also produced several economic bills of rights. They share many of the same commitments, as a comparison of Figures 6.1 and 6.2 will demonstrate. Figure 6.1 is a proposed congressional resolution offered by Carnoy, Shearer, and Rumberger. Figure 6.2 is the statement of purposes of the proposed Recovery and Full Employment Planning Act of 1984, sponsored by Representative John Conyers. But these do not by themselves represent solutions. They need to be expanded and developed and then applied through political action.

An expanded version of the social wage would reorder the taxing and spending priorities of the national government. A truly progressive tax system is needed to replace the inequitable and regressive system now in effect. In particular the taxes on the rich and the corporations eliminated in 1981 need to be restored. Spending for military purposes should be drastically cut back, both to reduce the dangers of the arms race and to make funds available for social needs.

Sec. 2.   The major purposes of this Act are to

   (1) develop a nation-wide commitment to democratic planning for the establishment of an enforceable right to earn a living at real earnings high enough to provide the purchasing power required for sustainable recovery and a full employment society,

   (2) through both market and non-market processes, expand useful employment toward the goal of sustainable recovery and full employment,

   (3) enlarge productive capacity by improving the infrastructure of the nation's public works, human services and private industries and developing natural resources in a manner consistent with the maintenance of environmental quality,

   (4) match enlarged productive capacity with the higher real wages and salaries needed by both middle and lower income people to buy goods and services and invest in the productive capacity of the country,

   (5) provide thereby larger markets and better opportunities for enterprises with smaller unit profit margins to earn larger, more stable and less subsidized total profits on invested capital,

   (6) prevent or counterbalance undue concentration of corporate and federal planning power by fostering recovery and full employment planning by

        (a) labor, the unemployed, racial and ethnic minorities, women, small and large profit-seeking enterprises, and cooperative, non-profit and voluntary organizations, and

        (b) town, city, county and state governments in urban, suburban, rural and agricultural areas,

   (7) establish a full employment context for the preparation of and action on the many local, state and federal laws and executive policies required for recovery and full employment

   (8) reduce economic dependence on military outlays and promote conversion from military to civilian goods and services,

   (9) provide for greater accountability to the American people by elected and appointed government officials and by the directors and executives of corporations and other organizations operating under public charters,

   (10) create conditions for more self-empowerment by people victimized by discrimination in hiring, training, wages, salaries, fringe benefits or promotion on the basis of prejudice concerning race, ethnic background, religion, sex, age, political or sexual preferences or personal disability, and

   (11) in doing all these things, promote greater activism by all Americans in decisionmaking affecting themselves, their families, workplaces, communities, states and nation and their country's place in the world community.

FIGURE 6.2   The Recovery and Full Employment Planning Act (Draft Version, Statement of Purposes)

The next task would be to begin to redirect private investment toward social concerns instead of profit maximizing at the expense of workers and communities. The principal means to this end is plant-closing legislation. This would require corporations to give notice of their intent to close and/or move plants from one community to another. In some versions, corporations would have to provide moving or retraining allowances to workers, community compensation, or opportunities for the community or workers to buy the plant and operate it themselves.

Once these basic protections have been secured, restructuring of the economy can begin. Growth is essential to provide for full employment. But it must be growth without the recurring threats of inflation or unemployment and without destruction of the environment. This combination of priorities means that planning and a major role for the national government in controlling the rate and character of growth are imperative. The full employment side of economic democracy sees a necessary major role for government, in opposition to the still-dominant free market principle. The Full Employment Action Council again offers a good example:

> While the market can be a marvel at promoting short-run efficiency, it cannot solve larger problems. Markets by themselves cannot protect the environment, secure the health and safety of workers, eliminate discrimination, promote equal opportunities and adequate income levels for households, foster long-run basic research and innovation, and ensure national security.[14]

Broad democratic participation in an elaborate new planning system, reaching from the lowest levels of local jurisdictions to the heights of national decision making, will be required. New institutions for planning will probably have to be created at the local level, perhaps with the incentive of federal funding. Either new or newly democratized national institutions will be required to synthesize and implement the local recommendations. An example would be a newly democratized Federal Reserve Board in which representatives of workers and consumers would break the bankers' monopoly, giving the public genuine control over the value and availability of money and credit.

How would such a national planning system seek to achieve growth and full employment? In part the answer lies in massive public investment, for example, in public works programs. Far from being of a make-work nature, the programs would permit the badly needed development of roads, mass transit systems, and terminals that make all the rest of the economy and society able to function. In addition, investments in training, education, environmental quality, work safety, and the like would require many new social service workers and give all people a better chance for personal development. And many new public enterprises would compete effectively with private businesses, producing goods and services actually needed by people and steadily contributing to a rising standard of living.

As the economy boomed in response to this massive public investment, there would probably be need for assurance that inflation would be prevented. Economic democrats propose a control system over the key areas of inflation—food, energy, health care, and housing. With profit maximizing inhibited through public ownership and control, inflation would not develop anything like its 1970s momentum. If necessary, strict indexing or outright controls could be imposed. Under no circumstances, however, would the current tax-cutting or recession-promoting remedies be employed. The principle of equity requires that all share both burdens and benefits equally in the new democratic economy.

All economic democrats recognize that this program of sweeping change in social purpose and national policy is possible only in conjunction with equally profound changes in political thought and practice on the part of millions of Americans. New voting alignments and the participation of many of those who do not now vote regularly will be required—as will reconstruction of existing political institutions.

However, only a relatively few economic democrats address the actual problems involved in developing such a political movement or holding it together long enough to accomplish its ends. Many seem to feel that the Democratic Party is the best vehicle for achieving such reforms, without much regard for the fact that the Democrats are only slightly less strongly linked to big business than the Republicans. Others are vehement in urging that a new third party be established to press their claims, free of the encumbrances of the Democratic Party. The Citizens Party of 1980, for example, was programmatically linked to economic democracy, although its national top-down character violated basic principles of the movement.

One major work that fully expresses the economic democracy hopes for developing a political base capable of bringing it to power is Harry Boyte's *The Backyard Revolution: Understanding the New Citizen Movement.* Boyte argues that an unrecognized grass-roots movement, "different from liberal, progressive, or left traditions," is a rapidly growing and already significant force in American politics. He argues:

> The citizen movement represents, indeed, an alternative popular democratic thread of insurgency in modern society—what I believe can be called a "populist" heritage. . . . it incubates an alternative world view, different than the conventional vision of either left or right.[15]

The presence of a large and active social base in support of economic democracy's decidedly radical program would indeed make it a major new force in American politics. The possibility is worth further analysis.

IMPLICATIONS AND PROSPECTS

As we have seen, the economic democracy program essentially has five planks: full employment, race and sex equality, economic growth in balance with environmental protection, control of the arms race, and democratization of the economy. This last includes work place democracy, in plant and office; employee ownership; social control over capital investment decisions, probably by some combination of workers, communities, and the general public; and at least some degree of democratic planning.

Most Americans probably agree with the first four planks of that program, although they might have doubts about the specific forms or whether they are really practical and achievable. But the last plank poses a real challenge. History, habits of thinking, anxiety about the unknown — all contribute to the likelihood of support for what is sure to be determined resistance from the business community.

Americans are historically accustomed to thinking of economic and social life as one distinct sphere, where private property reigns supreme and individuals must rely on their own efforts to reach their own levels in the social pyramid. Politics is another sphere, where political-legal rights apply. The idea of "democracy" is linked to the second sphere only. The long-established notion of the free economic market helps to maintain the image of a wall of separation between the two worlds. And our capitalist economy, it is felt, is one of the reasons why the United States is the richest and most powerful nation in the world today.

All of these deeply grounded habits of mind stand stonily in economic democracy's path, almost daring it to try to undo what history has taken three centuries to accomplish. But economic democracy is at least arguably an idea whose time might yet come. It is plausible and has a genuine logic to it. It can be made to fit in the American tradition. Moreover, it is beginning to pick up a number of advocates from a wide variety of sources, some quite unlikely.

Theorists of democracy who have focused on its close relationship to human aspirations are well aware of the logical indefensibility of a wall of separation between economics and politics. Capitalist democracy, in other words, is a contradiction in terms. Systematically produced and maintained inequalities cannot be made compatible with democracy in the full sense except by doing some form of violence to the idea or practice of democracy. Thus democracy is clearly incomplete without *economic* democracy.

Logic does not often win in politics, of course, but it does keep some ideas alive. The notion of economic democracy has more than that going for it today, however. It is intellectually attractive to many diverse elements across the American spectrum. The eminent political scientist Robert Dahl, for example, reflecting on the incompleteness of the American pluralist democracy that he has studied throughout his long and distinguished career, concludes that "an economic order fully under democratic controls"[16] must be explored in order to realize the potential of pluralist democracy in the United States. The originator of the idea of industrial policy, Robert Reich of Harvard, argues that the nation needs more, not less, democracy in its institutions and practices if it is to make the necessary economic adjustments in a just and peaceful manner. In particular, he insists upon democratizing a new economic planning system.[17]

And so the notion of economic democracy seems to have a lively new intellectual base. Its political base seems less firm, however, and dependent on continued economic crisis and hardship. There is continual tension among the disparate elements of the economic democracy movement, and their fragile coalition often seems about to break apart. Despite some powerful and persuasive arguments, particularly in Richard Grossman and Gail Daneker's *Energy, Jobs, and the Economy*,[18] some still see economic growth and protection of the environment as fundamentally opposed goals. Environmentalists and organized labor, two vital elements of the economic democracy coalition, have not fully come to terms with each other. Both minorities and womens' groups have a tendency to insist that their own needs must come first, minorities vie with one another, and mutual cancellation always seems a distinct possibility. Nuclear freeze and antiwar groups seem even more prone to a tunnel vision that elevates their concerns above the "everyday" issues that absorb others. Local organizations appear to have an infinite particularism that prevents coherent action with others except at the cost of extreme delays.

All of these familiar difficulties are the mark of a *coalition*, rather than a genuinely integrated body of people with an equally integrated belief system. Economic democracy, in the absence of the economic crisis and hardship that induces coalition among groups and movements with different premises, priorities, and goals, would be a small and quarrelsome movement with little future. If the 1980s prove to be a period of sustained economic problems, however, this coalition may become an integrated movement.

It seems clear that economic democracy has the potential to be a viable movement, particularly in view of its growing intellectual respectability. The fact that American businesses are increasingly experimenting with various forms of worker control suggests that the movement may be entering a stage where it is threatened with cooptation by employers. In the American system, when a movement has to worry about cooptation, it knows that it has arrived as a serious challenge to the established political-economic structure.

ADDITIONAL READINGS

Boyte, Harry. *The Backyard Revolution: Understanding the New Citizen Movement*. Philadelphia: Temple University Press, 1980.

Carnoy, Martin, and Shearer, Derek. *Economic Democracy: The Challenge of the 1980s*. White Plains, N.Y.: M.E. Sharpe, 1980.

Carnoy, Martin; Shearer, Derek; and Rumberger, Russell. *A New Social Contract: The Economy and Government After Reagan*. New York: Harper & Row, 1983.

Dahl, Robert A. *Dilemmas of Pluralist Democracy: Autonomy vs. Control*. New Haven: Yale, 1982.

Green, Mark. *Winning Back America*. New York: Bantam, 1982.

Grossman, Richard, and Daneker, Gail. *Energy, Jobs, and the Economy*. Boston: Alyson Publications, 1979.

Hayden, Tom. *The American Future: New Visions Beyond Old Frontiers*. Boston: South End Press, 1980.

Lekachman, Robert. *Greed Is Not Enough: Reaganomics*. New York: Pantheon Books, 1982.

Newfield, Jack, and Greenfield, Jeff. *A Populist Manifesto: The Making of a New Majority*. New York: Warner Paperback Library, 1972.

Rifkin, Jeremy. *Own Your Own Job: Economic Democracy for Working Americans*. New York: Bantam, 1977.

CHAPTER 7

American Democratic Socialism

Classic socialism originated almost immediately after capitalism crystallized as a set of beliefs. However, the body of ideas analyzed here — American democratic socialism — really took form only in the 1970s. It is a successor to and distinct from both the American socialist tradition and European Marxist socialism. It is a new synthesis original to the United States and not just another of Marxism's many forms.

Some democratic socialists no longer even refer to Karl Marx. His concepts and methods have been fully melded with the principles developed by the many American democratic socialist thinkers. Moreover, those who make their adaptations of Marxian ideas more explicit often take great pains to distinguish their beliefs from those of contemporary Marxists and today's socialist countries. In part they do so because in the United States a fair hearing for explicitly socialist beliefs is almost impossible unless advocates disassociate themselves from what Americans see as foreign ideas and repressive systems. But, at least in some cases, democratic socialists warmly welcome the opportunity. In a recent work entitled *Socialism Today and Tomorrow*, for example, the authors declare their distance in this way: "We can no longer be bound by a language incapable of expressing real situations. The litany that the Soviet Union, China, Cuba, or the Eastern Block countries are socialist societies is a lie."[1] While this may be a bit extreme, it is representative in its determination to sever any connection with sectarian Marxist-Leninist thought and to avoid association of the concept of socialism with the structures and practices of contemporary socialist countries. Once most American socialists viewed other countries as their models. Today's democratic socialists offer a fresh and distinctive modern vision applicable only to the United States at some future time.

Democratic socialism is readily distinguishable from economic democracy even though some socialists may employ the latter term in order to avoid the problems just noted. Democratic socialism is a holistic and integrated body of beliefs which sees all facets of a society as coherent and mutually supporting. The problems that generate change-seeking movements — feminist, minority, ecology, anti-war — are all one and the same. They form an interrelated package that can be addressed effectively only as a unit.

Democratic socialists acknowledge no threshold whatsoever between economics and politics. They do recognize, however, that part of their task is to help others break down the wall of separation that their society has erected. But that's not all. To reconstruct the economic and political system, one must also reconstruct the cultural base and personal identities that are produced within that society. Herbert Gintis clearly expresses this interpenetration of politics with all other aspects of social life:

> Individuals are themselves produced by the political practices they engage in. Just as work produces not only goods, but also transformed people with transformed capacities and social relations, so politics produces people as well as decisions. . . . Thus our first task will be to characterize politics in such a way that it becomes clear that it is not restricted to one sphere of social life, but is present at all sites of social activity — the state, the family, the economy, education, the scientific and cultural communities, the media, and the like.[2]

Most democratic socialists see economic democracy as a coalition of separate movements and individuals, anticapitalist but not yet socialist in their orientation. What makes the difference is the socialist's comprehensive grasp of the mutually reproducing nature of all the various parts of a society as it moves through time. Economic democrats would not normally see all of these interconnections or the cultural depths at which capitalism lives in all Americans. The economic democracy agenda is not as crowded and complex, and its demands are so specific and tangible that they are more readily subject to cooptation by a few successes.

Another distinguishing mark is that democratic socialists are more comfortable with the subtle concept of social class. Class has a reality for socialists. It expresses a relationship between people that is grounded in the way a society produces what it needs to maintain itself. Class is central to a society's tensions and dynamism and, most importantly, to how it changes. Though workers or laborers are generally the core, socialists might include groups that could perform equivalent functions in the process of social change.

Economic democrats, in contrast, tend to think of people in terms of their specific interests. They see the problem of change as one of organizing tactical coalitions among various groups. Economic democrats are less likely than socialists to think in terms of a theory of social change. And, finally, they would never use the word "socialism" in describing their beliefs.

ORIGINS AND EVOLUTION

American Socialism

Before the Civil War, socialism was essentially grounded in moral rejection of capitalism's practices — its greed, selfishness, and sharp dealings and, particularly, its treatment of workers. Long hours, low pay, and unsafe and authoritarian working conditions led many to look for alternatives; some embraced socialism. At this point, it meant public ownership of the means of production and an egalitarian sharing of both the burdens and benefits of the new industrial capacities. Some socialists sought to act out their beliefs in the form of experimental cooperative communities. For many reasons these were short lived, but ever since their sponsors have been known as "utopian socialists."

As industrialization proceeded, the contrast in the way owners and workers were affected by it led to a growing sense of two classes whose interests were directly opposed. Many workers were immigrants, and among them were Germans who had knowledge of Marx's writings and experience with socialist political activities. Socialism began to focus on building a mass working-class organization grounded in the developing labor movement. From the beginning, socialists were divided by controversies over tactics and routes to be followed.[3]

The Socialist Labor Party (SLP), formed in 1877, represented one major position. It was highly critical of the labor movement for being too ready to cooperate with capitalism. While led by Daniel DeLeon, an aristocrat of Spanish descent who joined the party in 1889, the SLP stood for an all-or-nothing transformation of the society. A particular target was the American Federation of Labor (AFL) under Samuel Gompers. However, the AFL remained the largest labor union and adhered to reformist goals in the characteristic manner of American interest groups.

A much more flexible position was maintained by the greatest of the early socialists, Eugene V. Debs of Indiana. Debs was originally a railroad union leader and was involved in several bitter strikes of the 1890s. He became a socialist while in jail for his part in the Pullman Strike of 1894. Debs believed in bringing together as many workers as possible to work for immediate improvements. In the process, he hoped that they, too, would come to see the necessity of socialism. He was a thoroughgoing democrat, and this was reflected in the Socialist Party which he was instrumental in forming in 1901. In part because of its pragmatic radicalism, the Socialist Party enjoyed much greater electoral success than the SLP ever did.

Another major issue dividing socialists in this period was the form of labor organization that would best serve the goals of building a working-class political base for socialism. One group wanted to work within the AFL. Hoping to rise to power in the trade union movement, they believed they could eventually bring the workers to socialism. The AFL was organized on the basis of distinct skilled crafts, however. This not only meant that its members had greater leverage against employers than did unskilled workers but also that they were better paid and, hence, less receptive to radical political programs.

Others wanted to form their own socialist unions and bring workers into them. Usually this meant organizing *industrial* unions, or a union of all workers in a given industry, from the most skilled to the ordinary laborers. Debs was committed to industrial unionism as the only way to effectively get socialism on the agenda of the trade union movement. He was initially a supporter of the International Workers of the World (IWW), a group dedicated to organizing the many workers in seasonal, migrant, and other hard-to-organize occupations. Despite some real successes, the IWW finally alienated many socialists with its violent rhetoric and sometimes violent practice.

Prior to World War I, American socialism was predominantly a democratic educational enterprise devoted to electoral efforts to build its strength. Debs and others often denounced the violence of some anarchists and IWW followers. In 1912, probably the high point of socialism in the United States, more than 1,200 elected public officials were socialists. That year socialists also made up almost one-third of the delegates at the AFL convention and hotly contested Gompers' reelection. Its own leadership elections repeatedly demonstrated socialism's commitment to racial and sexual equality.

But then came World War I. Socialist parties in Europe abandoned international workers' solidarity to vote support of their respective capitalist governments' war efforts. Millions of workers literally fought each other. But American socialists sought to preserve international working-class solidarity, vehemently opposing American involvement in the war. They called a convention in April 1917 and passed a resolution declaring the war "a crime against the people of the United States." They pledged that "in support of capitalism we will not willingly give a single life or a single dollar." At almost the same moment, the U.S. Congress declared war against Germany.

In the fall of that year, as part of its opposition, the Socialist Party ran several municipal and state candidates on peace platforms. Many of them did well, which seemed to promise a continuing effective socialist opposition to the war. But socialism was promptly overwhelmed by patriotic nationalism and forced on the defensive. New federal laws prohibited opposition to the draft. Local police and vigilantes joined in harassing socialists and the Immigration and Naturalization Service investigated and deported thousands of socialists as "alien agitators."

The success of the Bolsheviks in the Russian Revolution greatly complicated the situation for American socialists. Some socialists wanted to defend everything the Soviet Union did. This meant they had to suddenly reverse themselves, supporting the war against Germany so that the Soviets would be free to proceed with their experiment. More important, to many Americans it made the threat posed by American socialists seem greater. The U.S. government redoubled its efforts to jail, deport, and silence socialists. After the armistice, a major campaign was mounted to eliminate socialism as a force in American life.

Under these pressures and beset by internal disagreements, socialism began to dissolve. In 1920, although once again in jail, this time for speaking out against the war, Debs ran for president for the sixth time. In a remarkable individual tribute, he received nearly a million votes. However, socialism generally ceased to be a significant factor in American politics. Ever since, except for a short period in the depths of the depression of the 1930s, socialism has not approached its earlier role as an organized opponent of capitalism in the United States. It remains to be seen, of course, whether its current renascence can change this situation.

The Essence of Marxism

Few sets of ideas have had as much impact or been so variously understood as the principles developed by Karl Marx.[4] Since the 1850s, American socialists have wrestled with the problem of adapting Marx's ideas to the specific realities of the American social experience.[5] Some have tried to make direct applications in almost literal fashion. Others have made so many modifications their Marxism has not seemed distinguishable from standard American reform liberalism.

In this section, we shall briefly indicate some of the concepts and methods that Karl Marx contributed to the current versions of democratic socialism in the United States. By now, most democratic socialists perceive these basic analytic principles as a matter of common sense rather than as specifically Marxist in origin. They do, however, provide democratic socialists with a common core of ways of thinking about social life.

Marx was first and foremost a *comprehensive* thinker. He sought to grasp the entirety of a social order as it moved from one form through the present toward another form. Each new form was both old and new, a synthesis of past and future. If a society did not adapt to its changing environment in this way, it would not survive. Marx was specifically writing about industrial societies like those of Europe in the mid-nineteenth century. He believed capitalism to be a necessary prerequisite to the higher forms of socialism and communism.

Capitalism was in turn a higher form than feudalism because it generated improved material conditions. It possessed the productive capacity to raise everybody's standard of living far beyond the stage where people had to struggle for survival. But capitalism also produced greed, destructive competition and wars, and irrational abuse of natural resources; it denied people the opportunity to realize their innate potential as *human* beings. The profit motive compelled man's exploitation of his fellow man. But, in its turn, capitalism would create the economic conditions and social pressures that would make for its transformation to socialism.

However, Marx never believed the transition to socialism to be inevitable, mechanical, or necessary in the sense of being preordained. It was a highly desirable possibility, essential, in fact, if the world were to survive and progress. On the other hand, capitalism would not be the first social order to perish because of failure to change when conditions required it. Every society, like any complex situation, contains within it several possible futures.

Marx always emphasized the potential that situations or societies had for becoming something that they were not yet but could be. The purpose of philosophy was to find ways to bring about the better, more desirable potential. Socialism was important to Marx because it would create the conditions under which human beings could realize their true potential.

The essential factor was what human beings did with their opportunity to shape their future. Human agency determines which of several potential futures will actually come about, constrained only by the range of the possible set by surrounding historical conditions. In Marx's world, the historical agency of change was the working class. It would determine whether capitalism served as a prelude to socialism or to barbarism and eventual human extinction after a period of rigidification, fascism, war, etc. Marx saw class conflict as the source of change that led to the establishment of capitalism. The shift to socialism, the next possible and desirable form of social order, would only occur if that great opposition class, the working class, came to a consciousness of both the social imperative of forcing the change and its own strength and capacity to do so.

Marx's concept of class had both objective and subjective dimensions. Objectively, the working class was defined by its dependent relationship to the major means of production owned by the few capitalists. And it was the capitalists whose ideas and power dominated the society. In other words, all those who had no way to earn their living except by selling their labor power were objectively one class. Furthermore, their interests were opposed to those of the capitalists whether they realized it or not. When economic and social conditions made it possible, workers would become aware of their shared interests, conscious that such interests were irreconcilable with those of the capitalists, and determined to act on their own behalf. At this point, the subjective dimension of class would be reached. The working class would be *class conscious* and ready to fulfill its role as the historical agent of change to socialism.

Marx never underestimated the power of the ruling ideas within capitalist society. He was aware of their effectiveness in preventing workers from understanding their own true interest in forcing the change to socialism. He saw all people as *socially produced* in the sense that their language, values, concepts, ways of thinking, and even their personal identities were shaped by the society in which they grew up. People would see and understand their world as that world wanted them to. Wherever they looked they would find confirmation of the rightness, inevitability, and permanence of its particular distribution of wealth and power. Only dramatic changes in economic and social conditions would break the grip of the dominant ideology. At that point, knowledgeable socialists and a working class political party should be ready to help the class take power in the state. Only then could the working class as a whole begin to implement socialist reconstruction of the society, a process that would be long and arduous.

Marx emphasized thinking and acting in terms of a desirable future that was only a potential, neither predetermined nor inevitable. He was impatient with "utopians," by which he meant those who imagined and sought to bring about future societies that were not historically possible under existing conditions. Marx was always concerned with the range of the possible set by current economic and social circumstances. However, he always viewed those circumstances flexibly — in the light of what they would permit and could become, rather than what they were or how they might prevent change. This led him to intensive studies of contemporary conditions. He looked for the contradictions within them, the things that capitalism was doing that would lead to internal conflicts or opposition. But his search was always for the openings and opportunities that might allow for socialist advances.

With such a perspective, Marx was more interested in and optimistic about the prospect of social change than most other people in Western societies. Particularly in the United States, people tended and still tend to see the world exclusively in terms of tangible, measurable facts about its current situation. Any thoughts about change generally focus on one or two factors, with everything else perceived as remaining fixed. Far-reaching changes in the basic structures of the society thus seem both impossible and undesirable. It is hard for Americans to understand why Marxists do not like capitalist society. More importantly, it is difficult to believe things could ever be different from what they are today.

When recession or depression brings unemployment and hard times, however, many people become more receptive to Marx's advocacy of a more egalitarian and stable economic system. His most famous work, *Capital*, is a detailed critique of capitalism that contains explanations for many of the processes and results that regularly occur. At first, this was the only major work that socialists had as a source for understanding his ideas. Marx's earlier publications, *The Economic and Philosophical Manuscripts of 1844* and *The German Ideology*, became widely known to Americans only after World War II.[6] From these, it was possible to piece together Marx's humanism and his comprehensive image of the process and purpose of change. With so much more to go on, however, socialists began to disagree more. In addition, the experiences of successful socialist movements in other countries soon added to the principles that had to be considered, as well as to the resistance to Marxist ideas in the United States.

The Marxism that American democratic socialists employ is a synthesis around an economic core, thoroughly adapted to American realities. However, it is composed of many strands rather than a single agreed content. Academic and other economists have kept Marx's economic analysis of capitalism alive by applying it to explain downturns in the business cycle. Others have concentrated on merging Marx's methods and humanistic purposes with psychology and existentialism to produce a cultural critique of American society.

Many blacks and feminists who were dissatisfied with narrow reform movements have found this holistic approach to provide a better understanding and framework for action. A variety of other environmental, antiwar, and community activists have come to the same conclusion. They have joined with labor, academic, and other long-term socialists to bring revitalization and urgency to the new democratic socialism. It is not necessary in the eyes of any but a few diehards that the Marxist origins, texts, or categories be explicitly referenced in the process of seeking explanations and solutions. Democratic socialism has thus emerged in full possession of some powerful tools, free of many of the disabilities that their predecessors once carried, and ready for a much larger role in the American political dialogue.

BASIC VALUES

Today's revitalized democratic socialism is substantially reconstructing the basic American values, moving them (characteristically) toward becoming one coherent new package. The labels are the same, as is some of the content. But enough is different to give the whole a distinctive new set of implications. Before examining each, it will help to identify two major streams of thought and purpose that have played major roles in the reconstruction process.

The first started from the socialist tradition but sought to profoundly rework its economic and cultural components into a new American synthesis. The most traditional example is the cluster of economists and others around *Monthly Review*. Started during the cold war era, *Monthly Review* is an explicitly Marxist journal that has made an important place for itself on the American left. More iconoclastic are the chiefly academic economists and others associated with the Union for Radical Political Economy and the mostly ex–New Left activists associated with the periodical *Socialist Review*.

In every case, thinkers have two main goals. One is to appropriately apply modernized socialist concepts to the American experience, often casting them in familiar American democratic terms. The other is to integrate feminist, minority, antiwar, and environmental theory and analysis into the socialist core to create a single multidimensional framework and action agenda. This expansion of the socialist project has been carried furthest (and laced with a touch of anarchism or 'council cmmunism") by Michael Albert and Robin Hahnel, the authors of the book *Socialism Today and Tomorrow*. They call for a "totalist socialism," by which they mean "an attempt to evolve a new orientation suited to both our current situation and our socialist aims" that "emphasizes four spheres of daily life" (politics, economics, kinship, and community).[7]

The second perspective from which democratic socialism is being revitalized and American values reconstructed is that of the expansion of democracy. Sometimes covertly, but often quite explicitly, thinkers ask what democracy requires for its realization in the United States. And they conclude that the answer is democratic socialism. This is not the same as the economic democrats' assertion that democracy should be extended to the economy. In making that demand, economic democrats more or less assume that political democracy exists in a satisfactory form in the United States. All that is needed is its application "as is" to economic affairs.

Democratic socialists, in contrast, believe that political democracy in the United States is corrupt, degraded, and a sham. Inequalities of wealth and power, inherent in capitalism, make for domination of politics and people by corporations and the wealthy. To extend *this* sort of democracy is to foster illusions. In effect, these theorists start with the limitations and defects of political democracy today, searching for causes and solutions in order to maximize the democratic qualities of life for all citizens. It does not take long before their inquiry identifies capitalist social relationships as well as its inequalities, the profit motive, and unlimited corporate power as the seat of the problem.

For example, in an excellent little book with the disarming title *On Democracy*, the political theorist authors flatly declare:

> For its realization, democracy requires the abolition of capitalism. Again, this is not because of the materially unsatisfying character of life under capitalism, but because of its structural denial of freedom. To choose democracy is to choose against that denial.[8]

That is putting the matter rather bluntly. But the same message has been spelled out at greater length and with more detail by several other scholarly students of democracy in the United States.[9]

The advantage that socialists from this second group have, of course, is that they start with the well-accepted value of democracy. They then arrive at the necessity of socialism. Tactically, they are on stronger ground than their allies who start from the strengths of socialism and insist that democracy can be realized only in that context. But the two groups are saying exactly the same thing and their congruence helps to give democratic socialism its momentum in reshaping American values. What they share most clearly and explicitly is their commitment to democracy.

Democratic socialists have no sense of separation between politics and economics, much less of a wall between the two. But they recognize that to most Americans "democracy" is a term that applies only to politics. The first task, therefore, is to show that political democracy is incomplete without at least some measure of popular control over the uses of private wealth and power. They want to illuminate the fact of conflict between democracy (revered) and capitalism (questionable) in American life. If the wall of separation can be breached, many goals become possible. Changes in value definitions are only one of the possibilities. Changes in established conceptual assumptions, such as that of an inevitable conflict between equity and efficiency, are another. The economist Herbert Gintis declares the strategy as follows:

> We shall initially apply our conception to capitalist production, arguing that democratic production is not only more conducive to worker satisfaction and growth, but is also efficient and provides superior production. This is in direct contrast to traditional economic theory, which holds that through the logic of profit maximization, capitalist production is maximally efficient and worker satisfaction cannot be improved without lowering efficiency, wages, and product quality. We will then apply our conception of democracy to the organization of the family. . . . [10]

In other words, democracy is not only paramount as a value, but it is to be generalized to every aspect of social life, particularly including economic activities. The payoffs from institutionalizing democracy include popular control and personal development, familiar enough aspirations if always incompletely realized. But they also include improvement in every function — in the efficiency of the economy and the quality of its products, for example. This is a new, deeper, and more pervasive claim for democracy, well beyond the goals sought by multiplying rights or participatory mechanisms.

In democratic socialism, the realization of the individual's aspirations comes primarily through associations with other people. To develop oneself will mean to contribute successfully to the development of others, and vice versa. Individuals in a society are mutually interdependent. There will be ample room for initiative, responsibility, and distinctive achievement, but all of these will occur with and for others, in a spirit of solidarity.

The notion of community is a vital one for democratic socialists, both as a priority in its own right and as the arena for individual participation and development. In a major recent work entitled *The Deindustrialization of America*[11] the economists Barry Bluestone and Bennett Harrison focus on a concern for American communities. The subtitle of the book, for example, is "Plant Closings, Community Abandonment, and the Dismantling of Basic Industry," and the title of the first chapter is "Capital vs. Community." Communities are social as well as geographic entities; they are, in fact, the basic unit of social life, and as such they are entitled to protection and enhancement in every possible way. The authors go on to propose new powers for communities over corporations and their investment decisions. They also advocate a comprehensive community-based democratic planning system.

The traditional isolated individual of American thinking is thus to be replaced by a participating member of a community who derives his or her satisfactions from playing an integral part in this complex social web. Perhaps the single most important collective function for communities and for the public as a whole is social control over investment. This requires fundamental change in the notion of property rights, of course, as well as conversion from individualized to community-grounded thinking. Gintis urges that such change be viewed as the expansion of "personal rights" — life, liberty, pursuit of happiness — over mere "property rights." This is integral to his conception of democracy and socialism as an integrated whole, and his argument deserves to be quoted at length:

> We shall suggest that socialism be viewed as the abolition of property in the means of production, not its mere collectivization. This can be understood only if we view the economy as a political system in which property rights confer political power on owners. The abolition of property rights in the means of production involves vesting access to political participation in the economy directly and equally in all workers, communities, and consumers, on the basis of their rights as citizens in the economic community. More generally, socialism in America must be seen as the deepening of democratic practices in the state, and the extension of democratic practices to the economy and family life. For socialism to come about, Americans must come to see it not as the excision of democracy from the state but its expansion in the state and its intrusion into the economy, where the despotism of the capitalist now reigns supreme, and into the family, where male supremacy and authoritarianism regulate the relations among men, women, and children. . . .
>
> Our vision of the political structure of socialism derives from this struggle (between "person rights" and "property rights"). The demands of social groups for person rights — the right to vote, the right to organize and assemble, the right to a job, equal rights for women and minorities, the right to control one's body and one's personal relations with others, the right to education, health, and

welfare — are direct attacks on capitalist property rights. Socialism in America
can be conceived and achieved precisely in these terms: the full expression of
rights vested equally in persons in all spheres of life, property rights existing only
where they are instrumental to the securing of person rights.[12]

Gintis' argument demonstrates once again that democratic socialism's
values are so fully integrated that it is very difficult to speak of them separately. It is obvious that contracts and law will recede in importance with
property rights, leaving much greater flexibility (or freedom) for communities to devise methods to suit their goals. Indeed, freedom becomes
something like diversity of outcomes and opportunities. It is a concept that
describes what happens through community and public decisions rather
than a right of individuals against the community. Equality expands to involve redistribution and a range of individual entitlements that make genuine membership in the community possible.

The integrated nature of democratic socialist values — their mutually re-
inforcing character — means that they are often stated as a package. They
cannot be implemented as separate items. This is evident, for example, if we
look at the seven main institutional requirements for democracy identified
by Cohen and Rogers: civil rights and civil liberties, public subsidy for organized competitive political groups, egalitarian distributional measures,
public control of investment, work place democracy, equal opportunity, and
a foreign policy informed by the principles of democratic legitimacy that underlie the domestic system.[13] In a similar vein, Albert and Hahnel say:

> We believe that neither our community, kinship, political, or economic visions
> can stand alone. We don't see how it would be possible to move from a society
> like the one we endure in the United States to the goals we have outlined in one
> or two of these spheres alone. We are not going to overcome class division while
> preserving a sexual division of labor and a kinship process generating shattered
> personalities. Nor will we attain participatory democracy while pursuing ho-
> mogenization of different cultural heritages. . . . As the kinds of human traits
> which socialist kinship activity generates provide a basis for economic self-
> management, and as economic self-management propels participatory politics,
> and as participatory politics helps instill attitudes necessary for communities to
> learn from and appreciate one another, so the reverse is true as well . . . the
> core characteristics of oppression are mutually reproductive.[14]

In short, all or nothing — not out of a desire to be the most radical, but
out of necessity. In practice, democratic socialists will take whatever they
can get as a way of developing motion and support, but their goal is a rather
comprehensive reconstruction. At some point, of course, this integrated new
package becomes a substantively new set of values. The package may carry the old labels, but it will contain a transformed content — one amounting
to a synthesis of socialism and democracy. Cohen and Rogers assert, "The
democratic conception owes much to the socialist tradition within modern
politics . . . because the taking of profits under capitalism necessarily subor-
dinates one class of individuals to another." But they also hold that the dem-

ocratic conception owes much as well to the liberal tradition and that "individual liberties require some recognition not only in principle, but also in the actual institutional arrangements of political order."[15]

PROBLEMS AND POSSIBILITIES

The Problems

Democratic socialists believe that the U.S. economy is in serious trouble and that corporations and banks are determined to save all they can of their profit margins by seizing every opportunity to cut costs. The terms democratic socialists use to describe these processes include "deindustrialization," "capital flight," and "the attack on the working class." They see the corporate campaign as systematic, deliberate, and well organized. It amounts to nothing less than an attempt to roll back the bulk of labor's gains since World War II. With corporate influence over the national government at a postwar height, U.S. safety, environmental, and other regulations are rapidly disappearing, along with taxes and social services. International competition becomes another excuse to cut wages, institute automation in various forms, and promote union busting.

National government policy is part of the corporate program to discipline labor. To some extent policy is based on faulty analysis and advice from mainstream economists. Many such economists see inflation as the most serious problem facing the economy. They trace it to rising labor costs and/or reduced investment and low productivity. These conclusions are vigorously challenged by democratic socialists. However, their wide acceptance by policymakers leads to the implementation of one of two remedies, both of which are deplored by democratic socialists as unnecessary, callous, and dangerous.

The first of these remedies is the one preferred by monetarists. Monetarists believe that the way to cure inflation is to reduce the money supply, making money and credit less available and more costly. Essentially their remedy for inflation is a recession brought about by raising interest rates so high that businesses contract and lay off workers. If the inflation is high and sustained, a long and severe recession is necessary to fully eliminate it. Democratic socialists argue that other means of controlling inflation are readily available. The monetarists' remedy is not only unnecessary but forces working people to absorb almost all the costs of halting inflation through reduced wages and joblessness.

The second remedy is the "supply side" approach. This justifies cutting taxes for corporations and the rich on the grounds that they are the only sources of the new investment essential to increasing productivity and profits. When they invest in new plants and other facilities on a massive scale, the new productivity and increased economic activity have two vital effects.

Productivity increases so much more rapidly than other costs that inflation is actually reduced. So much more economic activity is generated that more taxes are returned to the federal treasury than it would have received without the tax cuts. To democratic socialists, this is sheer "voodoo economics." They deny that tax cuts result in either new investment in productive facilities or revenues that are anything but drastically lower than before.

According to democratic socialists, what really occurs amidst all this scientific analysis and prescription is a deliberate and systematic upward redistribution of wealth and power. While working people suffer, the rich really do get richer — and it is all celebrated as being for the good of the whole! Worse, the suffering endured cannot yield a permanent cure for the economic ills of the country because the remedies are intended only to aid the wealthy. They are not aimed at real, underlying economic problems. And it is very dangerous. A deep recession, however deliberately started, can always turn into something policymakers cannot control, such as a serious depression.

Democratic socialists make a special point of refuting the standard explanations for the economy's problems of inflation, unemployment, low profitability, and low productivity. Standard explanations often focus on American workers, the power of unions, excessive wages, or too much government aid to the unemployed and indigent. Alternatively, blame is placed on the government, excessive regulations, excessive taxes, or too much social spending. Democratic socialists deny each and every one of these allegations. They point out that the real wages of American workers declined throughout the 1970s. Several countries' wage levels now exceed those of the United States.

Moreover, in other countries, unions include a much larger proportion of the work force, have many more protections against employers, and play a larger role in government policies. All the major industrial nations that are our competitors have higher taxes and levels of government support for the unemployed or indigent. And governments elsewhere play a much larger part in directing the economy. Our economic difficulties can be traced to neither the failure of the American worker nor too much government, democratic socialists insist. It is the wrong uses of government, together with short-sighted corporate behavior, that have brought about the acute American problems.

The Possibilities

The future looks even less promising than the present. Democratic socialists insist that the economy's structural problems are such that recoveries will be only temporary periods preceding the return of inflation. Furthermore, recoveries are highly segmented: they reward upper-middle-class people but have little constructive impact on ordinary workers, minorities, women, or those who are steadily dropping out of the middle class to which they once belonged.

Without adoption of their own program for economic and political renewal, most democratic socialists see two basic alternatives ahead for the United States. One is continued drift and chaos. There will be occasional illusory recoveries but longer and more frequent recessions. Reagan-like free market policies or Carter-like drift will both fail to deal with the sources of contemporary problems. Conditions will worsen until action becomes unavoidable. If the delay is too long the action likely to be taken is institution of an American brand of neofascism.

The second basic alternative is a more direct movement toward that same neofascism starting with the corporatism currently proposed in the neoliberal industrial policy solutions. This characterization is applied to industrial policy proposals because of the new cooperation between business, labor, and government that they call for and the new institutions they propose for achieving it. Corporatism means the integration of once-separate major interests of a society into one unified body that, though it purports to represent the whole, actually speaks and acts on behalf of big business. Corporatism can take the next step toward a form of fascism should implementation of its decisions become urgent or difficult.

Democratic socialists agree with some of the neoliberals that the United States now has an irrational industrial policy, one that is increasingly out of touch with the needs of national industries in an internationalizing world. Without some substantial change in national macroeconomic policy, the United States will continue its decline and drifting transformation. Sooner or later it will be forced to cope with the chaos flowing from sustained high unemployment and the rising pressures of the new world economy. At such a time, democratic socialists fear, there will be a strong temptation on the part of dominant neoliberals to institute something like an American brand of neofascism. Current proposals for industrial policy are only a preview—but a dangerous one—of what lies in store.

Democratic socialists stress only the *potential* that current proposals and trends have to eventuate in a uniquely American form of neofascism. They do not suggest that the United States presently has such a system in place or that it is inevitable. In *Friendly Fascism: The New Face of Power in America*, for example, Bertram Gross shows the many ways governing elites can manage information and opinion to their advantage without ever resorting to outright coercion. However, he also emphasizes that democratic rights and procedures may make it possible to avoid a final coalescence of American neofascism.[16]

In *Beyond the Waste Land*, Bowles, Gordon, and Weisskopf make an argument similar to that which we have outlined. They see the "megacorporations" as engaged in a campaign for upward redistribution of wealth and power, insulation of the corporations from accountability to the public, and vast increase in military power for use abroad. All of these changes will come at the expense of democracy. The authors cite various sources to show that business executives define excessive democracy as a major obstacle to their dominance. They point out that industrial policy proposals would further increase the leverage corporations have in the society, enabling them to become even freer of public control. They conclude:

> Democracy thus may hang even more critically in the balance than it did in the 1890s and 1930s. . . . Capital has won in the past not from omnipotence, but on

the basis of its ability to define alternatives, and to pose continued economic stagnation as the price of democracy.[17]

Democratic Socialist Programs

Most democratic socialists start from two conceptual premises that make their program seem much less impractical than socialism is often alleged to be. The first reverses the capitalist premise that equity and efficiency are opposed. Democratic socialists argue that the new socialist economy can be *more* productive and efficient precisely *because* it stresses equity and democracy. For example, the authors just cited argue against the claims made by business by presenting "an alternative program that can provide both economic recovery *and* more democracy." They add, "We are convinced that a more democratic and egalitarian economy will work better, not worse, than our present system."[18]

Next, the same authors deny that the costs of the new programs they propose present insuperable obstacles. They develop the concept of waste and misuse of resources into a major thesis, finding such enormous waste in the current capitalist economy that all their alternative programs can be implemented without financial strain. *Beyond the Waste Land* identifies the various kinds of waste and estimates their value in both dollars and proportion of annual gross national product. The analysis is based on the general premise that the heavy hand of corporate power has many costly effects on the economy, not least of which is the resistance it provokes from workers. Corporations waste much time and money in supervising, reorganizing, and otherwise trying to overcome workers' resistance — an investment that would not be needed if workers were free to organize and manage production as they felt proper.

Another tremendous waste is the advertising necessary to sell unwanted goods. Then there is overpriced and unnecessary health care, food, energy, and military spending, as well as money spent in control of crime inspired by joblessness, destitution, and advertising. The authors arrive at a total waste per year of more than $1.2 *trillion*, or nearly half the GNP in 1980.[19] And this estimate does not attempt to include the unmeasurable costs in human resources under- or unutilized, in personal alienation on the job, or other similar wastes of resources. The estimate of current waste in the American economy supports the argument that the democratic socialist program — despite vast expenditures for public works and other social needs — does not involve excessive or unbearable costs for the economy.

Armed with these two empowering concepts — of the positive relationship between equity and efficiency and of current unnecessary waste — democratic socialists offer a variety of proposals for democratizing the economy, promoting equality, and providing for social control over investment through decentralized planning systems. Many sound much like those of the economic democrats, although they eventually go much further. Several democratic socialist programs start with an economic bill of rights.

I. **Right to economic security and equity**
1. Right to a decent job
2. Solidarity wages, comparable pay, and equal employment opportunity
3. Public child care and community service centers
4. A shorter standard work week and flexible work hours
5. Flexible price controls

II. **Right to a democratic work place**
6. Public commitment to democratic trade unions
7. Workers' right to know and to decide
8. Democratic production incentives
9. Promoting community enterprises

III. **Right to chart our economic futures**
10. Planning to meet human needs
11. Democratizing investment
12. Democratic control of money
13. Promoting community life
14. Environmental democracy
15. Democratizing foreign trade

IV. **Right to a better way of life**
16. Reduced military spending
17. Conservation and safe energy
18. Good food
19. A national health policy
20. Lifetime learning and cultural opportunities
21. Payment for home child care in single-parent households
22. Community corrections and reduced crime control spending
23. Community needs information and reduced advertising expenditures
24. Equitable taxation and public allocation of resources

FIGURE 7.1 A Democratic Socialist Economic Bill of Rights

Source: Samuel Bowles, David M. Gordon, and Thomas E. Weisskopf, *Beyond the Waste Land: A Democratic Alternative to Economic Decline* (New York: Anchor Press, 1983), p. 294.

The 24-point economic bill of rights set forth by Bowles, Gordon, and Weisskopf is reproduced as Figure 7.1. It is organized in four categories reflecting their purposes: economic security and equity, democratic and productive work relations, democratic planning in a democratic economy, and the right to a better way of life.

Other democratic socialists employ more general principles and then proceed to illustrate them. For example, Bluestone and Harrison state their basic program this way:

First, there must be a rising standard of living for working people, more equally shared, and an adequate supply of useful goods and services, whether or not they can always be made at a profit . . . more hospitable, more interesting, less authoritarian, and safer work environments. . . . it will be necessary to radically transform the nature of active popular participation in the day-to-day running of the basic institutions of the economy and society.[20]

The democratic socialist programs proceed in three basic stages, consistent with the need to first defend workers and consumers against the corporate attack on their living standards and then reconstruct the society. Thus the restoration of the social safety net comes first, together with plant-closing legislation to prevent further deindustrialization. At the close of their critique in *The Deindustrialization of America*, for example, Bluestone and Harrison stress that job security, health care, and adequate retirement income are needed before other programs can go forward:

> Only as the fear of poverty, disease, and joblessness recedes can human energies be totally released for creative, truly productive effort. Thus, before Americans can embark on any major planned structural transformation of the economy, they must reject the claims of those who would promote insecurity as a matter of policy, find ways to re-establish the social safety net, and *extend* the range of the regulatory system to make that net even more secure for more groups in the population. These are the preconditions for any fundamental restructuring of the American economy.[21]

The second stage implements permanent recovery measures, particularly including full employment programs. Rebuilding the nation's infrastructure is high on the list, followed by health insurance, training, research and development, and other similar investments in human capital. Social control of investment and the planning system are reserved for the final stage, in part because they are the most politically controversial and difficult to achieve. Democratic socialists expect vigorous opposition, especially at the third stage, and have paid considerable attention to the strategy and tactics for accomplishing changes of this scope.

The Political Programs

One of the distinguishing features of democratic socialism is the historical depth and sensitivity of its political thinking. Indeed, there is some impatience with those who do not see economic renewal and social change irretrievably linked to political change. The basic point is well stated by Alan Wolfe, a democratic socialist and a political scientist:

> Americans who live with an economy that must throw people out of work in order to control inflation should not be surprised that they have a political system that must disenfranchise its citizens in order to choose its leaders. Much talk is heard in the 1980s of the need for a program of economic revitalization. Yet, as was true also in the 1940s, economic direction must come from the political system, and American politics is stagnant. America needs a program of political revitalization before its economy will begin to work again.[22]

This political revitalization is also sought by others. It crucially involves several different dimensions. One is the cultural change inherent in reunderstanding the notion of politics so that it includes the relationships between people in all of their activities. Again, we can turn to Gintis for a clear statement regarding this dimension:

> What is wrong with the political structure of capitalism is not simply that it often produces outcomes neither just nor favorable to the vast majority of citizens. Worse, it produces individuals whose depth of political experience and paucity of relevant information renders them barely capable of controlling their lives and regulating their relations with others to the benefit of all. A [good] political system, then, must produce not only democratic outcomes, but in the process reproduce relations among people conducive to their integrity and growth, and favorable to perpetuation of a democratic and classless society.[23]

Another important dimension of political revitalization is the formation of a new and class-based realignment of voters in electoral politics. Former nonvoters and regular voters alike, particularly women and minorities, must unite in a broad new coalition that sees economic and other national policies in terms of the *class* biases that they involve. The government under Reagan, for example, would be clearly recognized as an upper-class government, devoted to the redistribution of wealth and power from the poor to the rich. The same bias would be evident, though perhaps to a lesser degree, in other conventional American governments.

The new alternative would be the conviction that it is equally proper, and long overdue, for the government to act in accordance with the wishes of the great bulk of the people — whose class interests are openly opposed to those of the rich and powerful. This means thinking differently and acting differently than most Americans have in the past, but such a difference is essential to the kind of change that democratic socialists seek. Perhaps the best statement of this part of the argument comes from Frances Piven and Richard Cloward, both experienced political activists. They insist in *The New Class War* that Reagan has begun a "class war" that only a new class-based realignment can reverse.[24] And elsewhere they suggest how this realignment can be accomplished by a new voting coalition that incorporates nonvoters essentially through a massive registration campaign conducted by social service workers.[25]

Finally, the new ways of thinking and acting in politics must eventually focus on the reconstruction of political institutions. These must be made more democratic and more effective in serving public, rather than special, interests. Many democratic socialists argue that such reconstruction has now become more possible because of the very severity of our economic problems and the danger involved in the mainstream remedies. Alan Wolfe summarizes the situation well:

> Political revitalization — a path out of America's impasse — is possible, *if* it is based on three propositions. First, the American people must take whatever steps are necessary to guarantee their security: against inflation and unemployment at home and against the possibility of nuclear war and an uncontrolled arms race abroad. Second, Americans must create for themselves a public

authority that will help them achieve this security, which requires both a strong
government at home capable of planning and intervening in the public interest
and a strong international authority capable of countering the self-interest of
nation states. Third, the majority of the American people must recognize that
they have in common a class position and that they must be as willing to use government to support that position as business, in the past, has been willing to use
government to support its position.[26]

In other words, a self-conscious and class-based movement must hold together and act coherently to implement its will through the national government for a sustained period of time. Only in such a manner can democratic
socialism come to power and achieve its program.

Democratic socialists acknowledge that the working class has never
shown this solidarity and capability in American history. But they deny vigorously that this means that no such movement is possible. Michael Harrington,
one of the most prolific of democratic socialist writers, has argued consistently that "there is a massive objective basis for class politics in America today which *could* be actualized by political movements and economic
events."[27] Black and feminist socialists argue that minorities and women are
important potential components of an eventual socialist movement because
only socialism offers a genuine chance for realization of the goals of
minorities and women in the United States. Thus despite the past, democratic socialism remains convinced that it can successfully compete for power in
American politics.

IMPLICATIONS AND PROSPECTS

Just as the problem of designing routes by which democratic socialism might
rise to power dominates the political thinking of that body of beliefs, so it
looms large over the issue of democratic socialism's implications and prospects.
To be viable and credible as a set of beliefs, democratic socialism must establish that it has at least a chance of success. In this respect, it must pass a more
demanding test than other bodies of values and beliefs in the American context. Socialism has a history of impotence, failure, and vilification in the
United States. Many Americans carry mental defenses against understanding
or joining anything that sounds like socialism. Many others are actively opposed, responding enthusiastically to pleas to repel ideas labeled as socialist.
No other body of beliefs, current or developing, faces such obstacles.

As with economic democracy, improvement in the fortunes of democratic socialism seems to have as a precondition continued economic difficulties.
No democratic socialist believes that Americans will now or in the immediate future embrace socialist ideas. Thus, they concentrate on how to help
people cross the threshold once they have become convinced that problems
are too great for solution through any less drastic means. Albert and Hahnel,
for example, believe that a socialist movement must parallel more orthodox
reform movements:

> As the constituency for a left social democratic program grows in the eighties, it will certainly move left, developing new political skills and sophistication. But if the trend is to reach fruition in socialist progress, there will have to be a totalist socialist vision and movement constructed alongside the social democratic project. For without this, as women, minorities, and workers become frustrated with the limits of social democracy, they will have no place to go but out of the left. On the other hand, with a clear and viable socialist movement to enlarge and command, the left trend of this constituency will be able to continue toward socialism.[28]

Democratic socialists firmly dismiss all "vanguard" versions of the route to power, leaving those for the many small Leninist or Trotskyite sects that remain from the early days of Marxism in the United States. But they just as firmly reject coalition politics in which every component retains its particularistic premises and goals while joining in an alliance to seek power. Cohen and Rogers, for example, argue that coalition politics rests on the principle of fragmentation because it does not perceive a fundamental principle of agreement underlying everyday politics. Their strategy for democratic socialism in the present is to achieve broad new commitment to a democratic political order, "to accede to the principle of democracy itself."[29] This commitment will lead to the necessity for socialism, just as their argument unfolds from democracy to socialism.

But even if economic decline continues to create the necessary preconditions and people increasingly open up to the possibility of democratic socialism, the route to power still seems strewn with obstacles. Criticism would probably evolve into blunt attacks and even violent reactions as democratic socialism gained adherents. The most effective opposition would probably take the form of actual or threatened capital flight or a "capital strike." In the first case, investors and corporations would direct their capital overseas; in the second, they would simply refuse to make new investments in the United States. The result might well be depression and chaos, which would be blamed on democratic socialism and used as a means of inducing voters to abandon that movement. Only the complete lack of alternative uses for capital or voter awareness that such moves were deliberate attempts to coerce them would prevent capital flight and/or strike from standing in the way of democratic socialism's rise to legitimate governing power.

Nevertheless, democratic socialism counts on developing a broad base of support from current nonvoters and the many others who suffer from continued underemployment, unemployment, and sustained reductions in social services. Once the comprehensive nature of the attack on working people becomes clear and the unfairness of the deliberate redistribution of wealth from the poor to the rich builds resentment, democratic socialists expect to see a class-based realignment of voters. This would, of course, enable them to increase their ranks dramatically. There is a conflict among democratic socialists, as among economic democrats, over whether to promote their program through a third political party or to seek to make it the program of the Democratic Party. But most believe that the latter route is essential.

Many democratic socialists believe that there is widespread support for their program in the American public. What is needed is clear demonstration that it is really practical. The authors of *Beyond the Waste Land*, for example, argue that public knowledge of their analysis of the current waste and latent potential of the U.S. economy would make their program dramatically more viable:

> Some have doubted the feasibility of a democratic alternative, while others have assumed it would be too costly. Our program lifts the burden of defensiveness under which proponents of progressive change have had to labor in recent times. . . . Simply knowing that there is a democratic alternative to regressive redistribution, in the first instance, makes an enormous difference. Much more important, the possibility of real job security through active full-employment policies helps remove the occasion for much of the problem of fragmentation and mutual suspicion.[30]

If conditions permit, and the program can be brought to public attention, democratic socialism genuinely believes its chances are good. In the last instance, this confidence rests on the conviction that democratic socialism appropriately embodies America's past and offers the best hope for its future. Herbert Gintis sums it up as follows:

> Most of all this vision of socialism resonates to the progressive beat of a radical democratic America past and present. It is a vision of an American socialism, echoing the demands of workers, citizens, women, and minorities over the few centuries of our existence as a nation. Indeed, the democratic structures we have suggested are not novel forms requiring a radical cultural reconstruction of social life, but represent the logical culmination of a major strand of the demands of popular groups since the inception of capitalism.[31]

It seems clear that democratic socialism has in fact had a rebirth in the United States. The analyses being made today are historically informed and deeply sensitive to the current American context. They are broadly comprehensive in both economic and political terms and vigorously argued by a new generation that crosses race, sex, and class lines. Despite the obstacles, democratic socialism could well become a major competitor for popular support in the United States.

ADDITIONAL READINGS

Albert, Michael, and Hahnel, Robin. *Socialism Today and Tomorrow*. Boston: South End Press, 1983.

Bluestone, Barry, and Harrison, Bennett. *The Deindustrialization of America: Plant Closings, Community Abandonment, and the Dismantling of Basic Industry*. New York: Basic Books, 1982.

Bowles, Samuel; Gordon, David M.; and Weisskopf, Thomas E. *Beyond the waste*

Land: A Democratic Alternative to Economic Decline. New York: Anchor Press, 1983.

Cohen, Joshua, and Rogers, Joel. *On Democracy: Toward a Transformation of American Society*. Baltimore: Penguin Books, 1983.

Eisenstein, Zillah, ed. *Capitalist Patriarchy and the Case for Socialist Feminism*. New York: Monthly Review Press, 1979.

Gintis, Herbert. "A Socialist Democracy for the United States," in Stephen Rosskamm Shalom (ed.), *Socialist Visions*. Boston: South End Press, 1983.

Herreshoff, David. *The Origins of American Marxism: From the Transcendentalists to DeLeon*. New York: Pathfinder Press, 1973.

Marable, Manning. *How Capitalism Underdeveloped Black America*. Boston: South End Press, 1983.

Piven, Frances, and Cloward, Richard. *The New Class War*. New York: Pantheon Books, 1982.

Weinstein, James. *Ambiguous Legacy: The Left in American Politics*. New York: Franklin Watts, 1976.

_____. *The Decline of Socialism in America, 1912–1925*. New York: Vintage Books, 1963.

Wolfe, Alan. *America's Impasse: The Rise and Fall of the Politics of Growth*. Boston: South End Press, 1981.

_____. *The Limits of Legitimacy: Political Contradictions of Contemporary Capitalism*. New York: Free Press, 1977.

CHAPTER 8

Neoconservatism

We now turn to the belief systems that make up the conservative or right side of the American political spectrum, beginning with that closest to liberalism. Like neoliberalism, neoconservatism is long on intellectuals and their prolific pens but short on a popular following. Essentially the heir to the pessimistic, cautious side of liberal thought, it was the first major fragment to detach itself from the sinking post-1960s liberalism. But it was the last component to join the conservative coalition whose political success in 1980 ended almost five decades of liberal rule.

The dynamics of the decades of the 1970s and 1980s are clearly dominated by the rebirth of a robust American conservatism. During this period deep-running forces that had built over the preceding three decades converged and then transformed into a powerful new American version. Neoconservatism is a relatively minor but very vocal component of that new voice. We shall briefly sketch this simultaneous renascence and creation of conservatism so that the entire process is before us. However, we take up each of the major current strands in separate chapters.

In the immediate post–World War II period, what Americans called "conservatism" consisted of two sets of ideas that maintained an arms-length relationship with each other. One was an antistatist version of liberalism that emphasized individualism, strictly limited government, and the economic free market. This brand of liberalism, also known as Manchester liberalism after the English school of thought that gave it its clearest expression, was at its height in the 1890s. In the United States it was also associated with "Social Darwinism," a set of principles derived from Charles Darwin's biological theory of natural selection and applied to social life. In essence, Social Darwinism held that government assistance to disadvantaged people was undesirable because the human species was improved by the struggle to survive.

Antistatist, 1890s liberalism gained support in the postwar years because it warned against the very expansions of government activity that seemed to some to have led inexorably to fascist governments in Germany and Italy or to socialism elsewhere. Freedom, in the sense of freedom from government intervention, was the cornerstone of this brand of liberalism. In particular, the economic free market was held out as a neutral, efficient, and proper allocator of burdens and benefits in the society. Any increase of

130

government functions, particularly in economic affairs, touched off vigorous opposition from this corner as a threat to individual freedom.

The other version of conversatism was descended from the traditional organic conservatism identified with the eighteenth-century English thinker Edmund Burke. This set of beliefs if fundamentally different from liberalism. It does not focus primarily on the individual and his or her needs for fulfillment through various self-seeking activities. Instead, it starts with the society considered as a whole. Its primary concern is the improvement of the civilization represented by that society. The responsibility of leaders is to guide that society in ways consistent with its traditions, natural law, or some other public interest standard — not to seek favor with necessarily transitory majorities of individuals.

Organic conservatism is concerned with social and cultural dimensions of life, that is, with the moral values and religious or ethical spirit that suffuse the social order and give life meaning. Property rights are important because they assure stability. They also provide opportunity for some to cultivate their intellectual and artistic qualities, thus contributing to the civilization as a whole. Complete economic freedom for individual or corporate self-seeking, however, can be morally or physically damaging to the continued development of the society. The claims of business under 1890s liberalism's "laissez-faire" principles stand on no higher ground than the claims of individuals for some similar short-term advantages. Organic conservatism always keeps its eyes on long-term goals. Appetites must be curbed today so that needs of future generations may be considered.

The position of organic conservatives in the American context has always been an awkward one. Devoted to the preservation of the society's enduring traditions, they looked to the past for guidance but found only liberalism. Some observers argued that organic conservatism was really another foreign import or a romantic effort to reconstruct the American past and present. Moreover, the basic assumptions of an individualistic society stood squarely in the way of conservatives' efforts to achieve electoral success. One distinguished commentator described conservatism as "the thankless persuasion." Liberals generally dismissed it as a serious factor in American political thinking.[1]

What seems to have provided the impetus for uniting the two strands of conservatism was the anticommunism of the 1950s cold war. First came a genuine alliance and then their emergence and expansion as a major new force. Both strands believed the threat of Soviet military expansion abroad and internal subversion at home to be the most pressing issue facing the United States. Worse, it seemed to be one that liberals either did not understand or were unwilling or unable to address effectively. Patriotic, nationalist, economic, and religious attitudes merged into a sometimes strident movement seeking to restore pre–World War II values and conditions while eliminating current threats to American society.

One of the first expressions of these sentiments and evidence for their apparently wide appeal came in the early 1950s. Senator Joseph McCarthy of Wisconsin began a concerted campaign against alleged domestic subversives in and out of government. Liberals generally deplored McCarthy's "witch hunts" and saw his activities as cynical attacks on civil liberties. Conservatives, however, viewed his efforts and the liberal reaction as a clear indication of just how serious and deep the problem of communism was. They saw a nation that was spiritually rotting from within, that faced an implacable foreign enemy, and that was dominated by a ruling group whose complacency made them blind to these twin dangers.[2]

In 1955 the catalytic call to arms was sounded by a new conservative journal, which probably did more than any other single factor to unify, expand, and legitimate the new conservative movement. The journal was the *National Review*, its founder the uniquely capable William F. Buckley. Creative thinker, incisive writer, intimidating debater, indefatigable fund raiser, and urbanely witty in the bargain, Buckley is the most important individual figure in the rise of conservatism and perhaps in postwar American political thought. From his first book in 1951, *God and Man at Yale*, through *McCarthy and His Enemies* and a continuing series of other polemics and travelogues, Buckley kept the conservative viewpoint visible, always lively, and on top of every issue.[3]

The *National Review* opened its pages to all brands of conservatism, but emphasized anticommunism and the failures of liberalism. It symbolized a decisive shift in the orientation of conservatism, from a defensive posture to an offensive against the decadent liberal establishment. Conservatism no longer appeared resigned to the dominance of liberalism or to the role of a despairing critic on behalf of an old order. It now took on a much more aggressive approach, offering itself as the prospective replacement of liberalism and talking seriously in terms of achieving the strength to govern and redirect the country.

In a short time, other major publications followed Buckley's. First was Barry Goldwater's *Conscience of a Conservative*.[4] In it, Goldwater brought 1890s liberalism together with the notion of a powerful government for purposes of fighting communism throughout the world. It served as a rallying point for Goldwater's followers in 1960 and ultimately helped build the movement that achieved his nomination for the presidency in 1964. Another major work was Milton Friedman's *Capitalism and Freedom*, a clear and compelling call for pure laissez faire and the free market.[5]

The first plateau of the new conservatism as a real social movement was reached with the Goldwater nomination in 1964. Despite the view of some historians, both then and now, that this was simply a quixotic reactionary adventure, it stands as the moment when conservatism really coalesced in its new form.[6] The Goldwater following of 1964 was the form of the future, for the Republican Party and for the country as a whole. The death of John F. Kennedy together with Johnson's southern strength led to a reactive but temporary outpouring of Democratic votes which obscured the conservative consolidation. But the new conservatism gained in the South and West, eliminated some opposition within the Republican Party, and began a period of massive ferment in ideas *and* growth in numbers.

The minority, antiwar, student, and other change-oriented movements of the era (subsumed under the general label of the "New Left") claimed the headlines of the later 1960s. But the reality was a mounting reaction, one that grew steadily with every new success ("outrage," in conservative terms) on the part of the New Left. On the surface, the cauldron of the late 1960s continued to bubble, even beyond the presidency of Richard Nixon and the termination of the Vietnam War.

By the mid-1970s, conservatism had assumed a quite new three-component character, shown graphically in Figure 8.1. The purest and strictest of the 1890s liberals had detached themselves, reacting against the big-government (for military purposes) emphasis in the new conservatism. They took on an independent identity as a libertarian and even anarchist movement that we shall not encounter again until our last chapter. Conservatism's first element was a holdover from its postwar synthesis, an anticommunist and business-oriented fragment well grounded in the right wing of the Republican Party. It combined with some of the older aristocracy and organic conservative intellectuals to make up an Old Right grouping, which we shall examine in the next chapter.[7] A majoritarian, "populist conservative" movement, which became known as the New Right, is the second and really distinctive new element of today's reconstructed American conservatism. It will be explored in Chapter 10.[8] The third element is neoconservatism, to which we now turn our exclusive attention.

THE EVOLUTION OF NEOCONSERVATISM

Neoconservatism is a quite self-conscious movement of a small but highly visible number of intellectuals who are well grounded in the universities, the media, and the governing establishment.[9] Many of these leaders were once active supporters of the New Deal; some even thought of themselves as socialists. Their rupture with liberalism and coalescence in the neoconservative movement was both a reaction against what they saw as the excesses of the 1960s and an insistence on carrying forward some vital aspects of the older liberalism to which they were committed.

Neoconservatives reacted against the radical demands and behavior of the New Left, as well as the permissiveness and placating response of the liberals. They saw the civil rights and antiwar movements as representing excesses of democracy with far too little regard for authority. Moreover, government was trying to do too many things in the way of social policies, simply creating an "overload." Neoconservatives saw a "new class" of liberal social engineers as attempting through government the impossible and undesirable task of changing the way people lived.

Neoconservatives were also carrying forward some basic principles that liberals in government seemed to be forgetting. They focused on both the traditional concern for individual freedom and the necessary vigilant anticommunism of the cold war period. Freedom, it seemed, was being forced to

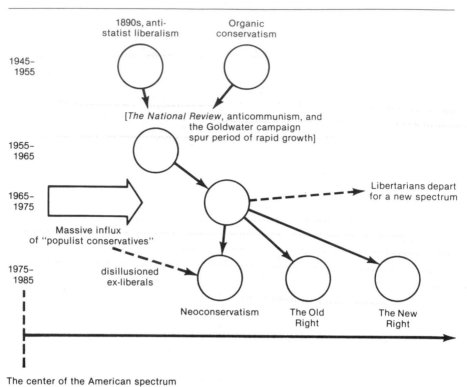

FIGURE 8.1   The Evolution of the Conservative Side of the American Political Spectrum, 1945–1980s

give way before an egalitarian onslaught. It needed defenders before it was smothered by government programs and regulations. Also, most neoconservatives were marked in some way by the cold war and struggles against domestic communist influence in the 1940s and 1950s. Liberals seemed to have forgotten all the lessons of that period. In particular, American foreign policy appeared to be lacking in firmness and political will in the aftermath of Vietnam. There was a real prospect that the carefully nurtured system for containing communism would crumble in the face of Soviet military strength and boldness given this failure of American resolve.

Irving Kristol, perhaps the leading symbol of neoconservatism, sums up the movement's "consensus" as support for the welfare state but opposition to bureaucratic intrusion and paternalism; respect for the economic market; support for traditional values and religion against the "counterculture" and its threats to order; opposition to egalitarianism in which "everyone ends up with equal shares of everything"; and insistence on a strong anticommunist foreign policy.[10] Using other terms, Midge Decter reaches much the same characterization:

> I would call it an intellectual movement which combines a very bitter disillusionment with socialism and hyperactive liberalism with a high degree of Amer-

ican patriotism. Many of us are former liberals or socialists who think of themselves as people who are trying to restore the country to a kind of intellectual and spiritual health.[11]

The beginnings of neoconservatism date from 1965–1966, but the movement did not reach its peak of visibility and strength until the early 1970s. In 1965, Irving Kristol and Daniel Bell, both leading social commentators, founded one of neoconservatism's two leading journals, *The Public Interest*. The other is *Commentary*, the long-established journal of the American Jewish Committee. Under the editorship of Norman Podhoretz it, too, began to develop the neoconservative position in the late 1960s. Together, the two journals served as a platform from which a corps of regular contributors attacked the New Left and liberalism's apparent acquiescence to its demands. These regulars included many leading social scientists and literary or political figures, such as Edward Banfield, Midge Decter, Martin Diamond, Nathan Glazer, Sidney Hook, Seymour Lipset, Daniel Moynihan, Robert Nisbet, Aaron Wildavsky, and James Q. Wilson.

The development of neoconservatism was rapid, in part because of its adherents' ready access to the media, particularly for the purpose of attacks on the left by people who seemed to have been former members of that very left. Most of the energies of neoconservatism in these early years were invested in vigorous polemics against individual radicals, their claims and actions, and the public policies of liberal government in the late 1960s. The conservative press, particularly *The Wall Street Journal*, helped to make Irving Kristol and Nathan Glazer into central figures in the new critique; the business community was generous in its praise and assistance. Established conservative think tanks gained new legitimacy from supporting the neoconservatives in a variety of ways. By the time of *The Public Interest's* bicentennial edition in 1976, neoconservatism had become well established as a major force on the American political spectrum.

BASIC VALUES: THE SHIFT TO THE RIGHT BEGINS

The fact that neoconservatism emerged from liberalism should serve to remind us that liberalism always had a pessimistic side, expressed most fully in the United States Constitution of 1787. Prominent here were concerns about the volatility of popular majorities and the felt need to create governing institutions where self-interested factions would cancel each other out. Cooler and wiser heads could then evolve public policies more genuinely in the public interest, preserving the basic values and traditions of the society as times changed. In particular, liberalism, both by definition and in practice, stood for liberty and the protection of individuals' freedoms and property rights. For neoconservatives in the 1960s, this meant protections against the redistributing thrust from the left and the confiscatory tendencies of governments, both of which neoconservatives saw as immediate threats.

But neoconservatism has also incorporated more than a touch of organic conservatism. Its emphasis on the need for deference to authority, acceptance of traditional ways, and respect for moral, religious, and spiritual values is squarely in the organic conservative model. More than any other contemporary belief system, neoconservatism stresses the need for coherence between the animating values of the economic order and the underlying culture. It finds this link in religious sources. Neoconservatives often use terms like "pragmatic," "realistic," and "practical," but they do not mean opportunistic, goal-maximizing practices, as liberals might. Instead, they mean considering the status quo very seriously and respectfully, taking only such steps as that status quo *should* take to preserve and enhance itself.

One of the major issues on which neoconservatives have taken a stand against both radicals and liberals concerns the changing meanings of equality and freedom. Neoconservatives are alarmed at the implications of expanding the notion of equality and determined to defend earlier definitions of freedom. They see equality of opportunity being pressed to absurd, equality-of-results lengths. This means not only vast new (and unworkable) expansion of government, but also bureaucratic intrusions into all spheres of personal life. The result is an intolerable reduction of personal freedom.

Irving Kristol has frequently argued the neoconservative position on the equality-freedom dichotomy. He insists that liberals and radicals have sought equality of results without any clear sense of what that would mean. Such vague yearnings result in policies that destroy liberty — the essence of a free society and Kristol's highest value. He declares that the distribution of income achieved by capitalism is right because it reflects a general belief that "it is better for society to be shaped by the interplay of people's free opinions and free preferences than by the enforcement of any one set of values by government."[12] For Kristol, the only alternatives to the distributions accomplished by capitalism inevitably involve intolerable coercion and sacrifice liberty. Speaking of the philosophy that prefers equality, he denies that it has an "authentic attachment to liberty" and says:

> It follows that "social justice" may require a people, whose preferences are corrupt (in that they prefer liberty to equality), to be coerced into equality. It is precisely because they define "social justice" and "fairness" in terms of equality that so many liberal thinkers find it so difficult to detest left-wing (i.e., egalitarian) authoritarian or totalitarian regimes. And, similarly, it is precisely because they are true believers in justice-as-equality that they dislike a free society, with all its inevitable inequalities.[13]

One example of how the liberal search for equality has gone awry may be found in the principle of affirmative action. Hardly any principle of domestic social policy has drawn as much bitter opposition or ridicule from neoconservatives as affirmative action. Nathan Glazer attacked the notion in 1975 in a book revealingly titled *Affirmative Discrimination*.[14] Midge Decter has led the attack on feminism and, particularly, on affirmative action, which she sees as "corrupting our society."

> Comparable worth is a vicious idea. . . . When female activists couldn't talk very well about equal pay for equal work, they invented comparable worth. The idea, if it gets established, is going to create a maelstrom in this society. It must not be allowed to happen.[15]

What both Glazer and Decter fear from affirmative action and other such policies is that they may lead to unreasonable expectations, governmental expansion, bureaucratic coercion, and an angry public reaction. These all add up to the unravelling of the society, a process they believe is already underway.

The way to avoid coercion, of course, is through greater reliance on the economic free market. Neoconservatism acknowledges some imperfections in the market's operations but sees these as vastly preferable to the only alternative — bureaucratic coercion forcing conformity to a single set of choices made by distant social engineers. Neoconservatives see government as inherently unable to perform functions as well as the apparently uncoordinated activity of people responding to market incentives. Liberals in government — the "new class" that we shall take up in the next section of this chapter — were misguided in their offer to perform all these functions, but even more in error when they encouraged people generally to expect so many things from government. In effect, liberals created expectations that no government could have even begun to fulfill. They thereby contributed to the crisis of authority that is the real American problem.

Neoconservatives firmly endorse a limited, procedural concept of democracy. Even this sort of democracy can get out of hand, however. Any major involvement of people in public decision making carries serious dangers. The unreasonable expectations and increased participation encouraged by liberals in the 1960s led directly to popular pressures for a wide variety of changes and to a general attitude of disrespect for established ways. It was as if people were led to challenge or doubt all the traditional ways and to withhold respect for governing institutions and officials.

This theme of the excesses of democracy and the loss of authority is one sounded by many neoconservatives. It is developed, for example, by Samuel Huntington, a political scientist, in his controversial essay in the bicentennial issue of *The Public Interest*.[16] Asserting that the problems of the 1960s stemmed primarily from too much popular participation and excessive expectations, Huntington called for greater power in government to enforce obedience and sacrifices where necessary. Robert Nisbet did much the same in *The Twilight of Authority*, a book whose title fully conveys its message.[17]

But there is even more involved in the decline of authority and legitimacy in the leading institutions and standards of the society. Basic moral commitments and traditional practices are also being undermined by this liberal pandering to majoritarian whims and special interest demands. Religion, the family, and social morality in general are falling before the rise of self-gratification and hedonistic short-term indulgence that liberalism has encouraged. Michael Novak in particular has argued strongly for a rebirth of religious and spiritual grounding for the basic institutions of the society, seeing this as the necessary foundation of faith in democratic capitalism.[18]

Perhaps the worst effect of the loss of moral fiber that neoconservatives see in the United States today is the failure to stand up for basic principles — particularly in international affairs. Neoconservatism sees the Soviet Union as an implacable enemy covertly building up its strength and waiting for the moment to attack vital American interests. Third World countries are hypocritically demanding assistance and playing self-interested, nationalistic games without regard for the stakes involved. Only firm assertion of the rightness of capitalist democracy and determined anticommunist vigilance can maintain freedom's shrinking domain around the world. An American isolationism or failure of will at this point in history amounts to consigning billions of people to the equivalent of slavery for the foreseeable future.

The neoconservative approach to contracts and law, and to individualism, fits within the context of the high-priority concerns just described. Both are seen, in other words, in the organic conservative sense. Contracts and law, in the form of regular procedures, are highly valued. But courts should observe traditional limits in the scope of their decisions; they should reject liberal efforts to involve them in social engineering. The image of "the imperial judiciary," of judges deeply involved in implementing social change, invokes invective from many neoconservatives.

On the other hand, individuals' self-help efforts are highly valued. These should occur in the private sphere, not take the form of demands for government assistance. Nor are individual wants particularly important indicators of what the society should do at any given time; they are much too likely to be expressions of mere self-indulgence. Instead, individuals should accept guidance from the established moral standards of the society. Western civilization, as represented by the traditions and values of the United States, has a prior claim on people. Its survival and development are more important than the wants of any transitory majority of individuals.

It seems clear that neoconservatism has reverted to some older definitions of basic values. At that, they have given them a more consistently conservative character than was ever the case in traditional liberal thought. Social and economic inequality is a necessary accompaniment of freedom, which has paramount priority. The separation of social and economic life from political affairs is not only obvious but a necessary and desirable way of giving primacy to the private sector. Problems in the United States are more the result of people's personal failures, or their excessive expectations, or the faulty ways that they seek social change, than they are the result of structural flaws in the social, economic, or political systems. Neoconservatism may have originated in liberalism, but has more than made up for such early sins by the warmth of its current embrace with conservatism.

PROBLEMS AND POSSIBILITIES: CONTROLLING THE "NEW CLASS"

The problems that neoconservatism sees as most important are not rooted in economic conditions or social structures. Rather, they lie in the values and beliefs of leaders and followers in the American social system. In other words, with the exception of Soviet military strength and worldwide subversive activities, problems do not have objective content. They are quite real, but they take the form of willfulness or error in people's minds. The remedies that appeal to neoconservatives are therefore directed partly at the replacement or conversion of governing elites and partly at the restoration of certain habits and beliefs among the masses.

Problems

In the eyes of neoconservatives, the key to the failures of American leadership and the decline of the American civilization is the rise of a "new class" of middle-class professionals opposed to the basic values of the society that nurtured them. This new class started at an unprecedented level of affluence, encountered little in the way of character-building hardship to struggle against, and had easy access to higher education. It then directed its energies into the effort to enable everybody to enjoy the same opportunities, with little or no realization of how difficult that would be or why many people might not desire such ends. Most damaging of all, this class, whether in government positions or in private life, was proegalitarian and antibusiness.

Once again, it is Irving Kristol who mounts the attack most vigorously. In his relentless critique of those who seek equality, he uncovers "an intelligentsia which so despises the ethos of bourgeois society, and which is so guilt-ridden at being implicated in the life of this society" that it despairs of American ways and has a fatal attraction for totalitarian regimes. He goes on to say:

> We have a "New Class" of self-designated "intellectuals" who share much of this basic attitude . . . [and] pursue power in the name of equality. And then we have the ordinary people, working-class and lower-middle-class, basically loyal to the bourgeois order but confused and apprehensive at the lack of clear meaning in this order—a lack derived from the increasing bureaucratization (and accompanying impersonalization) of political and economic life. All of these discontents tend to express themselves in terms of "equality"—which is in itself a quintessentially bourgeois ideal and slogan.[19]

The false god of equality has combined with the rise of self-indulgence and the decline of religion to make for a basic cultural opposition to capitalist-liberal society. Some neoconservatives term this "an adversary culture," and they locate its basic source in the "new class" of antibusiness professionals. The exact composition and nature of this new class is not easy to pin down, in part because neoconservatives variously see it as intellectuals, or intellectuals and professionals, or government workers, or all college-educated people. Peter Steinfels, the leading student of neoconservatism, says: "In neoconservative writings, references to the 'new class' make up in frequency and vehemence what they lack in precision."[20]

But it is certainly clear that neoconservatism has identified a significant problem. It is partly people—the new class, whether defined and located specifically or broadly—but more particularly the beliefs that they hold. The problem is located in the egalitarianism and antibusiness attitudes of this new class. It is here that the efforts for change should focus.

The second major problem that neoconservatism identifies is located, by contrast, in mass publics. Several neoconservative thinkers, notably Daniel Bell and Michael Novak, have characterized contemporary society in terms of three components, each with a dominant principle.[21] When these principles are not in harmony, the society experiences tensions and potential disintegration. The first and most basic component, according to Bell, is the technological order, in which the dominant principle is that of efficiency. The next most vital component is the polity, where the energizing principle is equality. (These principles could be seen as antagonistic, but the potential problem is resolved by giving precedence to efficiency.)

The third component of society is the underlying culture. Essentially, the problem in recent years is that the dominant cultural principle has not been supportive of or even compatible with the others. The dominant principle generated by American cultural dynamics in the period from the 1960s to the present is one of indulgence and self-gratification. This is the "Me Decade," in which everyone's demands on the economy and society simply cannot be met. And yet they have actually been encouraged by the new class, with its continuing emphasis on the right to equality. The decisive weakness of contemporary elites, in other words, has combined with the dominant inclination of masses of people in an incendiary mixture.

A society in which everybody seeks the maximum possible benefit for himself or herself without regard to others is not a pleasant or even governable society. Somehow, this basic cultural principle has to be harmonized with the others. If necessary, it has to be controlled, so that the appetites unleashed do not tear the society apart. The civility of the future depends on solving this problem.

Possibilities

As we have seen, the reputation of neoconservatives has largely been built on the style and acerbity of their critique of the New Left and the liberal effort to propitiate all its demands. If there had not been an apparent threat from the left, neoconservatism might never have achieved its media visibility or its business support. Neoconservatism has not really proposed a program for governing, but only outlined a critique of those who do.

Nonetheless, an alternative program can be inferred from the criteria used against liberalism. Not surprisingly, it reflects fundamental neoconservative principles. First is the pervasive notion of limits to social possibility. Neoconservatives are much impressed with how very difficult it is to accomplish change in any important social relationships by deliberate action, and particularly by means of public policies. One of the major documents of neoliberalism is Nathan Glazer's article "The Limits of Social Policy." In it, Glazer argues that many goals involving change in social and economic conditions are simply beyond the capabilities of governments.[22]

If the possibilities are so limited, what are the real alternatives? Neoconservatives see two leading possibilities. One is to depress public expectations, bringing about a return to realism in the people's public aspirations. The other is to replace or reconstruct the governing elite so as to install a new sense of the limits of government capabilities and a chastened vision of the importance of equality. This latter principle — equality — is really at the heart of the problem. Attempts to focus on and achieve equality are the death warrant of free society. Thus nothing is more important than controlling the thrust toward equality.

The other half of the neoconservative program is aimed at revitalizing the religious grounding of today's capitalist order. Michael Novak has led the way in trying to provide a new justification for capitalism that could harmonize the dominant principles of the three major sectors of social life. He begins *The Spirit of Democratic Capitalism* with the premise that no system of political economy has so improved the quality of life and yet been so lacking in theological justification as democratic capitalism. The latter term is intended to include the familiar three sectors, here identified as "three dynamic and converging systems functioning as one: a democratic polity, an economy based on markets and incentives, and a moral-cultural system which is pluralistic and, in the largest sense, liberal."[23]

What distinguishes Novak's argument is his premise that the combination of a capitalist market economy and political democracy is not an historical accident but rather a necessary relationship — one in which democracy depends on the existence of capitalism. He declares that "economic liberties without political liberties are inherently unstable. Citizens economically free soon demand political freedoms."[24] Free markets are the necessary condition precedent to democracy; democracy does not occur without them. To have and to hold political democracy, one must protect and preserve capitalism.

Once this link is established, Novak takes the next step in building capitalist imperatives into the democratic polity that it generates. Democracy is made dependent on economic growth. He says:

> Democratic polities depend on the reality of economic growth. No traditional society, no socialist society — indeed, no society in history — has ever produced strict equality among individuals or classes. Real differences in talent, aspiration, and application inexorably individuate humans. Given the diversity and liberty of human life, no fair and free system can possibly guarantee equal outcomes. A democratic system depends for its legitimacy, therefore, not upon equal results but upon a sense of equal opportunity. Such legitimacy flows from the belief of all individuals that they can better their condition. This belief can be realized only under conditions of economic growth. Liberty requires expanse and openness.[25]

The problem, Novak admits, is that "throughout the world, capitalism evokes hatred. . . . Even at home, within the United States, . . . the Achilles' heel of democratic capitalism is that for two centuries now it has appealed so little to the human spirit."[26] Mere acquisitiveness is not an uplifting principle of life. It has so many destructive consequences that most people turn away in revulsion when the moral basis of capitalism is seen to consist of little else. In fact, Novak claims, there are genuinely uplifting moral values underlying capitalism. Specifically, democratic capitalism is distinguished by pluralism, the multiplicity of sets of relationships which assures that no single group of authorities will make all the decisions in the society. It is this differentiation of systems that protects all against unitary (and therefore arbitrary) power.

Novak then proceeds to show the support for pluralism in Christian doctrine, as well as the deep connection between Jewish-Christian culture, values, and experience and democratic capitalism. The ideals of democratic capitalism, he insists, are the very bedrock ideals of Christianity itself. He concludes:

> Almighty God did not make creation coercive, but designed it as an arena of liberty. Within that arena, God has called for individuals and peoples to live according to His law and inspiration. Democratic capitalism has been designed to permit them, sinners all, to follow this free pattern. It creates a noncoercive society as an arena of liberty, within which individuals and people are called to realize, through democratic methods, the vocations to which they believe they are called.[27]

Novak then adds that God will judge whether people have in fact accomplished their tasks. By implication, democratic capitalism should be judged in terms of whether or not it has permitted them to do so.

This argument is neoconservatism's best effort to revive capitalism's underlying moral basis. It is not a program for new public policies. Rather it is a program for wholesale moral regeneration of millions of people. Its appeal to conservative intellectuals, and perhaps to theologians, seems clear. But its capacity to gain acceptance at the level of mass culture remains to be seen.

There is one area, however, where neoconservatism has a very concrete program for new public policy. This is the field of international relations, particularly relations with the Soviet Union. Neoconservatism stands for vigorous development of American military power and a readiness to use it around the world to counter continuing Soviet expansionism. In terms of visibility, Jeanne Kirkpatrick has been the outstanding neoconservative advocate of an interventionist posture for the United States, particularly in Latin America. But her position is widely shared among neoconservatives. Close relations with Israel are a cornerstone of Middle East policy thinking. A generally hard line in any future arms limitation negotiations fits this perspective as well. What all this adds up to is a frank commitment to serving American national interests throughout the world, in confidence that by doing so the cause of freedom and democracy will simultaneously be served.

IMPLICATIONS AND PROSPECTS

What explains the sudden appearance of neoconservatism, and what is its long-term significance likely to be? It is easy to overestimate the importance of this movement: its intellectuals are prolific, and they occupy highly visible positions. Peter Steinfels, an otherwise skeptical expert on neoconservatism, seems to succumb to the temptation in titling his excellent study *The Neoconservatives: The Men Who Are Changing America's Politics*. There is certainly no mass following behind neoconservatism, not even as much as may have once existed for organic conservatism. The Old Right and the New Right, particularly the latter, have all the troops that fill the ranks of conservatism today.

But just as certainly, there is a significant audience among American intellectuals and policy-oriented elites and technicians. Between the universities, semipopular policy journals, business press, foundations, and conservative think tanks, neoconservatives are assured of a ready platform and a powerful audience in a way that other forms of conservatism are not. For this reason, at least, neoconservatism's opportunity is great. The question seems to be whether it can make good on that opportunity. On this point, Steinfels believes that neoconservatism may be its own worst enemy:

> Neoconservatism has made itself hostage to those it so relentlessly criticizes. Its victories can only be as substantial as its adversaries, and it has tended, in its crusade against cant, to choose the most insubstantial targets. . . . *The most debilitating intellectual weakness of neoconservatism is its lack of respect for its political opponents.* In this it resembles, not surprisingly, the New Left against which it first mobilized — the old tale of enemies mirroring each other.[28]

Steinfels sees neoconservatism as too willing to exaggerate the sins of its opponents in order to castigate them with devastating style and wit. In his eyes, this does more to expose neoconservatism than to denigrate its targets. He declares:

> To acclaim civility, and yet treat one's adversaries as ignorant, neurotic, or power-driven totalitarians, to honor complexity, and yet divide the intellectual world into two camps and set out to police it on behalf of one; to profess independence of mind, and yet insist on a new conformity; to reject the tyranny of "fashion," and yet rehearse another set of shibboleths — in so doing, neoconservatism threatens to discredit the very values it aspires to serve.[29]

This seems to raise the question of what neoconservatism really seeks. Is its aim merely to do away with the New Left and "hyperliberalism," returning the country to where it was before liberalism went wrong? Or does it have longer-range goals? In turn, this seems to make its origins important, as whatever led to its emergence may eventually shape the substance of a new agenda. Most neoconservatives insist that they remained true to the basics of the old liberalism, while liberalism itself fell victim to its own incessant search for equality and latent radicalism. It is other people who have changed, while neoconservatism is bedrock-constant. As we have seen, this has some validity. But neoconservatism has also incorporated a strong dose of organic conservatism and the defensive elitism that goes with that perspective.

Other explanations for the rise of neoconservatism tend to emphasize sociological and psychological dimensions of the life experiences of individual neoconservatives themselves. For example, they were vigorous cold warriors who were shunted aside by the antiwar movement in the 1960s and are now seeking revenge. Or, as many neoconservatives are Jewish, they are reacting to their fears of anti-Semitism in the radical movements and the increased vulnerability of Israel under conditions of American withdrawal from a world-policing role. Or they are simply self-made people who rose from the ranks of the poor through hard work and now demand that others earn their privileges in a similar manner.

We are uncomfortable with such explanations. They are not readily subject to proof and they downgrade the importance of ideas. Moreover, there is one explanation that links the origins of neoconservatism and its inclusion of organic conservatism with one of the main lines of its explicit argument. This is the notion that neoconservatism is really an intraelite argument over the criteria to be employed in shaping public policy. Neoconservation arose in rejection of the radical-liberal equality-promoting approach. It argued the case for limits—limits to promises, expectations, and government expansion. Its images of the good society were developed in order to support these policy criteria. It purposefully addressed only a policy-oriented audience and did so effectively. Its principal target was the "new class" and its beliefs.

Neoconservatism arose from, and has taken as its mission, the imperative of replacing or converting the policy-making stratum of American society. In other words, neoconservatism is about the loyalties and beliefs of the new class—its reconstruction, in fundamental ways, so that it will act on the correct (neoconservative) values and principles. This explanation makes the most sense and also clearly points toward a continuing agenda and role for neoconservatism. Furthermore, this role does not depend at all on developing a mass following. Neoconservatism addresses only the governing class, because in its view of the world that is the only group that matters. And there is every reason to believe that neoconservatism will continue to play an important role in educating that new class of policy-oriented leaders. In time it could come to serve as the rationale or ideology of governing in the United States.

Should this occur at least two different scenarios are possible. Peter Steinfels expresses one such scenario:

> The great danger posed by and to neoconservatism is that it will become nothing more than the legitimating and lubricating ideology of an oligarchic America where essential decisions are made by corporate elites, where great inequalities are rationalized by straitened circumstances and a system of meritocratic hierarchy, and where democracy becomes an occasional, ritualistic gesture.[30]

The alternative scenario involves the reintegration of neoconservatism with a future version of liberalism in a reconstituted center of the American political spectrum. With its self-limited focus on elite attitudes and behavior, and almost deliberate avoidance of efforts to gain a mass following, neoconservatism must always take its stance from where governing elites seem to be heading. And that, in turn, depends ultimately on what numbers of Americans believe and are willing to support. Working through the operational practices of governing elites seems to be neoconservatism's best hope for continued impact on American life.

ADDITIONAL READINGS

Bell, Daniel. *The Cultural Contradictions of Capitalism*. New York: Basic Books, 1976.

Coser, Lewis, and Howe, Irving, eds. *The New Conservatives: A Critique From the Left*. New York: Quadrangle/New York Times Book Co., 1974.

Croly, Herbert. *The Promise of American Life*. New York: Dutton, 1963.

Glazer, Nathan. *Affirmative Discrimination: Ethnic Inequality and Public Policy*. New York: Basic Books, 1975.

Glazer, Nathan, and Kristol, Irving, eds. *The American Commonwealth — 1976*. New York: Basic Books, 1976.

Green, Philip. *The Pursuit of Inequality*. New York: Pantheon Books, 1981.

Kristol, Irving. *On the Democratic Idea in America*. New York: Harper & Row, 1972.

_____. *Two Cheers for Capitalism*. New York: Basic Books, 1978.

Moynihan, Daniel P. *The Politics of a Guaranteed Annual Income*. New York: Random House, 1973.

Nash, George H. *The Conservative Intellectual Movement in America Since 1945*. New York: Basic Books, 1976.

Nisbet, Robert. *The Twilight of Authority*. New York: Basic Books, 1972.

Novak, Michael. *The Spirit of Democratic Capitalism*. New York: Simon and Schuster, 1982.

Podhoretz, Norman. *Making It*. New York: Random House, 1967.

Wilson, James Q. *Thinking About Crime*. New York: Basic Books, 1975.

CHAPTER 9

Conservatism: The Old Right in New Labels

We began the last chapter with a historical sketch of the evolution of post–World War II conservatism. In it we described the central core of conservatism as the heir to an alliance between traditional organic conservatism and 1890s antistatist liberalism. We noted that a strong anticommunism, and eventually a commitment to big government for fighting communism around the world, enabled that alliance to be forged. That early alliance has since moved toward something like synthesis. While the two major strands are still readily discernible, and sometimes even at odds with each other, they share considerable common ground. To understand their potential impact in America, we must explore this still-incomplete synthesis in some detail. Our first section, therefore, combines historical evolution with deeper analysis of the two strands and the glue that has brought them together.

THE EVOLVING SYNTHESIS: TRADITIONALISM AND ANTISTATIST LIBERALISM

The heart of the early differences between traditional conservatism and anti-statist liberalism lay in their contrasting attitudes toward government. "Traditionalism" is actually traditional only in the sense that it followed the classic organic conservatism closely identified with Edmund Burke. It is traditional *conservatism*, not traditional American thinking. Government, in the eyes of traditional conservatives, had many important functions to perform. Firmly in the hands of talented elites, its job was to guide the society in the correct direction. Government should exercise its powers to teach morality and to articulate and implement the public interest. It should consistently wield its authority on behalf of the society's goals at home and abroad.

Liberalism in some form, of course, has always dominated in the United States. Antistatist, or 1890s, liberalism represents the right wing of liberalism. It strongly advocates unlimited individualism, the economic free market, and strictly limited government. Freedom, its central value, exists precisely to the extent that government is limited. There is no "public interest"except in the sense of many individual interests aggregated in some manner, such as through the economic free market.

Throughout the twentieth century, however, mainstream liberalism had steadily enlarged the state apparatus in order to serve both economic growth and welfare needs. And 1890s liberalism had just as steadfastly opposed such expansion. After the New Deal and World War II, antistatist liberalism was defined almost entirely by its freedom-defending opposition to government action. Its constant defense of the free market earned it continuing strong support from the business community, large and small businesses alike.

Thus, in the immediate postwar years, the two strands of conservatism had in common only their defensive posture on behalf of some older American values and the fact that each stood firmly against the mainstream liberal tide. Their critiques of liberalism rested on quite different grounds. However, their apparently shared backward-looking orientation earned them the collective title of the Old Right. They found some mutual support in their opposition to the dominant trend of belief and practice, but agreed on little else — until the 1950s. Anticommunism, the cold war, and their shared sense of the need for a powerful American military and political presence around the world provided the initial basis for alliance. This foundation proved to be a strong and compelling one. Furthermore, it enabled conservatives to draw new support — and not only from the business community.

Now allied, opponents of liberalism could rally others with concerns about the direction that American society was taking. Liberalism was no longer solving problems, it was creating them. And as the problems grew, so did the ranks of opponents. Conservatives took considerable pleasure in stressing their differences from liberalism.

At first, the antistatist liberals insisted that they were the true liberals. In a way, they were correct. They argued that those in government were misguided egalitarians who had been led to support big government by wrongly blaming the free market for the Depression. But now the line had to be drawn. As Milton Friedman's *Capitalism and Freedom*, the leading 1890s liberal tract of the times, declared:

> The liberal will therefore distinguish sharply between equality of rights and equality of opportunity, on the one hand, and material equality or equality of outcome on the other. . . . But [the egalitarian] will defend taking from some to give to others, not as a more effective means whereby the "some" can achieve an objective they want to achieve, but on the grounds of "justice." At this point, equality comes sharply into conflict with freedom; one must choose. One cannot be both an egalitarian, and a liberal.[1]

Traditional conservatives saw the contrast between themselves and mainstream liberals in even more sweeping terms. They complained that liberalism wrongly thinks of the world as a rational, controllable place in which all problems have solutions. A metaphor used recently by George Will, a leading organic conservative, clearly states the contrast perceived:

> Liberalism is political astronomy — anachronistic astronomy, unaware that even the planets do more wobbling and wandering and banging about than the eighteenth century thought. Conservatism is political biology. It emphasizes the indeterminateness, the complexity of things, and the fact that there is more to a social system than meets the eye.[2]

At some point in the mid-1960s, conservatives of both varieties began to realize that they were not necessarily a permanent minority standing in isolated opposition to an inexorable liberalism. The Goldwater campaign of 1964 is probably the best point from which to date the conservative shift away from a defensive posture. Conservatism was melding the bulk of the business community, the right wing of the Republican Party, and new constituents from other sectors into a significant force. To take the offensive, however, requires both the sense that it is possible to become a majority and contend for the right to govern *and* a more positive shared program. It was essential to be *for* some things as well as against many others. And it was important to be against a number of different things for the same reasons and with the same remedies in mind.

Many conservatives were quite self-conscious about this threshold. Organic conservatives began at this point to talk in terms of their own vision of an appropriate welfare state, grounded in a transcendant concept of social justice.[3] The most visible 1890s liberal, Ronald Reagan, regularly used the term "social safety net" to refer to legitimate government protections for disadvantaged people. In looking back at this period from the vantage point of 1983, George Will aptly states the issue that had to be faced:

> For nearly half a century, conservatism was, or felt itself to be, in the political wilderness. . . . conservatism generally was a doctrine in, and of, opposition. During this period it became cranky and recriminatory. Therefore, a question posed by the coming to power of self-conscious conservatism is this: Can there be conservatism with a kindly face?[4]

The awareness of the potential of majoritarian appeal is itself a powerful force strengthening the synthesis between the two versions of conservatism. Hope for power creates not only strange bedfellows, but also more tolerant roommates. It is true that for many the Soviet threat remained alive and dangerous despite its eclipse in official liberal perceptions. Opposition to liberalism was exacerbated by the failure to effectively pursue the war in Vietnam and by apparently unparalleled growth in Soviet military power. But during this period at least three other very important convictions came to be shared with increasing enthusiasm. Each added new layers of strength to the basic foundation already in place.

First, conservatives believed that liberal social engineering and welfarism were undermining absolutely fundamental American values associated with family, religion, and work. For the organic conservatives, such values were deep cultural traditions. They provided the source of the American spirit and the basic social ties that knit the society into an organic unit.

They are the values at the very core of the civilization, the essence that conservatism seeks to conserve and enhance.

The 1890s liberals also believed such values were basic building blocks. For them, family, religion, and work were roots of self-reliance and individualism, the essential ingredients of a working free market and good society. All that 1890s liberals opposed most fiercely about government intrusion into the realm of personal freedom seemed typified by the substitution of bureaucratic intervention for the roles once played by family and religion in American life. Characteristic of the many statements from this perspective is that of Senator Paul Laxalt. He warns of

> the growing threats to our traditional values and institutions and the resulting assault upon the American spirit. I speak of the American family. Under attack though it is, the American family must survive. I firmly believe that, if the family is destroyed, our society as we know it will follow.[5]

Second, beginning about 1968, the American economy began to decline; unemployment and inflation became simultaneous problems. None of the liberal remedies celebrated as capable of "fine tuning" the economy seemed to work at all. Organic conservatives as well as 1890s liberals began to identify the same causes behind these problems: excessive spending, taxes, and regulation on the part of government. Organic conservatives had always believed in a frugal, prudent government of modest size, with a balanced budget and a small deficit. Military needs were one category of priority, but expensive social programs and the taxes required to sustain them were another matter.

The 1890s liberals were even more outraged at the ever-expanding scope of government intervention. They saw mounting levels of spending and taxes as the measures of this expansion. The taxes required to sustain social programs were drawn from an increasingly hard-pressed private economy. The geometrically multiplying regulations added significantly to the cost of doing business. Between taxes and regulations, businesses were neither free nor, in many cases, profitable. Moreover, unbalanced budgets led to inflation and the destruction of predictability in the market economy.

Third, the economy and society were dominated by self-interested behavior on the part of businesses, groups, and individuals alike. Everybody was not only out for themselves but out to get all they could. This self-aggrandizing took the form of battling over subsidies, concessions, and other supports from government. It had nothing to do with the competition appropriate to a free market situation. There was no regard for a public interest, whether articulated explicitly by government or silently by the automatic workings of the free market.

Both organic conservatives and 1890s liberals saw businesses, particularly big businesses, seeking to avoid competition. Such businesses claimed special favors on the grounds of the widespread public hardship that would otherwise result from their reduced profitability. One of the purest of free-market 1890s liberals put the matter this way:

> Although most businessmen publicly proclaim their devotion to the free market, they always do so with a big "but." The "but" is usually followed by some explanation about how their situation is different, about how they are faced with "unfair" competition, or how the "national interest" demands that they receive government help.[6]

Not only businesses but also powerful lobbies and special interest groups were subjected to this criticism. Obviously, none had any concern for the general welfare of the economy as a whole. Liberalism was blamed for having encouraged such assertiveness. Furthermore, liberalism had no standards other than relative political power for determining whether or not a claimant was entitled to help.

Consistent principles were impossible amidst these swarming self-seekers. No moral spirit animated either people or business in such a context. Notions of honor, integrity, and other sound principles of social and economic life were lost. In particular, the sense of creativity and satisfaction in capitalist entrepreneurship was missing. And again, liberalism was to blame for encouraging such a self-interested society in which so many were unwilling to be exposed to the risks requisite to growth and progress. One of the leading publicists of the conservative "return to capitalism" of the early 1980s was George Gilder. In his popular *Wealth and Poverty*, he argued:

> Liberals seems to want wealth without the rich. Yet most real wealth originates in individual minds in unpredictable and uncontrollable ways. A successful economy depends on the proliferation of the rich, on creating a large class of risk-taking men who are willing to shun the easy channels of a comfortable life in order to create new enterprise, win huge profits, and invest them again. . . . They are the heroes of economic life, and those who begrudge them their rewards demonstrate a failure to understand their role and their promise.[7]

In each of these three areas, the alliance of organic conservatism and 1890s liberalism encountered the happy fact of popular support. People rallied in large numbers to the arguments that the values of family, religion, and work were being undermined; that the government was too big, intrusive, and costly; and that one key cause was excessive self-interest on the part of everybody besides themselves. The alliance grew stronger, becoming almost a synthesis. Tensions still exist, however, as we shall see throughout this analysis.

THE BASIC VALUES OF A
NOT-YET-INTEGRATED CONSERVATISM

Spurred by the realities of popular support and possible power, the two distinct strands of the earlier conservatism moved from strange bedfellows to tolerant roommates and then on toward wedded bliss. But along the way, changes were inevitable. Some values and beliefs allied themselves easily;

others merged and became something new; still others struggled for independent survival. Conservatism, in other words, has been going through a process of reconstitution and regeneration. The organic conservative George Will welcomes this development. Speaking of the inevitable and appropriate "clustering" of ideas that, once they take distinct shape, lead to useful labels, Will says:

> There are moments, and this is one, when it is particularly important to suggest alternative clusterings. Specifically, the cluster of ideas that is commonly thought to constitute conservatism should be pried apart and reconstituted. . . . My aim is to recast conservatism in a form compatible with the broad popular imperatives of the day, but also to change somewhat the agenda and even the vocabulary of contemporary politics.[8]

What we shall see in this section is a belief system undergoing a variety of changes. Components of the two major strands are moving in all directions and new principles are taking shape in their midst. In this survey, we can no longer be limited to the values that define the liberal mainstream, even in new definitions. We must include distinctly conservative values. The most prominent are actually two sides of the same principle: the scope and power of government and the role of the economic free market.

Equality and Freedom

Perhaps the traditional value of equality best illustrates the complexity of the emerging conservatism's principles. All conservatives agree that equality should mean only equality of opportunity. Liberalism has done great damage by its incessant efforts to achieve a much-expanded version. For most conservatives, what liberalism seeks is nothing less than equality of outcomes. Further, in seeking such an impossible goal, liberalism has been obliged to create and empower a government of vast and inevitably freedom-destroying scope.

Beyond this point, however, conservative reasoning and remedies begin to diverge in ways that show the synthesis to be still incomplete. For the organic conservatives, the problem caused by the liberal commitment to excessive equality is not the size of the government. The problem is that governmental authority has been destroyed. For the 1890s liberals, the problem is precisely the government's massive size. It crushes freedom and individual initiative while creating a new kind of inequality in the form of a "new class" of power holders.

At stake in the continuing tension over definitions of equality and freedom is a newly independent issue—the character and function of government itself. Liberals reach judgments about how the state should be structured and employed from their prior principles about what it should be doing. But conservatives *start* with principles about the power and functions of government. Once again, it is George Will who incisively articulates the organic conservative position. In a few short sentences, he illustrates each of the foregoing points:

> The fundamental goal of modern liberalism has been equality, and it has given us government that believes in the moral equality of appetites. The result is a government that is big but not strong; fat but flabby; capable of giving but not leading. It is invertebrate government. . . . Leadership is, among other things, the ability to inflict pain and get away with it—short-term pain for long-term gain. Liberalism, which is the politics of the pleasure principle, has made government the servant of consumption and, not coincidentally, the enemy of investment, which is the deferral of gratification. The one thing we do not have is strong government.[9]

From the perspective of the 1890s liberal, equality of opportunity is the only version of equality that is consistent with freedom. Every advance beyond it diminishes freedom by exactly the same amount. Many are so adamant about this point that they tend to see any extension of equality of opportunity as amounting to an extreme kind of homogenization of all outcomes and conditions. For some publicists, this may be a deliberate creation of a "straw man" that can be painted in threatening colors. For others it seems to be their genuine perception. Milton and Rose Friedman have been leading economists and persuasive advocates of the 1890s liberal position for more than three decades. After speaking of the service rendered to the individual by the harmonious relationship of liberty and equality of opportunity, they add:

> A very different meaning of equality has emerged in the United States in recent decades—equality of outcome. Everyone should have the same level of living or of income, should finish the race at the same time. Equality of outcome is in clear conflict with liberty. The attempt to promote it has been a major source of bigger and bigger government, and of government-imposed restrictions on our liberty.[10]

For the 1890s liberals, in other words, *any* expansion beyond the minimal government required to enforce contracts and punish crime is a potential threat to freedom. Vast military expenditures and the government-business establishment that goes with it are necessary but potentially dangerous evils. Underlying such attitudes is the 1890s liberal's complete conviction that only the free economic market can direct resources toward their best usage. Only the free market can allocate burdens and benefits in a noncoercive and maximally efficient manner. The market can reward and punish in a way that maintains social harmony, if only government will leave it alone.

Thus, there remains a continuing fissure in conservatism with respect to the appropriate form and function of government. Organic conservatives are willing to use government, and even expand it if necessary, to assure the kind of social welfare that they consider morally justified in the current context. They want a government capable of doing many things, as we shall see later. The free market is useful, when it does its job, but it cannot be left in charge when important goals are at stake. On the other hand, 1890s liberals insist on the free market as the sole allocator of important values in the society. They demand a strictly limited government.

To understand the conservative position with regard to the definitions of equality and freedom, therefore, we must be prepared to do two things. First we must add another value — the scope and power of government and its impact on the free market. Then we must distinguish between (*a*) a surface level of agreement between the two major strands on liberalism's errors (e.g., in expanding equality and thereby expanding government) and on what equality and freedom should mean and (*b*) the deeper but divergent reasons behind those positions. This is a pattern that will be repeated with respect to other important values. Surface agreement rests on different reasons for a shared position, complicated by tension over the proper form and function of government and its impact on the market.

Individualism

The differences evident with respect to equality and liberty shade directly into some contrasting understandings of the key value of individualism. For the 1890s liberals, the individual is the focus of all concerns. Speaking of the traditional importance of the right and power of individuals to shape their own lives as they wish, the Freidmans say:

> Equality and liberty were two faces of the same basic value — that every individual should be regarded as an end in himself. . . . Equality before God — personal equality — is important precisely because people are not identical. Their different values, their different tastes, their different capacities will lead them to want to lead very different lives. Personal equality requires respect for their right to do so, not the imposition on them of someone else's values or judgment.[11]

The image here, then, is of a body of autonomous individuals whose satisfaction-seeking needs, harmonized through the free economic market, in essence define the good society. Equality of opportunity means equality before the law — equality of chances — and is thus at once the means of implementing "personal equality" and an essential component of liberty.[12] All of these values are bound together in one indivisible whole. The consequence, of course, is to place the individual and his or her needs at the center of political thinking and adapt all other definitions and priorities to that first principle.

For organic conservatives, this simply will not do. Let George Will speak one more time:

> Once politics is defined negatively, as an enterprise for drawing a protective circle around the individual's sphere of self-interested action, then public concerns are by definition distinct from, and secondary to, private concerns. Regardless of democratic forms, when people are taught by philosophy (and the social climate) that they need not govern their actions by calculations of public good, they will come to blame all social shortcomings on the agency of collective considerations, the government, and will absolve themselves.[13]

Individualism of the Freidmans' variety is part of the problem that once-dominant liberalism has created. A system where everybody puts individual interest foremost has no concept of the public interest, let alone the capacity to implement one if it were found. If individuals are encouraged to think that they should always get whatever they want, they may well come to blame government for not providing it. And organic conservatives see disaffection from government as one of the worst maladies of contemporary society.

Organic conservatives mean something quite distinct by individualism. For them, individuals are important only as members of the community. The individual should be guided toward making contributions to the society's preservation and development. By making such contributions, individuals earn both immediate satisfaction from doing what is right and entitlement to share in the social justice that is appropriate for all in the community.

A Digression.   In its notions of the individual and the society, organic conservatism shares something important with economic democracy and democratic socialism. This strand of conservatism, like the radicals, would convert the American notion of individualism to a much more social or organic concept. In other words, the individual would be embedded in and draw his or her identity from a web of social relations with other individuals. Through these social relations—that is, through contributing to and receiving support from other people—the individual would realize his or her human potential. All together would constitute a community.

Whereas the left belief systems add full equality and substantive democracy to this goal, organic conservatism, of course, posits natural inequality and elite guidance. For conservatives, a community implies obligation, where the few with the greatest wisdom teach moral standards and behavior to the multitude of others. Only 1890s liberals (and the bulk of Americans) continue to think of the individual as an isolated social unit whose self-seeking should give the society all its important dynamics and priorities.

One more similarity between the radical belief systems and organic conservatism, together with the conversion of individualism to community, helps explain the occasional agreements between them. They share a sense of the entirely mythological nature of any separation between economics and politics. Neither believes for a moment that the unequal wealth, status, and power of the private sphere could possibly fail to translate directly into analogous inequalities of political power. The difference between them on this point is simple: radicals think the situation is wrong, organic conservatives think it is natural and right. Only liberals of various kinds (and the bulk of Americans) believe there can and should be separation between a private sphere where inequality is evident and acceptable and a public sphere where equality prevails.

From the foregoing, it should be obvious that organic conservatism and 1890s liberalism have not yet consummated their marriage. Their synthesis is an ongoing process that will require more time. Perhaps experience in power will help to shift their focus away from the precision possible only in rhetoric toward the practical accommodations necessary to devise and justify new public policies. It may also help that the powerful business support behind their joint rise to control of the national government is quite impatient with meticulously principled arguments, devoted instead to what works to stay in power. In any event, their alliance should be facilitated by the fact that their beliefs regarding the remaining basic values are shared.

Democracy, Property, and Contracts/Law

The conservative synthesis is quite evident in their shared attitudes toward democracy, as well as their strong concern for the regular procedures symbolized by contracts and law. The most complete agreement, however, occurs with regard to their highest value, property.

Most conservatives have little good to say about democracy in its current form in the United States. They see it as giving rise to special interest self-seeking and a set of mounting demands that government simply cannot begin to fulfill. As we shall see in the next section, organic conservatives define the loss of authority in government as one of the major problems of our times. Consequently, they have designed a program to reduce democratic participation and restore authority in government. The 1890s liberals are totally committed to the procedural definition of democracy, the more limited the better. The greatest possible room must be left for the free market to control allocations within the society. With their firm sense of a wall of separation between economic conditions and the political world, and their devotion to the principle of limited government, they could hardly believe otherwise.

The conservative penchant for order and regular procedures is reflected in their endorsement of a central role for contracts and the law. Both strands oppose the proliferation of litigation, which has, in their view, been encouraged by the liberal emphasis on self-seeking claims. Both are certain that liberal judges have taken the courts far too deeply into the social engineering business. But contracts stand on high ground and embody the honor and integrity with which a good society should conduct its affairs. The law is the basis for order. It is the necessary cement for a social system that shows far too many centrifugal tendencies. For organic conservatives law is value-laden and purposeful, whereas 1890s liberals have a sense of the law as a neutral machine not unlike the free market in its workings. But such differences are not very important in the context of essentially full support by each to the established legal system.

The most unequivocal commitment that conservatives share, however, is to the value of property. The right to gain, hold, and use property is the first component of their definition of a good society. For organic conservatives, property is imbued with a moral base. Property gives one a stake in the society. It enables one to act with some responsibility as a citizen. And it allows some members of society the time to develop their talents and wisdom for governing well. The fact that property can be used wrongly or sought too avidly does not detract from its central role in making possible a good society and thus good government.

The 1890s liberal is equally committed to the importance of property rights, but for different reasons. Individual wealth is the necessary and appropriate way to reward risk taking. The society always benefits more than the man from the activities that made him personally rich. Incentives are what make the market work effectively. Any effort to tax or otherwise limit wealth derived from economic activities reduces those incentives and warps the market's operation. George Gilder argues that "all the values of advanced culture—equality, bureaucratic rationality, predictability, sexual liberation, political 'populism,' and the pursuit of pleasure" inspire modern governments to intrude on the free use of property that spells economic growth and progress. He adds:

> Material progress is ineluctably elitist: it makes the rich richer and increases their numbers, exalting the few extraordinary men who can produce wealth over the democratic masses who consume it. . . . Material progress is difficult: it requires from its protagonists long years of diligence and sacrifice, devotion and risk that can be elicited only with high rewards, not "the average return on capital."[14]

Conservatism has thus put its stamp of definition and priority on the standard basic values. But it has also looked at them through a special lens, an overlay made from other value(s) — the form and function of government and the extent to which the free market is unhampered by that government. What emerges, though still incomplete, is a complex and somewhat inconsistent belief system searching for a lasting synthesis.

PROBLEMS AND POSSIBILITIES: THE CONSERVATIVE PROGRAM

As might be expected, the differences between the two strands of conservatism fade into the background as they analyze today's problems and begin to work out possible solutions. Each strand has some particular priorities, but neither denies the importance of the other's proposals. In some cases, notably foreign policy, they stand firmly together on what is wrong and what should be done about it. Economic concerns generally predominate, no doubt reflecting the circumstances of the 1980s. In turn, such priorities (and the remedies that flow naturally from 1890s liberalism's principles) help to explain continued strong business support for conservatism.

Problems

The most broadly shared concern that conservatives have is the rise of Soviet power and the advance of communism in the world. Some see the United States on the verge of falling behind the Soviet Union in strategic military capabilities and therefore entering a period of extreme vulnerability and danger. Others are less alarmist, but still believe in the need to substantially boost American strength. Almost all agree that the United States must get over its post-Vietnam reluctance to employ its military, economic, and ideological strengths on behalf of American national interests everywhere in the world.

Conservatives thus see a dual problem in restoring the United States to its rightful dominant role in world affairs. One part of the problem is quite tangible, namely, rebuilding the American military machine to make it efficient, mobile, and strong enough to at least fully balance the Soviet Union. Some still seek military superiority, but probably most acknowledge that nuclear parity is all that today's technological conditions make possible. The other, much less tangible, part of the problem is that of restoring the political will and popular support necessary for regular exercises of U.S. power to aid friendly governments, prevent communist advances, and serve American economic interests around the world.

For most conservatives, therefore, the problem is not just an external one. It is closely connected to what is happening in the United States. A leading conservative defense expert, Samuel Huntington, argues that efforts to expand democracy and egalitarianism at home effectively reduced freedom abroad because they limited the use of American power overseas:

> The strong recommitment to democratic, liberal, and populist values that occurred during these years [1960s and 1970s] eventually generated efforts to limit, constrain, and reduce American military, political, and economic power abroad. . . . The decline in American power abroad weakened the support for liberty and democracy abroad. American democracy and foreign democracy may be inversely related.[15]

The implication is that, in order to promote American versions of liberty and democracy abroad, efforts to promote the same values at home will have to be tempered. If true, this is a real contradiction whose resolution could have profound significance.

In the 1970s and 1980s, however, the most immediately visible problem for all Americans was that of economic decline. The problem has several facets, changing over time, but all adding up to declining economic growth and general performance when compared with the American past or other industrial countries today. At one point, the problem seemed to be defined by inflation and low productivity, at another by unemployment and low profitability. At all times, the American economy seemed to be losing the competitive advantages it had so long enjoyed. This is the problem that the 1890s liberals have been most concerned to analyze.

The 1980s liberals did not lack for an explanation of what was happening: the problem was excessive government. Too much spending, taxing, regulating, subsidizing, etc., was undermining incentives and work habits and imposing too heavy a burden on business. The Friedmans sum up the situation this way:

> The experience of recent years — slowing growth and declining productivity — raises a doubt whether private ingenuity can continue to overcome the

deadening effects of government control if we continue to grant ever more power to government, to authorize a "new class" of civil servants to spend ever larger
fractions of our income supposedly on our behalf. Sooner or later — and perhaps
sooner than many of us expect — an ever bigger government would destroy both
the prosperity that we owe to the free market and the human freedom proclaimed
so eloquently in the Declaration of Independence.[16]

Although their immediate concern is with economic freedom as the remedy
for economic decline, economic freedom is indivisible from human freedoms. Thus, for the Friedmans, more is at stake in freeing the market from
government intervention than merely the rejuvenation of the American
economy.

The 1890s liberals agree that excessively self-interested actions by
many, including business, is part of the American economic problem. However, they believe that such actions, too, can be traced to big government
and egalitarianism. The heart of the problem is the size of the national government — the total revenue that it is forced to draw out of the private economy to fulfill its functions. Size, then, is the issue, and *not* whether the federal
budget is balanced. Also burdensome on the market are the rapidly increasing numbers of regulations, as well as government interference with its
operations in the form of subsidies, trade protection, and "bailouts" of failing corporations.

The last major problem is one that particularly concerns former organic
conservatives: the loss of authority in government as a result of too much
democracy and rampant self-interest. A serious consequence is that government is simply unable to define, and act decisively on behalf of, the long-
term good of the society as a whole. In some ways, this is a problem inherent
in the American polity, a problem to which conservatives acknowledge there
is no real solution. One of the best recent statements of this dilemma is Huntington's *American Politics: The Promise of Disharmony*. Huntington argues
that the United States is distinguished by a set of values (essentially those we
have identified as the basic American values) so strongly held as to constitute
a "creed." Instead of ranking these values, Americans simply endorse them
all and expect them all to be fully realized. But governing institutions can
never live up to such ideals. There will always be a gap between the aspirations of the creed and the realities of power. If the creedal values are actually
sought, then the result is necessarily an attack on the (essential, and constitutionally provided) power and autonomy of governing institutions.

Huntington interprets American history in four cycles of "creedal passion," of which the 1960s and 1970s are the latest example and the Populist-
Progressive Era the last before that. During such periods, Americans seek
realization of their creed with special moralistic vigor and end up reducing
the power of government. Huntington sums up the results of the 1960s and
1970s in this way:

In the 1960s, when Americans became concerned about the gap between their
political ideals and their political institutions, they began to eviscerate the polit-

ical and governmental institutions that had been developed to deal with foreign enemies. . . . The S&S Years [the sixties and seventies] thus left the United States with a more equitable society, a more open politics, a more cynical public, and a less authoritative and effective government. They left the American people confronting foreign and domestic challenges that required the exercise of power, yet still unwilling to legitimize power.[17]

This loss of governmental power and authority is a recurrent problem in the United States. In European societies, conflicting ideologies are common and each finds primary expression in one set of governing institutions. Confidence and support are retained for *some* governing institutions no matter what the stage of the cycle of change may be. But in the United States, broad sharing of basic values means much less conflict between groupings of them. Instead, we have periods of "creedal passion," in which all are avidly sought at once, followed by periods of quiescence. We pay the price in loss of support for *all* governing institutions. Much of our politics consists of antigovernment belief and action:

> In the United States the gap between political ideal and political reality is a weapon always available for use by social groups against those who control the state. The dominant political creed constitutes a standing challenge to the power of government and the legitimacy of political institutions. Political authority is vulnerable in America as it is nowhere else.[18]

In other words, the problem is acute, distinctively American, and probably insoluble without fundamental change in the essence of American values and beliefs. In this pessimistic attitude, Huntington faithfully represents the characteristic organic conservative resignation to the imperfectability of humankind.

Possibilities

Pessimism and resignation are characteristic of conservatism, in contrast to the optimism and faith in progress that historically came with liberalism. It was quite in character, therefore, for conservative political scientist Andrew Hacker to publish a major work entitled *The End of the American Era* as early as 1971. Like other conservatives, Hacker considers it likely that the United States has embarked on its permanent decline. He sees egalitarianism and the expansion of democracy as having transformed American character: traditional deference is lacking now, and the emphasis is on personal pleasures rather than mutual sacrifice and national grandeur. He sets the American adventure in historical context:

> If every nation has a history, so has each nation its course to run, its age of ascendancy, and its time of decline. Most experience at least one epoch of exhilarating self-confidence when the country seems embarked on a mission carrying a moral for humanity. But, long or short, every such epoch must come to an end. The United States is about to join other nations of the world which were once prepossessing and are now little more than plots of bounded terrain.[19]

Hacker offers the usual conservative list of problems: loss of authority in government, failure of leadership and refusal of followership, the replacement of religion by skepticism, excessive hedonism and refusal of sacrifice, and loss of both patriotism and the sense of the United States as setting a moral and practical example for the world. He says simply, "America's history as a nation has reached its end" and decline is a condition we must learn to endure. It will not be cataclysmic, because "Americans will learn to live with danger and discomfort, for this condition is the inevitable accompaniment of democracy in its declining years."[20] However, it is the end of any serious effort to restore American world stature or to reconstruct conditions at home so as to restart American social and economic engines.

But most conservatives are far from ready to concede that there are no effective means by which American greatness can be restored. Some of these remedies have already been suggested in discussing the analyses of economic problems made by the 1890s liberals. They may be summarized as drastic reduction in the size of government and withdrawal of government from interference of any kind with the operations of the economic free market. Reliance is always placed on the capacity of the free market to energize the American economy, in clear contrast to the plans of neoliberals to use government as the vehicle of renewed growth.

Another set of remedies, once known as "supply-side economics," holds that tax cuts for the wealthy will spur investment, new productivity, jobs, and the return of competitiveness. But conservatism's commitment to rebuilding American military power imposes major spending, and hence revenue, needs. When these are added to basic social program costs, the tax load on the private economy has not lightened very much. The hope of supply-side theorists is that the new investments made possible by tax cuts will generate so much more productivity and competitiveness that the economy will boom. As a result, tax revenues will rise to new highs.

The supply-side theorists are quite willing to accept federal government budget deficits when they represent revenues foregone for purposes of productive new investment rather than mere consumption. Investment will mean production and jobs and revenues in the future, whereas consumption means only future inflation. Traditional conservatives, however, tend to see deficits as profligate burdens on future generations. They seek, as a matter of principle, to assure balanced budgets. Most Americans seem to agree with the traditionalists, and supply-siders have yet to gain even a near majority for their views.

Conservatives see an economic bill of rights as a major way to create a popular image of the kind of society they seek. A characteristic version, drawn from the constitutional amendments proposed in the Friedmans' *Free to Choose*, is presented as Figure 9.1. The fact that conservatives also think in terms of "bills of rights" is itself testimony to the strength of the beliefs among Americans in individual rights and limitations on governments. The basic rationale behind a bill of rights of this sort is quite consistent with 1890s liberal principles: preserving economic freedoms is prerequisite to enjoying all other human freedoms.

As the figure indicates, the Friedmans' first priority is (predictably) reduction of the total federal "take" from the private economy. After that, they would free all forms of economic activity from the prospect of government interference through four specific limitations on the national and state governments. Next, they provide for flat rate taxation, continued sound money, and protection against inflation. Regardless of whether such proposed amendments ever even receive serious public consideration, they serve to exemplify in a clear-cut way the principles for which this brand of conservatism stands. Nor are such principles unique to the Friedmans: quite similar prescriptions can be found in other major conservative works.[21]

Similarly, the organic conservatives' concern for restoring authority in government has been spelled out in some detail and yet may be the kind of goal that nobody really expects to achieve. George Will, among others, has suggested what a government should be like:

> The best government exists to frame arrangements in order that they may, over time, become matters of trust. . . .[that] does conduce to an increasingly comfortable fit between institutions and the public, which, like a flowing river, is both a shaper of and shaped by the institutional "banks" between which it flows. A river does not chafe against its banks, except in flood, when it is deformed by unnatural forces. Indeed, a river without banks is incomprehensible; it is a contradiction in terms; it is a lake or a swamp. A river is made by, defined by, whatever keeps it to its course.[22]

But Huntington warns us that popular support and trust is not a likely prospect. Americans must first learn to live with "the agony and the promise" of the conflict between the liberal ideal and the institutional reality, our distinguishing cleavage. They can only try "to reduce the gap between their ideals and their institutions, accepting the fact that the imperfections of human nature mean the gap can never be eliminated."[23]

George Will's answer is that politics itself must first be restored so that it can be rescued "from the stale, false notion that government is always and only an instrument of coercion, making disagreeable (even when necessary) excisions from freedom. . . . "[24] He argues that we have "lived improvidently off a dwindling legacy of cultural capital . . . that legacy is a renewable resource, but it will not regenerate spontaneously. Regeneration is a political choice, a political chore." Will's use of the word "choice" has quite different implications than does the Friedmans', suggesting instead of free market analogies a conscious and continuing effort at "cooperation" and "collaboration" to bring about a return to civility.[25] It seems clear that if the organic conservatives were to solve their problem of governmental authority, they might well encounter determined resistance from their current allies, the 1890s liberals.

IMPLICATIONS AND PROSPECTS

Throughout this chapter, we have stressed the incompleteness of the synthesis between organic conservatism and 1890s antistatist liberalism. The impli-

I. Limits on Federal Spending

Section 1. To protect the people against excessive governmental burdens and to promote sound fiscal and monetary policies, total outlays of the Government of the United States shall be limited.

(a) Total outlays in any fiscal year shall not increase by a percentage greater than the percentage increase in nominal gross national product in the last calendar year ending prior to the beginning of said fiscal year. Total outlays shall include budget and off-budget outlays, and exclude redemptions of the public debt and emergency outlays.

(b) If inflation for the last calendar year ending prior to the beginning of any fiscal year is more than 3 percent, the permissible percentage increase in total outlays for that fiscal year shall be reduced by one-fourth of the excess of inflation over 3 percent. Inflation shall be measured by the difference between the percentage increase in nominal gross national product and the percentage increase in real gross national product.

Section 2. When, for any fiscal year, total revenues received by the Government of the United States exceed total outlays, the surplus shall be used to reduce the public debt of the United States until such debt is eliminated.

Section 3. Following declaration of an emergency by the President, Congress may authorize, by a two-thirds vote of both Houses, a specified amount of emergency outlays in excess of the limit for the current fiscal year.

Section 4. The limit on total outlays may be changed by a specified amount by a three-fourths vote of both Houses of Congress when approved by the Legislatures of a majority of the several States. The change shall become effective for the fiscal year following approval.

Section 5. For each of the first six fiscal years after ratification of this article, total grants to States and local governments shall not be a smaller fraction of total outlays than in the three fiscal years prior to the ratification of this article. Thereafter, if grants are less than that fraction of total outlays, the limit on total outlays shall be decreased by an equivalent amount.

Section 6. The Government of the United States shall not require, directly or indirectly, that States or local governments engage in additional or expanded activities without compensation equal to the necessary costs.

Section 7. This article may be enforced by one or more Members of Congress in an action brought in the United States District Court for the District of Columbia, and by no other persons. The action shall name as defendant the Treasurer of the United States, who shall have authority over outlays by any agency or unit of the Government of the United States when required by a court order enforcing the provisions of this article. The order of the court shall not specify the particular outlays to be made or reduced. Changes in outlays necessary to comply with the order of the court shall be made no later than the end of the third full fiscal year following the court order.

II. International Trade

Congress shall not lay any imposts or duties on imports or exports, except what may be absolutely necessary for executing its inspection laws.

III. Wage and Price Controls

Congress shall make no laws abridging the freedom of sellers of goods or labor to price their products or services.

IV. Occupational Licensure

No State shall make or impose any law which shall abridge the right of any citizen of the United States to follow any occupation or profession of his choice.

V. Free Trade

The right of the people to buy and sell legitimate goods and services at mutually acceptable terms shall not be infringed by Congress or any of the States.

VI. Income Taxation

Section 1. Amendment XVI to this Constitution pertaining to income taxation is hereby repealed.

Section 2. The Congress shall have power to lay and collect taxes on income of persons, from whatever sources derived, without apportionment among the several States, and without regard to any census or enumeration, provided that the same tax rate is applied to all income in excess of occupational and business expenses and a personal allowance of a fixed amount. The word "person" shall exclude corporations and other artificial persons.

VII. Sound Money

Congress shall have the power to authorize non-interest-bearing obligations of the Government in the form of currency or book entries, provided that the total dollar amount outstanding increases by no more than 5 percent per year and no less than 3 percent.

VIII. Inflation Protection

All contracts between the United States Government and other parties stated in dollars, and all other dollar sums stated in federal laws, shall be adjusted annually to allow for the change in the general level of prices during the prior year.

FIGURE 9.1 A Conservative Bill of Rights (Proposed Constitutional Amendments)

Source: Derived from Milton Friedman and Rose Friedman, *Free to Choose* (New York: Harcourt Brace Jovanovich, 1979), pp. 289–297 and Appendix B. The first article is the text of a proposed amendment prepared by the National Tax Limitation Committee and incorporated by the Friedmans in their proposals.

cation, which we have often stated explicitly, is that conservatism could well divide again, leaving the minority organic conservatives once again in isolated intellectual splendor. Probably the most decisive factor in shaping the outcome wil be the future evolution of the New Right and the pressure it imposes on the conservative alliance.

Currently, the Republican Party seems to have room for all three versions of conservatism. But the New Right is the strongest and most adamant of the three. At some point, it could either reject or take over the Republican Party. In that case, the other two strands of conservatism would have to decide whether or not to follow. It is hard to imagine organic conservatism staying with the New Right in any such situation. The result might well be a rupture with 1890s liberalism. This speculation, however, can only be meaningful when we have explored the New Right in some depth. We shall therefore defer consideration of the prospects of conservatism until the concluding section of the next chapter.

ADDITIONAL READINGS

Bartlett, Bruce R. *Reagonomics: Supply-Side Economics in Action*. New York: Quyill, 1982.

Friedman, Milton. *Capitalism and Freedom*. Chicago: University of Chicago Press, 1962.

Friedman, Milton, and Friedman, Rose. *Free to Choose*. New York: Harcourt Brace Jovanovich, 1980.

Gilder, George. *Wealth and Poverty*. New York: Basic Books, 1981.

Hacker, Andrew. *The End of the American Era*. New York: Atheneum, 1971.

Huntington, Samuel P. *American Politics: The Promise of Disharmony*. Cambridge, Mass.: Belknap Press, 1981.

Laxalt, Paul, and Williamson, Richard S. *A Changing America: Conservatives View the 1980s from the United States Senate*. South Bend, Ind.: Regnery/Gateway, 1980.

Miles, Michael W. *The Odyssey of the American Right*. New York: Oxford University Press, 1980.

Nash, George H. *The Conservative Intellectual Movement in America Since 1945*. New York: Basic Books, 1976.

Sullivan, William M. *Reconstructing Public Philosophy*. Berkeley and Los Angeles: University of California Press, 1982.

Will, George F. *Statecraft as Soulcraft: What Government Does*. New York: Simon and Schuster, 1983.

CHAPTER 10

The New Right: "Populist Conservatism"

The New Right is clearly the most significant new force in American politics in half a century, and quite possibly the full one hundred years. Not since farmers and workers surged into politics, generating the turmoil of the late 1880s and 1890s, have the established powers and habits of American politics been so profoundly disrupted. In the mid-1980s, the ultimate role of the New Right is far from clear. It could remain within, or fragment, the Republican Party. It could become the nucleus of a major new lower-middle class party of the right *or* left or turn away from electoral politics entirely (perhaps toward more drastic alternatives). Whatever the route the New Right takes, it seems certain to play a major role in reshaping the American political spectrum.

The New Right is quite different from the seven belief systems we have considered so far. It is not only the newest and probably most powerful, but it is distinctively a social movement and not really a belief system in the way that we have been using the term. A social movement is composed of millions of people who share certain basic views, are actually mobilized, and are taking major steps to realize their goals. By contrast, belief systems have a few recognized thinkers and a body of loosely identified people holding common values and beliefs who, perhaps, would be willing to consider acting upon them at some future time.

The social movement known as the New Right has a closely linked network of issue-oriented organizations with overlapping leaders. These leaders and their organizations maintain close face-to-face communication with each other, and, through newsletters, journals, and direct mail, with a constituency of millions who strongly support one or more of the specific issues involved. These issues almost uniformly pit the New Right against national policies implemented or seriously considered since the early 1960s. The New Right stands for tax reduction, restoration of religious values and practices, a more nationalistic foreign policy, control of labor unions, "profamily" actions (defeat of the Equal Rights Amendment, prohibitions on abortions and pornography, etc.), opposition to gun control, and support for a variety of more drastic efforts at reducing crime.

The popular base of the New Right is made up primarily of two important and overlapping types of Americans. One is the fundamentalist religious groups, now numbering in the tens of millions, located chiefly in the South and Midwest. The other is the nationally distributed population group now coming to be know as "Middle American Radicals" (MARs), after a well-documented study by the Michigan sociologist Donald Warren.[1]

Middle American Radicals make up perhaps 25 percent of the American population according to Warren's analysis. They are the lower-middle class people who feel that they are being forced by government to bear an unfair share of the burden of social change, despite their hard work and loyalty to American ideals. More specifically, they feel that the complacent rich are using government to make them pay for the advances demanded by the militant poor and minorities. The solution lies in political action to get rid of those currently in power and install public officials who will follow the New Right majority's wishes. It is this democratic and antiwealthy attitude that leads the conservative commentator Kevin Phillips to characterize the New Right as "populist conservatives."[2]

This is an important insight for understanding the New Right. To be radical, majoritarian, lower-middle class, and conservative at the same time is completely unprecedented in modern American politics. And yet the combination is a logical one. When liberals control things, there is no reason to accept the status quo. There is also no way to change it except by majority action—hence the conjunction of radicalism with conservatism. Paul Weyrich, one of the key leaders of the New Right, makes the point as follows:

> We are radicals who want to change the existing power structure. We are not conservatives in the sense that conservatism means accepting the status quo. We cannot accept the status quo. . . . We have to take a turn in the other direction. The New Right does not want to conserve, we want to change—we *are* the forces of change. And if people are sick and tired of things in this country, then they had best look to conservative leadership for that change.[3]

And the way to change things is through mass political action. Thus, "populist conservative" is the way to understand all these characteristics in an incisive manner.

In this analysis, we shall make repeated adjustments in our standard approach in order to address the New Right as a social movement as well as a belief system. For example, we shall examine specific leaders and organizations, analyze issues more than values, and undertake some social analysis of the mass base of the movement. We do so because of the distinctive nature of the movement, not through any sense that this movement consists of people who can only be understood through sociological or psychological analysis. It is well past time to take the New Right seriously as a body of people in motion around a set of valid and strongly felt principles. They may well hold the key to the American future.

ORIGINS: THE RISE OF THE NEW RIGHT

The New Right developed as an identifiable movement in 1974–1975, in part in reaction to President Ford's appointment of Nelson Rockefeller (the embodiment of wealthy, liberal Republicanism) as vice president.[4] A group of young conservative activists, experienced in Republican politics, resolved to put principles before party. It was time to organize the constituency they were sure was available for a consistently conservative program. The appointment of Rockefeller was the final provocation in a long series of moderate Republican accommodations with big government and free-spending liberalism evident even in the Nixon administration. At the center of this new group of activists were four men.

Paul Weyrich, with the financial support of the wealthy Joseph Coors, had already been instrumental in starting or reshaping several conservative organizations. For example, he had helped revitalize the Heritage Foundation, a think tank that publishes policy-oriented work by conservative scholars. And he had made the American Legislative Exchange Council, originally a clearinghouse for information for state legislators, into the principal means of providing these legislators with the conservative viewpoint on issues. In 1974, again with help from Coors, he started the Committee for the Survival of a Free Congress (CSFC). This organization raises funds and supports conservative candidates for Congress, providing extensive training in the techniques of campaigning as well as financial help.

Howard Phillips founded the Conservative Caucus (CC) in 1975 as a way to mobilize constituents in as many congressional districts as possible to keep conservative pressure on elected representatives and senators. By 1980, the Conservative Caucus had hundreds of thousands of contributors, a budget upwards of $3 million, and organizations in 250 districts. It had spun off a research foundation, sponsored several newsletters reporting on legislators' actions, and developed a speakers' bureau and a number of other services for conservative candidates and officeholders.

John (Terry) Dolan helped to start and became the chairman of the National Conservative Political Action Committee (NCPAC) in 1975. NCPAC collects campaign funds and channels them to conservative candidates and causes. Taking advantage of the opportunities available to political action committees (PACS) under current laws, NCPAC runs advertising campaigns aimed at defeating liberal elected officials who are on the wrong side of issues such as abortion and the Panama Canal treaties. It was particularly successful in targeting and helping to defeat liberal senators in 1978 and 1980. Dolan also serves as chairman of the Washington Legal Foundation, which sponsors litigation for conservative purposes, and Conservatives Against Liberal Legislation (CALL), a lobbying group.

Richard Viguerie is the publisher of *Conservative Digest*, a monthly journal reporting on all New Right activities through original articles and reprints of important speeches or statements. He is also the head of the Richard A. Viguerie Company (RAVCO), a sophisticated and totally computerized direct-mail operation that handles the fund-raising and communications system for all the other conservative organizations. Viguerie is widely credited with having mobilized money and people behind the New Right organizations with an effectiveness previously unknown in American politics.

With these four men and their organizations at the center, the New Right was launched. In his words, Viguerie perceived that they shared the following characteristics:

1. A developing technical ability — in direct mail, in mass media, in practical politics.
2. A willingness to work together for the common good.
3. A commitment to put philosophy before political party.
4. An optimism and a conviction that we had the ability to win and to lead America.[5]

The label "New Right" was first applied by the sympathetic conservative columnist Kevin Phillips in 1975 in the course of an assessment emphasizing the "social conservatism" of the groups. Phillips made the point that the New Right represented a significant departure in American politics. They stressed cultural and social issues instead of the almost exclusively economic issues of the Old Right. He argued that if the New Right was able to make a firm link with that Old Right, the combination of issues would be very powerful.[6] In an important book, the devoted conservative William A. Rusher, publisher of *National Review*, made a similar argument. Social conservatives, many of whom were former Democrats, should seek alliance with the economic conservatives of the Republican Party, if necessary through a "new majority party."[7]

The New Right has moved in that direction throughout its brief existence. Its first task, however, was to mobilize a significant "social conservative" constituency; making itself felt in Congress and in presidential politics would follow. In addition to the key groups discussed, several other groups have played important secondary roles in this mobilization process. Richard Viguerie's widely distributed *The New Right: We're Ready to Lead* lists the more important ones as the following:[8]

Citizens Committee for the Right to Keep and Bear Arms (and the associated Second Amendment Foundation)
Coalition for Peace Through Strength
National Right to Work Committee
Heritage Foundation (and the associated publication *Policy Review*)
Washington Legal Foundation
American Legislative Exchange Council
Committee for Responsible Youth Politics
Conservative Victory Fund
Life Amendment Political Action Committee
American Life Lobby
National Pro-Life Political Action Committee
Public Service Research Council

Conservatives Against Liberal Legislation
National Tax Limitation Committee
Stop ERA
American Security Council
Council on Inter-American Security

The New Right gained its first victory in 1977 with a well-coordinated campaign to stop changes in the election laws. From the summer of 1977 to April 1978, it took the leadership that the Republican Party was unwilling to exercise in opposition to the Panama Canal treaties. That campaign nearly succeeded and added 400,000 new names to the New Right mailing lists. Another result was that eight senators who voted for ratification were defeated in the November 1978 elections. Five others did not seek reelection — in part because of New Right opposition.

Perhaps more important in the long run, in 1977 and 1978 the New Right began to build a "profamily" coalition. Antiabortion groups, the "Stop ERA" campaign, and organizations opposing pornography, gay rights, and childrens' services were all either started or extensively supported by New Right activists. At about this same time, the tax revolt, symbolized by the success of Proposition 13 in California, began to spread — also with heavy support from New Right money and campaign personnel.

Finally, in 1979 the decision was made to try to incorporate the "religious right" within the network of organizations and direct mail communication that is the heart and soul of the New Right. Several groups were founded for this purpose. First came Christian Voice, based in Los Angeles, which brings a New Right perspective on legislative voting records to the attention of tens of thousands of ministers and many more regular members. The next group founded was the Moral Majority, under Jerry Falwell. The Reverend Falwell was already well known for his "Old Time Gospel Hour," which reaches as many as 50 million people per week. The Moral Majority was credited with defeating several liberal senators in 1980. It also probably provided Ronald Reagan with a significant portion of his winning electoral margin. The third group, also begun in 1979, was the Religious Roundtable. It brings thousands of ministers together four or more times a year to hear a variety of New Right speakers.

By 1080, the organizational structure of the New Right had reached out to its full range of social and religious issues. It had prepared the way for a right-wing conservative triumph of major proportions. In its own eyes, it required only a consolidation period to become as permanent a governing majority as the American political system has ever known. The potential of the New Right is well summarized by Kevin Phillips:

> I submit that the New Right combines three powerful trend patterns that recur in American history and politics. First, to some measure it is an extension of the Wallace movement, and as such represents a current expression of the ongoing populism of the white lower middle classes, principally in the South and West.

All the right symbols are present: antimetropolitanism, antielitism, cultural fundamentalism. Second, the New Right is closely allied with the sometimes potent right-to-life or antiabortion movement, the current version, perhaps, of the great one-issue moral crusades of the American past — the pre-Civil War abolitionists and the early-twentieth-century prohibitionists. And this one-issue element, in turn, folds into the third phenomenon — the possible fourth occurrence of the religious revivals or "Great Awakenings" that have swept across the land since the middle of the eighteenth century. If so, the *religious* wing of the New Right may be the *political* wind of a major national "awakening."[9]

Whether this potential will be realized depends on the extent to which consolidation can be accomplished behind a president not just rhetorically sympathetic to, but willing to act in accordance with, New Right principles. But before we assess the prospects, we must explore those principles in somewhat more detail.

NEW RIGHT ISSUE POSITIONS AND UNDERLYING VALUES

The issue-oriented approach of the New Right has led to the formation of many "single-issue" affiliate organizations, often with distinct political action committees or lobbying arms and tax-free foundations for research and educational support. At the leadership level, there are close connections between the single-issue organizations and the four core groups. But each issue area has a distinct constituency whose members may not be actively involved in any other issue. We shall survey the range of major issues and the New Right positions with respect to them. From that survey, we can derive definitions and priorities concerning basic values. Although we shall group issues together in distinct categories, there are important overlaps between the categories, as will be noted.

Taxation

One of the New Right's central themes has been that of excessive taxation. Pointing to the steady increase in the total national budget and the national debt, the New Right has endorsed both the supply-side approach of massive tax cutting and Milton Friedman's concept of strict limits on government taxing and spending. As Viguerie says, "Frankly, what we must do is stop socialism."[10]

Drawing on the success of Proposition 13 (which limited state property tax capacity) in California in 1978, the New Right has endorsed the tax limitation amendment drafted by the National Tax Limitation Committee (see Item I in Figure 9.1). It has also cosponsored the National Taxpayers Union's efforts to have state legislatures pass resolutions petitioning Congress to call a constitutional convention for the purpose of passing an amendment to the

Constitution to require balanced national budgets. To make lower government revenues practical, the New Right has called for drastic cutbacks in the scope of government regulations of business, limits on federal salaries and pensions, and an end to government "handouts" to welfare recipients.

Profamily

The New Right entered the profamily field in an explicit manner in 1979 through the "Library Court" umbrella of organizations. The Library Court group, named for the street in Washington, D.C., where the organizers first met, includes representatives of the Family Policy Division of the Free Congress Foundation, Citizens for Educational Freedom, Moral Majority, American Life Lobby, the Religious Roundtable, the American Association of Christian Schools, Conservatives Against Liberal Legislation, Family America, and the Christian Coalition for Legislative Action. Paul Weyrich is often credited with the insight that in the 1980s family issues might carry some of the same importance that Vietnam did in the 1960s or environmental and consumer issues did in the 1970s. He says, "In sheer numbers, the potential outreach of the Library Court group is greater than the whole range of conservative groups."[11]

The National Organization of Women and the Equal Rights Amendment are special targets. However, liberals generally are blamed for a wide variety of conditions such as the high divorce rate, the number of women with school-age children who work, and the high annual numbers of abortion, venereal disease cases, and illegitimate births. The focus of New Right efforts has been the Family Protection Act. Introduced by Senator Paul Laxalt in 1979, the act seeks to reassert the rights of parents in rearing and educating their children, protect private (Christian) schools, give parents the power of textbook review (to eliminate materials that are objectionable on religious grounds or because they belittle the traditional role of women), deny government protections to homosexuals, promote in home care of elderly parents, and deny food stamps to college students.

The profamily movement is a broad and inclusive one, even though some components are themselves single-issue movements. The Right-to-Life movement, for example, is one of the most powerful of all current New Right-affiliated groups but forms only a part of the broader profamily coalition. Some supporters of Right-to-Life efforts have no immediate links to the New Right, of course. The chances are very good, however, that their organizations do, and that member mailboxes will be the ultimate destination of many New Right communications.

It would be hard to overestimate the strength of the profamily issues for New Right supporters. Some Southerners in particular see this principle as the conservative root of social order itself. For example, Thomas Fleming declares:

> If we cannot keep the government out of our homes and out of our families, then freedom will cease to exist. I do not mean the paltry right to vote of which we

are so proud. In a society like our own, suffrage is only the right to collaborate with our captors. It is the high privilege of stool pigeons and prison trusties. Real freedom is the right to think our own thoughts, lead our own lifes, and rear our own children. Most men are only free when they are with their families.[12]

Foreign and Military

The New Right believes that American military defenses have collapsed and that liberals have lost all semblance of the political will necessary to stand up to communism. Viguerie says, "Liberal presidents and liberal Congresses have deliberately put us in second place, believing that America's over-whelming strength was a threat to the Soviets and world peace," and adds simply, "Our goal: military superiority."[13] New Right leaders are convinced that we are locked in a worldwide struggle to the death with communism. In effect World War III has been underway since before World War II ended.

A great number of policies have helped to put us in such desperate straits in this struggle. These include the development of trade relations, particularly technology transfers; acquiescence in such Soviet aggressions as Afghanistan; strategic arms limitation talks and treaties; failure to support Taiwan; the Panama Canal "giveaway to a Marxist dictator"; and the general loss of will suggested by the policy of "detente." The New Right advocates regaining military superiority on an emergency schedule, increasing efforts to disseminate anticommunist propaganda worldwide, rebuilding and deploying intelligence capabilities, and undertaking an offensive in the United Nations to focus attention on Soviet occupation of Eastern European and other satellite countries. As Viguerie concludes, "The alternative to such an all-out all-American effort is simple. The Soviets will either force us into a war we will lose or we will be forced to surrender."[14]

Religious

This category clearly overlaps with both profamily and school-related issues but has a large independent constituency. The focus is on the role of religion in public life generally, and more specifically the question of Christian morality as a driving force in the United States. Specific issues include the right to have prayers in schools and other public buildings, to have religious ceremonies and displays on public property, and to have religious criteria applied to education in a variety of ways. This last in turn includes parental rights to exclude textbooks that offend by teaching only the scientific doctrine of evolution and not "creationism" (the divine origin of life on earth). It also includes the right of parents to educate their children at home (along Christian lines) or to place them in private Christian schools that are free from state supervision and from federal income tax and affirmative action regulations.

New Right religious organizations also work for the elimination of profanity and sexually suggestive behavior from national television. Boycotts have been organized to discourage corporations from advertising on offending programs. As a way of bringing all these efforts to a single focus, a National Day of Prayer and Fasting has also been proposed to the Congress. This day would occur on the Sunday before Thanksgiving. All Americans would be asked to give thanks to God for their many advantages and to rededicate themselves to restoring the religious values that brought about these advantages in the first place.

Control of Labor Unions

Working through the National Right to Work Committee, the New Right has taken aim at the power of the "labor bosses" and their unions. Campaigns are overtly focused on the unrepresentativeness and raw power of labor leaders. However, in practice their result is often to severely weaken trade unions generally. One major tactic has been to promote passage of "right to work" laws (statutes prohibiting collective bargaining agreements from requiring that all employees join the recognized union at a particular site). Such laws have been enacted in several states. They effectively undercut union financial support and membership strength, making organization much more difficult. At the national level, the New Right has succeeded in cutting back union-supporting legislation.

Paul Weyrich explains these motivations by linking "big labor" with "big business." He says:

> Most of our fathers belonged to unions. We are anti-big business. The problem is that big unions turned into part of the problem. The New Right does not believe that unions *per se* are evil, as did the economic purist conservatives of the 1930s; we do not want to abolish unions. We merely recognize that today's big union leadership is unrepresentative of union membership, and, worse, uncaring of membership's concerns. We see that the big union bosses abuse members' hard-earned contributions.[18]

The New Right has also been strongly opposed to the formation of unions of public employees. The grounds are twofold: it is inappropriate for such workers to be unionized, and unionization here adds to the total cost of government.

Race and Crime

Crime has been another major focus of New Right energies. Racial antagonisms and fear often lie unacknowledged in the background of their discussions about the problem of crime in the United States. The New Right has endorsed any number of stricter punishments, including capital punishment, for various forms of crime. Much of its activity has taken the form of attacks on courts and judges for showing such great regard for the rights of accused defendants that convictions become very difficult and for imposing excessively light sentences when convictions *are* obtained.

Racial antagonisms are closer to the surface in such issues as school busing for purposes of integration. The New Right has regularly supported antibusing groups and promoted legislation to prohibit busing. However, it argues that such activity is not racially motivated but based in its belief in the principle of "neighborhood schools."

Opposition to the proposed constitutional amendment to give the District of Columbia the same voting rights in Congress as states enjoy again reveals this combination of racial and other concerns. It is the linkage with other issues that makes the D.C. amendment seem so threatening to New Right aims and generates such vigorous opposition. As an editorial in *Conservative Digest* advised:

> If you want to add to the United States Senate two more sure votes against a strong national defense, against effective internal security measures, against tax cuts, for gun control, for publicly financed abortions, for homosexual privileges, for ERA, for Big Labor, and above all, for big government, then support the proposed constitutional amendment to give the District of Columbia full voting privileges.[16]

Gun Control

The issue of registering, controlling, or outlawing certain kinds of guns is surely among the most explosive in American politics today. The National Rifle Association, though a very effective opponent of gun control, has maintained at least some distance from the New Right. But several similar organizations are closely linked with it. The Firearms Lobby of America and the American Legislative Exchange Council, for example, have carried much of the responsibility for opposition to the D.C. amendment as well as gun control legislation.

More narrowly focused on gun control alone are the Citizens Committee for the Right to Keep and Bear Arms and Gun Owners of America, both with state affiliates and/or tax-deductible legal and educational foundations. All of these groups oppose all forms of gun control. They argue that guns represent the last line of defense of individual rights and freedoms. Hundreds of thousands of Americans stand with them on these questions.

The Underlying Values and Beliefs

The New Right adheres to the basic American values in earlier and perhaps simpler forms. It also reflects a new religious dimension as well as containing some distinctive internal contradictions. There is a strong streak of orthodox individualism, for example, with a kind of John Wayne version of self-reliance, work, and sacrifice held up as a model. Much as the New Right endorses unfettered individualism and free enterprise, however, it retains a sense that some standards and guidance are appropriate. Public morality and public responsibility, in their definitions, are vital:

Free enterprise is not an absolute. It is a means, not an end. New Rightists, including those who devote their lives productively to free enterprise, do not intend to establish a religion of the dollar bill. This clearly distinguishes them from certain elements of the Old Right and from libertarians. New Rightists have no intention of having their neighborhoods turned over to pornographers and dope peddlers, their natural resources controlled by foreign corporations, their national honor understood chiefly as a matter of dollars and cents, their labor cheapened and culture undermined by the removal of barriers to immigration, all in the name of the free market.[17]

Other values are upheld in their older forms, including religion, family, and race. A genuine conservative theme with deep antipathies to equality runs through New Right thinking. A Southern New Right leader says:

The worst effect of the craze for equal opportunity lies in the curious phenomenon of women's rights. Leaving aside the whole question of inequality of ability, let us consider equal opportunity's effect on the family, when a mother decides that the family income and her own "self-fulfillment" take precedence over her maternal duties. Whatever a woman's reasons for going to work — economic necessity, greed, selfishness — the law guarantees her an opportunity for employment equal to any male head of the house. . . . When men and women are free to choose their own "life styles," and to decide what image of humanity they wish to represent, their children must be left increasingly to the protection of the State, which either operates or oversees the schools, childrens' homes, and day care centers that are replacing the family.[18]

The author's thesis is that equality of opportunity only widens the gap between people. The only eventual cure is therefore equality of condition, or socialism. That too is impossible, leading, as it does, to the corruption of the state. The only way out is to abandon the notion of rights altogether and to trust organic units such as the family and the church — and the patriarchal guidance that goes with them.

Similarly, the New Right is not an advocate of limited government along 1890s liberal lines. Government is a necessity, particularly in regard to the provision of economic security. The New Right does not attack social security or economic assistance. And it is decidedly antagonistic to big business and its use of government:

The truth is that big business has become too cozy with big government. In fact, big government protects big business. It's a sweetheart arrangement. Big business is comfortable with red tape, regulations, bureaucracy — it holds down competition. . . . Big business can no longer take the support of conservatives for granted. In the future, they must earn it and they have a lot of changing to do before they get it.[19]

In other words, government is an appropriate vehicle for helping people, including helping them to control other kinds of bigness in their worlds. What is essential is that government be responsive — democratically responsive — to the Middle American Radical majority that the New Right embodies. Who these otherwise neglected people are forms an important part of the New Right definition of current problems.

PROBLEMS AND POSSIBILITIES: THE NEW RIGHT AND ITS PROGRAM

Problems

The New Right sees itself as representative of a neglected middle class under extreme pressure from a combination of other sectors of the population — the rich, the militant minorities and poor, and the "new class" of government bureaucrats and allied professionals. This last group uses the power of government to make the powerless, hard-working middle pay the costs of the gains demanded by the poor and minorities and supinely granted by the controlling rich. It is as if the three groups worked together to make Middle Americans pay. Furthermore, none of them have any respect for *either* Middle Americans *or* their traditional values.

In New Right thinking, a new elite came into power in the 1930s. Steadily multiplying itself, it has dominated the executive branch and the judiciary ever since. This elite is cosmopolitan, amoral, self-indulgent, and materialistic. It acknowledges no limits and is contemptuous of families, work, self-sacrifice, community, and the moral and social order. In New Right eyes:

> Its ideology. . . is liberalism — a set of ideas and values that ostensibly upholds equality, liberty, and the brotherhood of man but which is amazingly congruent with and adaptable to the political, economic, and social interests (the structural interests) of the groups that espouse it. . . . Liberalism flourishes almost entirely because it reflects the material and psychological interests of a privileged, power-holding, and power-seeking sector of American society.[20]

It is not just the dismissal and denigration of families and communities that the New Right resents about the new class of federal bureaucrats and professionals managing the government. What also triggers bitter and active resistance is the *attitude* with which that new class goes about its work. Here is how the matter is perceived by another New Right leader:

> Nothing has contributed more to white populist disillusionment than the breathtaking hypocrisy and condescending arrogance shown by the establishment over the race issue. . . . While the wealthy remained immune (because they could afford to send their children to private schools), populist Americans have been expected to welcome the social and racial experimentation which bodes only disaster for themselves and their communities.[21]

Who are the Middle Americans thus neglected? Two major studies provide a social analysis that converges with the New Right's self-image and has been embraced by New Right thinkers. One is Donald Warren's *The Radical*

Center: Middle Americans and the Politics of Alienation, from which, as mentioned earlier, the term "Middle American Radicals" originated. The other is Kevin Phillips' *Post-Conservative America: People, Politics, and Ideology in a Time of Crisis*, which effectively combines public opinion survey data, electoral results in key counties, and shrewd insight.

Warren identifies the Middle American Radical from resentful attitudes expressed in answer to survey questions. He finds these attitudes clustered among people with high school or lower educations who hold nonmanagerial jobs and earn incomes that place them in the lower-middle category. He asserts that they feel threatened by the way that government responds to the combination of militant minorities/poor and the rich. They see their traditional values being altered or eliminated without their consent. All their lives, they have done what was supposedly expected — worked hard, tried to raise their children properly, had faith in the United States — and now they are not only unrewarded but positively denigrated.

Warren sees such people as victims of social change and the transformation of government-society relations. They are not so much racists, for example, as people who feel that they have been asked to pay the lion's share of the costs (financial and social) for the government-sponsored advancement of minorities. They continue to have pride in the United States, even though they profoundly distrust its current leaders. Warren estimates that 25 percent of Americans fit into the category of Middle American Radicals, whose resentments are potentially articulable by the New Right package of issues and values.

Kevin Phillips believes that Warren's analysis is plausible. And he sees two parallel ways of understanding the rise of the New Right. One is "center extremism," the move toward radical solutions (neither left nor right) that occurs when traditional politics breaks down. Another is "revolutionary conservatism," the European version of conservative attack on modernization in the name of religion, ethnicity, and nationalism. This radicalized middle, Phillips argues, amounts to "right-wing populism" or "populist conservatism." It is a version American observers never anticipated and therefore failed to recognize when it arose. After reviewing the European experience, Phillips raises the possibility, quite sincerely, that the United States could be headed for an authoritarian solution not unlike pre–World War II fascism.[22]

The point of these analyses is not to suggest, however indirectly, that the New Right should be viewed as the product of sociological or psychological aberrations or personal maladjustments. The point is that the New Right's collective self-image as people with grievances about the United States is confirmed by the research of respected observers of different perspectives. New Right supporters seem to think and feel precisely the way that New Right leadership believes they do. According to the New Right, the most important problem to be solved is that the United States today is a country in which a significant segment of the population feels profoundly bypassed and denigrated.

There are other problems of major stature, of course, such as the threat posed by Soviet expansion. As Viguerie says, "Some things never change—like man's spiritual nature, the danger of a too powerful central government, Communism's unchanging goal of wanting to bury us."[23] But many of these problems can be traced back to the performance of the liberal "new class" over the past decades. The answer will be the same: replace that new class before they destroy the United States as we have known it.

Possibilities

What the New Right sees ahead are indeed apocalyptic alternatives. President Reagan or his Republican successor must consolidate support from New Right organizations and constituencies by implementing the appropriate policies to fulfill their aspirations. The Republican Party can thus effectively become a New Right vehicle. Otherwise, the New Right will form a conservative political party to the right of the Republicans and force a realignment of American political parties. The only other possibility is that the United States continue its decline until defeat in war or some form of internal self-destruction ensues.

There can be little doubt that the New Right is playing for the highest possible stakes in American politics. There is clear recognition among the leadership that much more than politics-as-usual is involved. One strategist, for example, declares that the New Right must go beyond narrow versions of politics and gain possession of the fundamental levers of social control and real social power. He argues:

> The New Right-MAR coalition must seek to dismantle or radically reform the managerial apparatus of social control, and this objective means a far more radical approach to political conflict and to contemporary institutions. The strategic objective of the New Right must be the localization, privatization, and decentralization of the managerial apparatus of power.[24]

The first goal clearly is to mobilize MARs and blue-collar workers behind the New Right position on the full spectrum of social issues. And if, as observers such as Phillips have suggested, this social issues constituency could be merged with those devoted to the cause of economic conservatism, the result would be a very powerful and possibly unstoppable force in American politics. New Right leadership is undoubtedly also aware that several of its key areas of concern are highly congruent with the interests of business (e.g., right to work laws, opposition to minimum wages and government regulation, tax reduction and limitation). If the New Right is successful in these areas, it should be able to expect business contributions to its campaigns.

One of the most intriguing possibilities surrounding the New Right is that it may become, as Phillips has suggested, the political arm of a massive new religious movement. Three "Great Awakenings" have characterized American social (and political) life: the First from 1730 to 1760; the Second from 1800 to 1830; and the Third, from 1890 to 1920. In each era, an intense religious revivalism gripped the country and undermined the rule of established social groups and practices. Phillips argues that populism has paralleled such revival periods and could ride to sustained power on the crest of a Fourth Great Awakening.[25]

The Reverend Jerry Falwell, president of Moral Majority, Inc., believes just such a moral and political rejuvenation is imminent. He points out that the basic conditions are very favorable: there are 110,000 fundamentalist-evangelical churches in the United States today, 1,600 Christian radio stations, 79 Christian television stations, and untold millions of people filled with moral revulsion at the materialism and decadence of the 1960s and 1970s. Perhaps 75 million people are members of, or sympathetic to, fundamentalist Protestant religious groups. According to Falwell, "America is on the threshold of a spiritual awakening."[26] If this should come about in anything like the manner of the previous versions, no present estimates of potential New Right impact would even begin to suggest the real possibilities.

IMPLICATIONS AND PROSPECTS: OLD RIGHT AND NEW RIGHT

The New Right is simultaneously liberal, radical, and conservative—a fitting bundle of apparent contradictions with which to conclude a book that argues, as one of its themes, that the old labels have lost their meaning. Perhaps most important, the New Right has some substantial differences with the Old Right in its current incarnation as mainstream conservatism. The implication is, as some New Right thinkers see very clearly, that the contest between the New Right and mainstream conservatism may have to be played out before a clear majoritarian direction for future conservatism is achieved.

The New Right's tensions with mainstream conservatism present some interesting complications. For example, the New Right not only includes certain principles that put it at odds with mainstream conservatism. It also contains some genuine threads, particularly those emanating from Southern organic conservatives, that are at odds with its dominant populist, antielite ethos.

As we have seen, mainstream conservatism is an incomplete synthesis of traditional conservatism and 1890s liberalism. However, imprecise it may be about its principles, it certainly has none of the New Right's antipathy to big business as such. It is not populist or majoritarian in the manner of the New Right. And it does not welcome the government assistance of the New Deal with the sense of need and approval that the New Right does. Where mainstream conservatism is anticommunist, the New Right is nationalistic—which makes for a greater number of enemies abroad and a more aggressive stance against immigration at home.

Above all, the New Right is grounded in the lower-middle and lower classes, mainstream conservatism in the business community and the upper-middle class. Thus, though there is some overlap here, the social center of gravity of the two political tendencies is distinctly different. And this difference is profoundly consequential in American politics. It means that, in the long run, it will be very difficult for mainstream conservatism and the New Right to continue in a workable alliance or coalition.

This raises the question of the New Right's own internal cohesion. If it contains significant elements of both conservatism and populism, what are the prospects that they will end up in a conflict that would rend or paralyze the New Right? Our impression is that the New Right has little to fear in this regard. The Southern conservative tradition has always included a populist streak. Its yearning for solid grounding in home, family, and church is perfectly consistent with basic New Right priorities. Moreover, the New Right is united in its self-concept and as a social movement. Few belief systems in the United States could approach its level of mobilization around shared principles.

Consider some appraisals from New Right leaders, first a Middle American Radical and then a Southern conservative:

> The New Right . . . is the political expression of a relatively new social movement that regards itself as the depository of traditional American values and as the exploited victim of the alliance between an entrenched elite and a ravenous proletariat. Viewed in this sociopolitical perspective, the New Right is not a conservative force but a radical or revolutionary one. It seeks the displacement of the entrenched elite, the discarding of its ideology of liberalism and cosmopolitanism, and its own victory as a new governing class in America.[27]

> Our social vision, fortunately, is not limited to a choice between economic theories of political life — capitalism and socialism — both reflexes of the same degraded, aluminum coin, both sound as the paper dollar. Traditional conservatism . . . is still waiting to be tried. The hardest task for conservatives will be to convince our capitalist allies that the common rights of humanity, as embodied in the family, and our civil rights . . . take precedence over our desire for profits and productivity. Southerners have been arguing for years . . . that the land, the home, and the church — not the marketplace — are the only proper foundations for a healthy society.[28]

The Southern New Right conservative concludes his argument with a ringing endorsement of the necessity for working people such as the MARs to become the basic core of the new conservative movement. In short, we see nothing incompatible between the MAR and Southern conservative elements. There is every reason to believe that they form a viable working combination.

The New Right is, however, a volatile population group. Some adherents are habitual nonvoters; others are on the verge of leaving the electorate in frustration. Nearly all feel quite strongly about the issues that brought them into the New Right and possibly about other issues that make up the New Right package. The question is, in what direction will such people head? What means will seem appropriate to them?

Just as Donald Warren warned of the dangers inherent in the level of dissatisfaction felt by the Americans who qualify as MARs, so do New Right leaders see their constituency as an explosive one. Robert J. Hoy, for example, talks of the importance of bringing New Right followers into electoral politics as a last chance to preserve stability in the political system. He says, "Populists are just as alienated and frustrated today as their forebears were in the years just preceding the American Revolution. Many are just as radical and ready for violence."[29]

This concern for potential violence and authoritarian solutions is widespread among observers who know the New Right best. Perhaps the most balanced assessment comes from Kevin Phillips, who concludes his analysis of the state of the New Right constituency with these words:

> The die is hardly cast. The larger question is whether the United States can regain yesteryear's easygoing middle-class confidence and optimism, both enemies of radicalism and the politics of cultural despair. So if our national leadership elites over time can restore our economy and our belief in the future, Middle American radicalization will slacken and ease. But if not, a major convergence of various radicalisms is possible. Whereupon the public mood could support a politics of national mythology, Social Darwinism, and charismatic leadership.[30]

What Phillips fears, of course, is something equivalent to a neofascist solution, in which a Hitler-like figure rises to power amidst sweeping promises to restore American greatness. He may be right in asserting that general economic improvement and restoration of confidence would lead to the easing of New Right tensions and demands. Under such circumstances, mainstream conservatives in the Republican Party could probably maintain some sort of accommodation with the New Right.

The more acute questions concern the future prospects of mainstream conservatism and the New Right under conditions of continued economic uncertainty, decline, and/or transformation. If the United States does not enjoy a period of sustained economic prosperity, what happens to the relationship of these two versions of conservatism? For that matter, what happens to the whole American political spectrum?

If economic conditions, such as serious inflation and/or unemployment, continue to impose pressures on the New Right constituency, and if there are no dramatic compensating achievements in the social issues, we do not believe the conservative side of the spectrum can hold together. The gulf, ideological and social, between the mainstream conservatives and the New Right is too great to be bridged by the fragile links that are available under such circumstances.

We view the stinging attack on the New Right by a long-term conservative activist in 1980 as an indication of what would ensue. Alan Crawford, a veteran of six years' work for the New Right (including terms with Young Americans for Freedom, *Conservative Digest*, and the Viguerie complex of organizations), wrote *Thunder on the Right: The "New Right" and the Politics of Resentment* to expose the dangers conservatives should see in the New Right. Despairing of New Right ideology, tactics, people, and manners, he ends up denouncing the movement as "government by rabble-rousing."[31]

We think, however, that a unified conservative movement is likely under adverse economic conditions if circumstances arise that call for a kind of "Fortress America." That is, should a president be able to define our world position as one in which the United States was pitted against many other nations, in a kind of national struggle for survival, all brands of conservatives would rally to his support. Patriotism and nationalism and anticommunism would provide all the glue necessary to hold the variety of conservatives firmly in line.

In the absence of Fortress America, the most likely prospect is such pressure from the New Right that mainstream conservatives will be split apart. The more militant advocates, particularly among 1890s liberals, might find a home among the New Right. The Republican Party would either be captured by the New Right or fragmented by its departure. In either case, the New Right would have forced some (unpredictable) kind of realignment on the American political spectrum. The big losers would be the mainstream conservatives. Many of them would be forced to choose between the special brand of conservatism and militancy represented by the New Right and some kind of accommodation with former liberals — or face another period of irrelevancy.

These scenarios imply an ongoing polarization of people and ideas in the United States, one in which realignment occurs on both sides of a reconstituting political spectrum. This may well be the shape of things to come, but given present uncertainties, any attempt to see into the future becomes much too speculative. For example, it is even possible that some part of the New Right could end up in an alliance grounded in social class interests with what used to be thought of as "left" beliefs. What we are suggesting is that the New Right may be the catalyst, the final disintegrating force. Once released, it may have a fragmenting impact not just on its nearest ideological relatives but on the whole range of American political belief systems.

The New Right is clearly the single most powerful movement in American politics today. There is no comparable social grouping with the potential to force fundamental change on the rest of us. And the result of a New Right-triggered change process could be any number of new forms of social order — or chaos and anarchy. When such a process begins, there is no way to see its final form.

ADDITIONAL READINGS

Crawford, Alan. *Thunder on the Right: The "New Right" and the Politics of Resentment.* New York: Pantheon, 1980.

Hunter, William A. "The 'New Right': A Growing Force in State Politics." Washington, D. C.: Conference on Alternative State and Local Policies, 1980.

Phillips, Kevin P. *Post-Conservative America: People, Politics, and Ideology in a Time of Crisis.* New York: Random House, 1982.

Rusher, William A. *The Making of the New Majority Party*. New York: Sheed and
    Ward, 1975.
Viguerie, Richard A. *The New Right: We're Ready to Lead*. Falls Church, Va.:
    Viguerie Company, 1980.
Warren, Donald I. *The Radical Center: Middle Americans and the Politics of
    Alienation*. South Bend, Ind.: Notre Dame University Press, 1976.
Whitaker, Robert W. *The New Right Papers*. New York: St. Martin's Press, 1982.

Epilogue

We began by hypothesizing that the values and beliefs making up the American political spectrum are in a process of change. Not surprisingly, our analysis seems to have confirmed that fact. We found significant change occurring in each of the seven belief systems with still more likely to flow from their interaction amidst changing social and economic conditions. Indeed, the entire American political spectrum is racked with pressures for change, both internal and external. Like our economic and social systems, our values and beliefs are undergoing a sustained and sometimes painful process of reconstitution.

But this emphatically does not mean that we are about to leap into some wholly new world — either of social and economic circumstances or of political ideas and practices. That is simply not the way societies evolve, although Americans often think and act as if it were. An enduring characteristic of American thinking is the assumption that fundamental values and beliefs can change instantaneously in one rolling wave sweeping across the country, like so many light bulbs popping on simultaneously in individual minds. If people just become *enlightened, convinced, come to see the world clearly and realistically*, Americans tend to think, then the necessary change will ensue. Any number of books advocating dramatic forms of change have been written at various times in our history, become widely celebrated, and then had no consequences whatsoever.

This is such a regular phenomenon in American experience that it deserves recognition, perhaps as part of the long-term process of change. In the Populist-Progressive Era, for example, there were two dramatic works with wide popularity and very modest, if any, real effect. One was Edward Bellamy's *Looking Backward*. This utopian novel purports to look back at the United States of the late 1880s from the vantage point of the year 2000. All the country's problems are cured by instantaneous adoption of a benevolent authoritarianism called "nationalism."[1] The other was Henry George's *Progress and Poverty*, an analysis of social problems that found them all soluble through institution of a simple remedy, the "single tax" on land.[2]

But one book really described what was happening, forecasting accurately the future forms that governing ideas and practices would take. It was not published until 1906, and then received only modest recognition. This was Herbert Croly's *The Promise of American Life*. It outlined the precise synthesis of Hamilton and Jefferson that was instituted in the Progressive Era and eventually implemented fully in the New Deal.[3] In our own recent times, we have had several very popular utopian assurances (or dystopian warnings), but perhaps not yet the accurate synthesizing forecast.

The lesson here is that, to be effective, ideas must have grounding in concrete social forces and personal social or economic interests. It is not easy to break the grip of established assumptions, expectations, and ideology. Books cannot do the job. Only sustained social and economic conditions, personally experienced as basically at odds with orthodox beliefs, can accomplish such changes. At times, however, books or speakers may serve to crystallize people's recognition that in fact their beliefs and goals have changed, that it is both possible and necessary to act in new ways.

Thus, ideas must have social reality in the willingness of many people to act on them, and this, in turn, is the result of specific circumstances in those people's lives. Those who wish to affect social outcomes or events must envision lengthy processes of conflict and change. Entrenched opponents give ground slowly before the weight of change-seeking forces. Things did not come to be as they are through happenstance. And some people find it to their advantage and satisfaction that things remain as they are. They are not likely to welcome any change that threatens their positions. Nobody willingly gives up hard-earned power and advantage, especially when the loss appears important and permanent.

Thus, whatever "instantaneous" transformations happen only appear instantaneous: their way has been paved by underlying cultural, social, and political changes over a period of years.

It is also important to make clear that exclusively cultural changes cannot suffice to solve the kinds of problems now facing the United States. Significant social change is first and foremost a political problem. Specifically *political* actions will be required to reach the accommodations that can solve today's deeply grounded and multidimensional problems. These problems may be of a quite different order from those with which we are familiar, but they nevertheless are quite political in nature. Most fundamental political changes, to be sure, require profound cultural changes both before and after they occur. But their essence is political. They involve changing the ways of organizing and using power in the society, the actions of many people in search of shared goals, a high probability of conflict (and the need for ways of containing it short of violence), and the emergence of a new sense of the community and its priorities. These are the very considerations that are missing from most of the future-oriented writing now available in the United States.

These are the reasons why we have not made much use of certain kinds of popular materials in this book. Much of what passes for new ideas, and many prescriptions for change, are completely apolitical. Their proponents pay no attention to the present structure of power and priorities in the United States. They ignore the problem of how such deeply rooted social relationships are to be modified so as to permit the policy changes they advocate. It is as if a wand were to be waved and everything would be different thereafter. In illustrating this and other points made in this Epilogue, we shall draw only from the *best* of the current American materials. Far more egregious examples could be found, but we are interested in the way in which even the best of our future-oriented writers fall subject to the American penchant for transcending the political realities.

One way that authors get where they want to be in the way of social change is to simply assume that we are already there. For example, the widely acclaimed *Entropy: A New World View* says simply:

> Now that we are witnessing the transition from an energy environment built upon nonrenewable resources to one built on solar flow and renewable energy sources, great personal and institutional changes will sweep over our society. The questions that confront us are: How long will the transition take? How will it be accomplished? What will be our individual roles?[4]

It is as if there must be hope to go with the sobering analysis of the book — the chapter title is "From Despair to Hope" — and nothing can be allowed to get in the way.

Another route is to first posit the necessity of a complete change in how people understand their world and then to assume it has been accomplished.

> First, the most important prerequisite for constructive change is a new world view based on, or at least compatible with, the realities of the human ecological predicament. The ecological crisis is in large part a perceptual crisis: ordinary human beings simply do not see that they are part of a delicate web of life that their own actions are destroying, yet any viable solution will require them to see this. Once such a "paradigm" change has occurred — once people have chosen to accept ecological limitations deliberately as a consequence of their new understanding — then practical and humane solutions will be found in abundance.[5]

At the present time, there is broad agreement among thinkers and writers on the *necessity* of new social and political structures, institutions, values, and priorities. Almost everybody agrees that existing governing arrangements and social priorities are outmoded. And there is near unanimity of belief that the established categories of thought (liberal, conservative, etc.) are no longer viable. But after this point two unfortunate things happen. First, the agreement dissipates, and advocates head off in at least three distinct directions. That might be expected and perhaps even encouraged. Much worse is the second fact. In practically every case, and despite the most penetrating and insightful analyses of the problems, advocates' prescriptions evaporate into wishful, apolitical utopias.

LIBERTARIAN DIRECTIONS

The first direction is toward a libertarian or radical individualist kind of solution. The suggestion here seems to be that if only individuals will change their thoughts or act in a certain way the problem will be solved. No collective action, no struggle against those who prefer other ways, no use of government will be required — only the mental transformation of millions of isolated individuals. This approach is attractive along the entire length of the American political spectrum. It does not seem to matter what set of beliefs people hold about the world and how it should be. As Americans, they remain susceptible to the appeal of an individualized solution. Sometimes this takes the form of seeing the world differently. At others, one can somehow signal one's change of mind without leaving one's living room or suffering any inconvenience. Or it may be a more basic sort of spiritual awakening felt by individuals, and not just those of the religious New Right.

One of the most perceptive and persuasive libertarians is Murray Bookchin. His recent *The Ecology of Freedom: The Emergence and Dissolution of Hierarchy* has been rightfully recognized as a provocative synthesis of ecological and anarchist thought. He is content, however, perhaps necessarily so, with advocating merely a change in the way one sees the world: "The 'Ecology of Freedom' is meant to express the reconciliation of nature and human society in a new ecological sensibility and a new ecological society — a reharmonization of nature and humanity through a reharmonization of human with human."[6]

Sometimes instantaneous transformation is advocated just because the problems are so compelling. Thought is merely a delaying action:

> Because everything we do and everthing we are is in jeopardy, and because the peril is immediate and unremitting, every person is the right person to act and every moment is the right moment to begin, starting with the present moment. . . . Whatever the eventual shape of a world that has been reinvented for the sake of survival, the first, urgent, immediate step, which requires no deep thought or long reflection, is for each person to make known, visibly and unmistakably, his desire that the species survive. . . . And the place for rebellion to start is in our daily lives. We can each perform a turnabout right where we are.[7]

Just about the closest this individualist approach gets to a collective sense of purpose is indicated by Jeremy Rifkin's *Entropy: A New World View.* In it, individual transformation is linked loosely with that of other individuals:

> Unless we, individually and in unity with others, discard our Newtonian world view, there is no hope that a movement will develop that can revolutionize our society. The first step in this historic process is to fully comprehend what it is, as people, that we believe. We must voluntarily reformulate our lives so that they reflect the new paradigm. But that is not enough. We must also join together, in a popular, grassroots social force, to begin the dismantling of the existing high-energy infrastructure. At the same time, we must build our new society based on a new set of values which reflect our awareness of the entropy process.[8]

Communitarian and Authoritarian Directions

These efforts involve some important distinctions that will connect intimately with the belief systems that we have analyzed. The authoritarian answers are readily visible in the fears of many participants and observers, as well as in the publications of the "doomsday" futurists, for example, the Club of Rome's *Limits to Growth*.[9] They have been aptly summarized by Bertram Gross in *Friendly Fascism: The New Face of Power in America*.[10] In effect, the authoritarian approach says that there is no way out of our current problems other than through the unfettered actions of an all-powerful government. Neoliberals and some populists are sometimes tempted by these sorts of solutions.

More important, although less familiar to Americans, are solutions that depend on a concept of community. These assume some shared sense of priority and purpose amongst a continuing group of people. Given such agreement, some talented and/or democratically selected group of individuals could reasonably exercise a trusteeship or stewardship over all others. This notion is most congenial to organic conservatives and democratic socialists. William Ophuls, for example, undertakes an ecological critique of American politics in which he concludes that adaptation of the program he sets forth requires dropping old paradigms and embracing values that "bear a particularly uncanny resemblance to the ideas of the British conservative thinker Edmund Burke."[11]

Finally, there is the solution that says essentially "a plague on both your houses." It seeks to find the possible answer that includes some of all the others but rises above their internecine conflict. This kind of solution is the basis for our earlier suggestion that liberalism might not be dead at all. It is only awaiting an opportunity to locate itself in a middle ground between warring polar alternatives.

An example is the collective product of the Stanford Research Institutes entitled *Seven Tomorrows: Toward A Voluntary History*. This work essentially condemns "both" sides and offers a transcending synthesis a "Voluntary History" which is the product of knowing humans with a respect for diversity. All analyses and alternatives are cast in terms of avoiding every extreme — "Right or Left, optimistic or pessimistic, utopian or dystopian." The principles that are to guide action are never clearly stated, except in contrast to what others seek. "With respect to energy and the environment, for example, we can improve upon the adversarial deadlock that now poses business against the environmentalists." The result, according to the authors, is "seeing through the fallacy of total victory in a diverse and pluralistic world."[12]

This sounds very much like liberalism to us. It may be that this version would have a qualitatively different character than anything that previously went under that label. But it would be ironic indeed if the "collapse" of liberalism in the 1980s were only the prelude to the refurbishment of liberalism as the wave of the future in the 1990s.

It does not yet appear that any "new" belief system has the coherence and appeal — or the political content — to be identifiable as a compelling direction for the future. More likely, we shall face a period of profound uncertainty in which unforseeable events will help to shape outcomes. And the New Right will serve as the trigger for the next round of reconstitution of values, beliefs, and perhaps the entire spectrum.

Notes

Introduction
[1] Robert A. Dahl, *Dilemmas of Pluralist Democracy* (New Haven: Yale University Press, 1982), p. 3.

[2] Gary Hart, *A New Democracy: A Democratic Vision for the 1980s and Beyond* (New York: Quill, 1983), p. 20.

Chapter 2
[1] Herbert Croly, *The Promise of American Life* (New York: Dutton, 1963), Chapter 7.

Chapter 3
[1] Louis Hartz, *The Liberal Tradition in America* (New York: Harcourt, Brace, 1955).

Chapter 4
[1] Paul Tsongas, *The Road From Here: Liberalism and Realities in the 1980s* (New York: Knopf, 1981), p. xiii.

[2] Alexander Hamilton, *Report on Manufactures*, 1791.

[3] Amitai Etzioni, *An Immodest Agenda: Rebuilding America Before the 21st Century* (New York: McGraw-Hill, 1983), p. ix.

[4] Paul Tsongas, "Address Before National Convention of Americans for Democratic Action, June 14, 1980," in Tsongas, *Road From Here*, pp. 253–256.

[5] Lester Thurow, *The Zero-Sum Society* (New York: Basic Books, 1980); Robert Reich and Ira Magaziner, *Minding America's Business: The Decline and Rise of the American Economy* (New York: Harcourt Brace Jovanovich, 1982); Robert Reich, *The Next American Frontier* (New York: Times Books, 1983); and Felix Rohatyn, *The New York Review of Books*, issues of January 22, 1981; February 5, 1981; April 16, 1981; April 29, 1982; November 4, 1982; and August 18, 1983.

[6] Charles Peters, "A Neoliberal's Manifesto," *The Washington Monthly*, May 1983, pp. 9–18; Gary Hart, *A New Democracy: A Democratic Vision for the 1980s and Beyond* (New York: Quill, 1983); Tsongas, *Road From Here*.

[7] Peters, "Neoliberal's Manifesto," pp. 10, 12, 13.

[8] *Ibid.*, p. 18.

[9] *Ibid.*, p. 10.

[10] Tsongas, *Road From Here*, p. 129

[11] Hart, *New Democracy*, pp. 10–11.

[12] Tsongas, *Road From Here*, p. 135.

[13] Peters, "Neoliberal's Manifesto," p. 12.

[14] Tsongas, *Road From Here*, p. 90.

[15] Hart, *New Democracy*, p. 13.

[16] Tsongas, *Road From Here*, pp. xiv, xv.

[17] Reich and Magaziner, *Minding America's Business*, p. 255.

[18] Peters, "Neoliberal's Manifesto," pp. 10–11.

[19] Tsongas, *Road From Here*, pp. 148–149.

[20] Peters, "Neoliberal's Manifesto," pp. 11, 13.

[21] Thurow, *Zero-Sum Society*, p. 194.

[22] Felix Rohatyn, "The Older America: Can It Survive?" *The New York Review of Books*, January 22, 1981, p. 19.

[23] Thurow, *Zero-Sum Society*, p. 206.

[24] Robert Reich, quoted in *The New York Times Magazine*, August 28, 1983, p. 63.

[25] Peters, "Neoliberal's Manifesto," p. 17.

Chapter 5

[1] This issue is fully explored in Hugh Hawkins, ed., *Booker T. Washington and His Critics* (Lexington, Mass.: D.C. Heath, 1974).

[2] The best source is Elizabeth Cady Stanton, Susan B. Anthony, and Matilda Joslin Gage, *History of Woman Suffrage*, 4 vols. (New York: Fowler & Wells, 1882).

[3] Betty Friedan, *The Feminine Mystique* (New York: Dell, 1970).

[4] See Sara Evans, *Personal Politics: The Roots of Women's Liberation in the Civil Rights Movement and the New Left* (New York: Knopf, 1979).

[5] William Graham Sumner, "The Conquest of the United States by Spain," *Yale Law Journal*, 8 (January 1899), pp. 168–193.

[6] See William Preston, *Aliens and Dissenters* (New York: Harper & Row, 1957) and James Weinstein, *The Decline of Socialism in America, 1912–1925* (New York: Vintage, 1963).

[7] This story is well told in Milton Viorst, *Fire in the Streets* (New York: Simon and Schuster, 1979).

[8] For a good summary of the environmental movement and its implications, see William Ophuls, *Ecology and the Politics of Scarcity* (San Francisco: Freeman, 1977). The antinuclear case is well made in Amory Lovins, *Soft Energy Paths* (New York: Harper & Row, 1979).

[9] Robert L. Allen, *Black Awakening in Capitalist America* (New York: Doubleday, 1969); Manning Marable, *How Capitalism Underdeveloped Black America* (Boston: South End Press, 1983); James Boggs and Grace Lee Boggs, *Revolution and Evolution in the Twentieth Century* (New York: Monthly Review Press, 1974); Zillah Eisenstein, ed., *Capitalist Patriarchy and the Case for Socialist Feminism* (New York: Monthly Review Press, 1979); Batya Weinbaum, *The Curious Courtship of Women's Liberation and Socialism* (Boston: South End Press, 1979).

[10] Ophuls, *Ecology*, p. 3.

[11] Jonathan Schell, *The Fate of the Earth* (New York: Knopf, 1982) pp. 226, 227.

Chapter 6

[1] Jack Newfield and Jeff Greenfield, *A Populist Manifesto: The Making of a New Majority* (New York: Warner Paperback Library, 1972), p. 9.

² Jeremy Rifkin, *Own Your Own Job: Economic Democracy for Working Americans* (New York: Bantam, 1977).

³ The "Founding Statement of the Campaign for Economic Democracy" appears as an appendix in Tom Hayden, *The American Future: New Visions Beyond Old Frontiers* (Boston: South End Press, 1980).

⁴ Martin Carnoy and Derek Shearer, *Economic Democracy: The Challenge of the 1980s* (White Plains, N.Y.: M. E. Sharpe, 1980).

⁵ See *An Economic Strategy for the 1980s* (Washington, D.C.: Full Employment Action Council and National Policy Exchange, 1982). The Full Employment Action Council is an umbrella organization of more than 80 trade union, civil rights, religious, and other organizations.

⁶ Martin Carnoy, Derek Shearer, and Russell Rumberger, *A New Social Contract: The Economy and Government After Reagan* (New York: Harper & Row, 1983), pp. 1–2.

⁷ See Sec. 2 (1) and Title I, Sec. 101.

⁸ Carnoy, Shearer, and Rumberger, *New Social Contract*, pp. 1–2.

⁹ Full Employment Action Council, *Economic Strategy for the 1980s*, p. 51.

¹⁰ Carnoy, Shearer, and Rumberger, *New Social Contract*, p. 2.

¹¹ *Ibid.*, p. 2.

¹² *Ibid.*

¹³ Ibid., p. 230.

¹⁴ Full Employment Action Council, *Economic Strategy for the 1980s*, p. 36.

¹⁵ Harry Boyte, *The Backyard Revolution: Understanding the New Citizen Movement* (Philadelphia: Temple University Press, 1980), p. xiv.

¹⁶ Robert Dahl, *Dilemmas of Pluralist Democracy: Autonomy vs. Control* (New Haven: Yale University Press, 1982), pp. 204–205.

¹⁷ Robert Reich, "Why Democracy Makes Economic Sense," *The New Republic*, December 19, 1983, pp. 30–32.

¹⁸ Richard Grossman and Gail Daneker, *Energy, Jobs, and the Economy* (Boston: Alyson Publications, 1979).

Chapter 7

¹ Michael Albert and Robin Hahnel, *Socialism Today and Tomorrow* (Boston: South End Press, 1983), p. 373.

² Herbert Gintis, "A Socialist Democracy for the United States," in Stephen Rosskamm Shalom, ed., *Socialist Visions* (Boston: South End Press, 1983), pp. 12–13.

³ Two useful surveys of the history of the American left are Milton Cantor, *The Divided Left: American Radicalism, 1900–1975* (New York: Hill and Wang, 1978) and James Weinstein, *Ambiguous Legacy: The Left in American Politics* (New York: Franklin Watts, 1976). Socialist history is best detailed in James Weinstein, *The Decline of Socialism in America, 1912–1925* (New York: Vintage, 1963).

⁴ The best single secondary source on the nature of Marxism is Shlomo Avineri, *The Social and Political Thought of Karl Marx* (New York: Cambridge University Press, 1969).

⁵ The early followers of Marx are characterized in David Herreshoff, *The Origins of American Marxism: From the Transcendentalists to DeLeon* (New York: Pathfinder Press, 1973).

⁶ The place to begin any effort to understand Marx is with Erich Fromm, *Marx's Concept of Man* (New York: Frederick Ungar, 1961), which contains the *Economic and Philosophical Manuscripts*.

[7] Albert and Hahnel, *Socialism Today and Tomorrow*, p. 376.

[8] Joshua Cohen and Joel Rogers, *On Democracy* (New York: Penguin Books, 1984), p. 169.

[9] Many good examples of applied scholarship may be found in the journal *democracy*.

[10] Gintis, "Socialist Democracy," pp. 13–14.

[11] Barry Bluestone and Bennett Harrison, *The Deindustrialization of America: Plant Closings, Community Abandonment, and the Dismantling of Basic Industry* (New York: Basic Books, 1982).

[12] Gintis, "Socialist Democracy," p. 12.

[13] Cohen and Rogers, *On Democracy*, p. 167.

[14] Albert and Hahnel, *Socialism Today and Tomorrow*, pp. 362–363.

[15] Cohen and Rogers, *On Democracy*, p. 148.

[16] Bertram Gross, *Friendly Fascism: The New Face of Power in America* (New York: M. Evans, 1980).

[17] Samuel Bowles, David M. Gordon, and Thomas E. Weisskopf, *Beyond the Waste Land: A Democratic Alternative to Economic Decline* (New York: Anchor Press, 1983), pp. 258–259.

[18] *Ibid.*, p. 13.

[19] *Ibid.*, p. 177.

[20] Bluestone and Harrison, *Deindustrialization of America*, pp. 244–245.

[21] *Ibid.*, p. 232.

[22] Alan Wolfe, *America's Impasse: The Rise and Fall of the Politics of Growth* (Boston: South End Press, 1981), p. 239.

[23] Gintis, "Socialist Democracy," p. 20.

[24] Frances Piven and Richard Cloward, *The New Class War* (New York: Pantheon Books, 1982).

[25] Frances Piven and Richard Cloward, "Toward a Class-Based Realignment of American Politics: A Movement Strategy," *Social Policy*, Winter 1983, pp. 3–14.

[26] Wolfe, *America's Impasse*, p. 246.

[27] Michael Harrington, *Decade of Decision: The Crisis of the American System* (New York: Simon and Schuster, 1980), p. 301.

[28] Albert and Hahnel, *Socialism Today and Tomorrow*, p. 371.

[29] Cohen and Rogers, *On Democracy*, p. 175.

[30] Bowles, Gordon, and Weisskopf, *Beyond the Waste Land*, p. 387.

[31] Gintis, "Socialist Democracy," p. 34.

Chapter 8

[1] Clinton Rossiter, *Conservatism in America: The Thankless Persuasion* (New York: Knopf, 1962).

[2] The best history of the evolution of conservatism in the three decades after World War II is George H. Nash, *The Conservative Intellectual Tradition in America Since 1945* (New York: Basic Books, 1976).

[3] William F. Buckley, Jr., *God and Man at Yale: The Superstitions of "Academic Freedom"* (Chicago: Regnery, 1951) and *McCarthy and His Enemies* (Chicago: Regnery, 1954).

[4] Barry Goldwater, *The Conscience of a Conservative* (Shepherdsville, Ky.: Victor, 1960).

[5] Milton Friedman, *Capitalism and Freedom* (Chicago: University of Chicago Press, 1962).

⁶ William A. Rusher, "The New Right: Past and Prospects," in Robert W. Whitaker, ed., *The New Right Papers* (New York: St. Martin's Press, 1982). See also Kevin P. Phillips, *Post-Conservative America: People, Politics, and Ideology in a Time of Crisis* (New York: Random House, 1982).

⁷ Rusher, "New Right," is an excellent short history by a participant.

⁸ The term was first coined by Phillips, in *Post-Conservative America*, p. xx.

⁹ An exhaustive and critical source is Peter Steinfels, *The Neoconservatives: The Men Who Are Changing America's Politics* (New York: Simon and Schuster, 1979).

¹⁰ Irving Kristol, "What Is a Neoconservative?" *Newsweek*, January 19, 1976, p. 87.

¹¹ Midge Decter, quoted in *The Weekly* (Seattle, Wash.), November 16, 1983, p. 12.

¹² Irving Kristol, *Two Cheers for Capitalism* (New York: Basic Books, 1978), p. 178.

¹³ *Ibid.*, p. 179.

¹⁴ Nathan Glazer, *Affirmative Discrimination: Ethnic Inequality and Public Policy* (New York: Basic Books, 1976).

¹⁵ Midge Decter, quoted in *The Weekly* (Seattle, Wash.) November 16, 1983, p. 13.

¹⁶ Samuel P. Huntington, "The United States," in Michael J. Crozier, Samuel P. Huntington, and Joji Watanuki, *The Crisis of Democracy* (New York: New York University Press, 1975). The same essay appears in the bicentennial edition of *The Public Interest*, published as Glazer and Kristol, eds., *The American Commonwealth — 1976*.

¹⁷ Robert Nisbet, *The Twilight of Authority* (New York: Basic Books, 1972).

¹⁸ Michael Novak, *The Spirit of Democratic Capitalism* (New York: Simon and Schuster, 1982).

¹⁹ Kristol, *Two Cheers for Capitalism*, p. 171.

²⁰ Steinfels, *Neoconservatives*, p. 56.

²¹ Daniel Bell, *The Cultural Contradictions of Capitalism*, (New York: Basic Books, 1976), and Michael Novak, *The Spirit of Democratic Capitalism* (New York: Simon and Schuster, 1982).

²² Nathan Glazer, "The Limits of Social Policy," *Commentary*, September 1971, pp. 51–58.

²³ Novak, *Spirit of Democratic Capitalism*, p. 14.

²⁴ *Ibid.*, p. 15.

²⁵ *Ibid.*

²⁶ *Ibid.*, p. 31.

²⁷ *Ibid.*, pp. 359–360.

²⁸ Steintels, *Neoconservatives*, p. 76.

²⁹ *Ibid.*, p. 79.

³⁰ *Ibid.*, p. 294.

Chapter 9

¹ Milton Friedman, *Capitalism and Freedom* (Chicago: University of Chicago Press, 1962), p. 195.

² George F. Will, *Statecraft as Soulcraft: What Government Does* (New York: Simon and Schuster, 1983), p. 156.

[3] *Ibid.*, p. 131.

[4] *Ibid.*, p. 130.

[5] Paul Laxalt, "Commentary," in Paul Laxalt and Richard S. Williamson, eds. *A Changing America: Conservatives View the '80s from the United States Senate* (South Bend, Ind.: Regnery/Gateway, 1980), p. xi.

[6] Bruce R. Bartlett, *Reaganomics: Supply-Side Economics in Action*, (New York: Quill, 1982), p. 207.

[7] George Gilder, *Wealth and Poverty* (New York: Basic Books, 1981), p. 245.

[8] Will, *Statecraft as Soulcraft, p. 12.*

[9] *Ibid.*, pp. 158–159.

[10] Milton Friedman and Rose Friedman, *Free to Choose* (New York: Harcourt Brace Jovanovich, 1980), pp. 119–120.

[11] *Ibid.*

[12] *Ibid.*, p. 123.

[13] Will, *Statecraft as Soulcraft*, p. 45.

[14] Gilder, *Wealth and Poverty*, p. 259.

[15] Samuel P. Huntington, *American Politics: The Promise of Disharmony* (Cambridge, Mass.: Belknap Press, 1981), p. 258.

[16] Friedman and Friedman, *Free to Choose*, p. xx.

[17] Huntington, *American Politics*, pp. 40, 220.

[18] *Ibid.*, p. 42.

[19] Andrew Hacker, *The End of the American Era*, (New York: Atheneum, 1971), pp. 5–6.

[20] *Ibid.*, pp. 230, 231.

[21] See, for examples, Bartlett, *Reaganomics*, pp. 208–209.

[22] Will, *Statecraft as Soulcraft*, p. 96.

[23] Huntington, *American Politics*, p. 261.

[24] Will, *Statecraft as Soulcraft*, p. 22.

[25] *Ibid.*, p. 165.

Chapter 10

[1] Donald I. Warren, *The Radical Center: Middle Americans and the Politics of Alienation* (South Bend, Ind.: University of Notre Dame Press, 1976).

[2] Kevin P. Phillips, *Post-Conservative America: People, Politics, and Ideology in a Time of Crisis* (New York: Random House, 1982), p. 195.

[3] Paul Weyrich, quoted in Richard A. Viguerie, *The New Right: We're Ready to Lead* (Falls Church, Va.: Viguerie Company, 1980), pp. 59–60.

[4] Viguerie, *New Right* is the best historical source and will be used as the basis of interpretation throughout this chapter unless otherwise noted.

[5] Viguerie, *New Right*, pp. 54–55.

[6] Phillips, *Post-Conservative America*, p. 47.

[7] William A. Rusher, *The Making of the New Majority Party* (New York: Sheed and Ward, 1980.)

[8] Viguerie, *New Right*, pp. 66–71 (author's order).

[9] Phillips, *Post-Conservative America*, p. 49.

[10] Viguerie, *New Right*, p. 178.

[11] *Ibid.*, p. 196.

[12] Thomas Fleming, "Old Rights and the New Right," in Robert W. Whitaker, ed., *The New Right Papers* (New York: St. Martin's, 1982), p. 191.

[13] Viguerie, *New Right*, pp. 135, 133.

[14] *Ibid.*, p. 154.

[15] Paul M. Weyrich, "Blue Collar or Blue Blood? The New Right Compared With the Old Right," in Whitaker, ed., *New Right Papers*, p. 60.

[16] *Conservative Digest*, editorial, November 1978.

[17] Clyde N. Wilson, "Citizens or Subjects?" in Whitaker, ed., *The New Right Papers*, pp. 123–124.

[18] Fleming, "Old Rights and New Right," p. 195.

[19] Viguerie, *New Right*, p. 146.

[20] Samuel T. Francis, "Message from MARs: The Social Politics of the New Right," in Whitaker, ed., *New Right Papers*, pp. 68–69.

[21] Robert J. Hoy, "Lid on a Boiling Pot," in Whitaker, ed., *New Right Papers*, p. 98.

[22] Phillips, *Post-Conservative America*, p. 203.

[23] Viguerie, *New Right*, p. 46.

[24] Francis, "Message From MARs," p. 74.

[25] Phillips, *Post-Conservative America*, pp. 181 ff.

[26] Jerry Falwell, interview in *USA Today*, December 30, 1983, p. 9A.

[27] Francis, "Message From MARs," p. 80.

[28] Fleming, "Old Rights and New Right," p. 200.

[29] Hoy, "Lid on a Boiling Pot," p. 103.

[30] Phillips, *Post-Conservative America*, p. 204.

[31] Alan Crawford, *Thunder on the Right: The "New Right" and the Politics of Resentment* (New York: Pantheon, 1980), p. 331.

Epilogue

[1] Edward Bellamy, *Looking Backward*, (New York: American Library, 1982).

[2] Henry George, *Progress and Poverty*, (New York: Schalkenback, 1983).

[3] Herbert Croly, *The Promise of American Life* (New York: Macmillan, 1906).

[4] Jeremy Rifkin, with Ted Howard, *Entropy: A New World View*, (New York: Viking, 1980), p. 249.

[5] William Ophuls, *Ecology and the Politics of Scarcity* (San Francisco: Freeman, 1977), p. 223.

[6] Murray Bookchin, *The Ecology of Freedom: The Emergence and Dissolution of Hierarchy* (Palo Alto, Calif.: Cheshire Books, 1982), p. 11.

[7] Jonathan Schell, *The Fate of the Earth* (New York: Knopf, 1982), pp. 226–227.

[8] Rifkin, *Entropy*, pp. 250–251.

[9] Dennis Meadows *et al.*, eds., *The Limits to Growth* (New York: Dutton/Readers Digest Press, 1971).

[10] Bertram Gross, *Friendly Fascism: The New Face of Power in America* (New York: M. Evans, 1980).

[11] Ophuls, *Ecology and Politics of Scarcity*, p. 233.

[12] Paul Hawken, James Ogilvy, and Peter Schwartz, eds., *Seven Tomorrows: Toward a Voluntary History* (New York: Bantam, 1982), pp. 222, 225, 228.

Glossary

The glossary presents in classic form the major isms applicable to the American experience. Here we use the language of political theory whereas in the text we follow ordinary American usage. There are some important differences between the two, as we shall see. *Liberalism*, *capitalism*, and *democracy* come first. They had the greatest impact on our nation's history and still dominate our political thought. Challengers, both historical and prospective, follow.

Liberalism

Liberalism comes first because that is where the United States starts and, some would add, very nearly ends. Its basic components were described in Chapter 2 as the basic elements of the American political belief system. The defining characteristics of liberalism are individualism; natural rights, with particular emphasis on property rights; and the contract as the source of social order. But despite their strength and depth in the United States, this particular combination of principles did not just happen to come together on the North American continent. They arose out of the transformation of English feudal society into what would ultimately be recognized as capitalist society.

Under feudalism, the great landowning families effectively ruled. Most people were born into the status of serf or peasant on a lord's manor. They owed that lord fealty and service for their entire lives; the lord owed them protection and work. The king and the church "owned" vast tracts of land and claimed fealty and service from the lords and nobles. However, in realistic terms, a system of varying degrees of influence reigned. Parochial, predictable, and stable, most people understood this world to be one organic whole with a proper place and role for everyone.

Into this ordered (and agricultural) world, the Protestant Reformation introduced the notion of individual responsibility for salvation. At the same time some people began to trade and sell fabricated goods. But those people involved in trade, finance, and early manufacture had no traditional status. They were neither serfs nor lords, but a class between the two. The church frowned on, even regulated or restrained, their commercial activities. Their earnings were subject to confiscation by any king or lord's arbitrary action.

Their property was often even in danger from mobs of propertyless serfs and peasants. Thus, this rising commercial middle class needed both a personal justification and protection for the property it was earning through commerce. The Protestant notion of individual responsibility and rights rooted in natural law met these needs.

By the late seventeenth century, the new middle class found its fullest expression in the writings of John Locke. In his *Second Treatise on Government*, Locke set forth a complete version of a society and government organized by individuals voluntarily coming together for that purpose. Locke argued that individuals are originally in a state of nature. Each individual possesses freedom and certain natural rights as well as the reason necessary to know them. He also possesses any property with which he has mixed his labor. However, possession is insecure; some individuals use superior force to infringe on others' rights—and most particularly, the right to the fruits of their labor, their property. Therefore, reasonable individuals *contract* to create a social and governmental order, ceding to it some of their natural rights, powers, and freedom in return for its protection of all the others. The basis of such social order rests with the individuals who compose it. It derives all its authority from their transfer of powers to it. Finally, and as a safeguard, if the government fails in its fundamental protective duty, those same contracting individuals have the right to change it.

In seventeenth century England, all this was highly controversial. It stood in stark contrast to previous beliefs and practices. Instead of an organic social whole with everyone in a divinely ordained place, individuals were assumed to be paramount and became the source of the society's entire existence. Further, individuals were not only free to seek property through commerce, but were encouraged to do so. They could even rise in wealth, power, and prestige until they rivaled members of the aristocracy themselves. Possessed of the reason capable of deciding when their government had violated their natural rights, these individuals were potentially subversive of all established authority. They were willing to take on themselves the decision of when to replace one government with another. Locke's work was published just after the Glorious Revolution of 1688, in which the British Parliament had removed one line of kings and installed another. On the surface, Locke's work appeared to be a justification of that revolution.

In England, Locke's notions met stern resistance from a still dominant aristocracy. But on the American continent the state of nature was all too obvious. Locke's assumptions fit perfectly with a living reality. People did in fact contract with each other to create churches and governments. The new world was predominantly populated by entrepreneurs, merchants, and others of the new middle class—or people who aspired to the middle class through the new possibility of land ownership. Few aristocrats in the English sense chose to emigrate. Some came briefly to Virginia or Maryland or served as royal governors, but few stayed. Similarly, there were no serfs or peasants. Indentured servants came the closest, but their labor was contracted for only a limited number of years. They, too, aspired to the readily available land ownership that distinguished the developing society.

The special features of the United States' birth established liberalism as not so much the predominant belief system as the *only* belief system. In his famous *The Liberal Tradition in America*, historian Louis Hartz argues that liberal tenets are so pervasive that Americans have lost the sense of their distinctiveness. With no significant challenges from other classes, middle-class American liberalism reigned supreme. Liberalism was tempered elsewhere by a conservatism grounded in a former aristocracy and socialism emerging from the lower classes. Such challenges were simply missing from the American scene. By now, liberalism is self-evident and often unrecognized. Hartz's analysis helps to explain why the debates within the American political belief system have been over definitions and priorities associated with shared values and assumptions. We are all liberals, Hartz says, of marginally different kinds.

Capitalism

The United States is unique among nations of the world in the strength of capitalism as a popular belief system. The powerful appeal of capitalism rests on its congruence with the very same values that are fundamental to liberalism. Individualism, property, and contract already served as the foundation of a moral social and political order. Capitalism merely gave them a more specifically economic expression. Essentially capitalism means private ownership of the means of production. It normally includes a profit-seeking system with unlimited exchange of goods and services. The closely associated notions of the free market and laissez faire again connect with liberal faith in the free, economically oriented individual.

The economic system preceding capitalism was mercantilism. Under mercantilism, economic activity was meant to serve national interests as defined by the state. This had the effect of restricting the expansion and profitability of private enterprises. Leading governments, such as Great Britain, simply drained colonial wealth into the national treasury. Favored companies were granted monopoly trading rights. Royal or semipublic corporations were allowed to develop the high-profit opportunities. National governments strictly enforced taxes, restricted trade, and centrally managed the currency and credit — all to their own advantage. Many would-be entrepreneurs, particularly on the American continent, saw profitable opportunities denied them by these mercantilist policies.

Their resentment was well represented in the powerful arguments of the Scottish philosopher Adam Smith. In the *Wealth of Nations* (1776), Smith argued for the elimination of all government restrictions on private business. He claimed that the dynamism thus released would generate much greater wealth. An unrestricted market system would harmonize the demands of buyers with the supply produced by profit-seeking sellers. Thus, all members of the society would be satisfied. The nation as a whole would benefit because the country's resources would be fully employed with the greatest efficiency. Americans were eager to develop and profit from a richly endowed continent. Chafing under mercantile restrictions, they found Smith's argument utterly compelling.

With the liberal foundation firmly in place, the new U.S. Constitution assured an open national market. No obstacles remained to capitalist economic development. What the country seemed to need most was a multitude of willing risk takers. A large number of speculators and entrepreneurs were more than ready to help out. As both capital formation and industrial techniques became more sophisticated in the early nineteenth century, capitalism thrived. Science and technology seemed to be in harness with nature to generate progress and prosperity, at least for some and perhaps soon for all. Although the road might be hard at times, America was indeed the land of opportunity. Individuals who worked hard and took risks would prosper. Capitalism and liberalism were precisely the right combination of beliefs and practices, in the right place at the right time. As America flourished and grew more powerful, so did they.

Democracy

Our discussion in Chapter 2 of the ways that Americans have understood democracy has wide applicability beyond the United States. Originally a derogatory term, "democracy" now carries a broad and powerful appeal in all western countries. Equally common is the conflict between procedural and substantive versions. Its very universality makes the concept extremely difficult to pin down. To associate it with one author, as can be done with Lockean liberalism or Adam Smith's capitalism, is impossible. We must try to distill from general aspirations some essential values.

Literally, democracy means government by the people. The American version — "government of the people, by the people, and for the people" — is attributed to Abraham Lincoln. That succinct phrase does capture the variety of possibilities in the concept of democracy. "Of" the people implies that office holders, rulers, governors, etc., should come from the ranks of the population, the commoners. "For" the people means that governmental policies should benefit the majority, or as close as possible to the totality, of the nations' population. But the crucial preposition is *by* the people. The others are possible without participation by the citizens at large. But *by* suggests that people generally are capable of making and should participate in those decisions that affect their lives. Fundamental to democracy is the promise of some degree of *control* of the conditions of one's existence.

Left unanswered by the basic definition, of course, is the crucial question of just how "the people" are to govern. A very substantive aspiration becomes a procedural puzzle. In a large country with many citizens, the direct participation of all people in all public decisions appears impossible. How to limit the nature of participation and/or which questions shall be open to public control provokes immediate disagreement. Some argue that participation and decision-making powers must be very broad if democracy is to have any real meaning. Others, also self-proclaimed democrats, believe participation and decision making need to be limited in keeping with the dictates of "practicality." Furthermore, certain areas of life, such as personal liberties or economic activities, should be off limits to popular preferences. Obviously, there can be any number of variations on the democratic theme.

For our purposes, the crucial fact is that liberalism was firmly grounded and capitalism taking shape on the same foundation before democracy gained acceptance in the United States. Thus, the dominant understanding of democracy eventually would have to conform to liberal-capitalist values and practices. Remaining from the founding period was the distrust of democracy as mob rule. The belief that the greatest danger to democractic government was the "tyranny of the majority" persisted. By the time democracy became generally accepted, the notion of "majority rule, minority rights" was taken for granted. Constitutionally erected barriers to popular majorities and protection of minority rights (particularly property rights) went unquestioned. This is, of course, the beginning of *procedural* democracy. Many social and economic dimensions of life are placed beyond the reach of public action — until substantive democracy claims the right to enter the arena.

The greatest problem in the use of classic labels to understand the evolution of American ideas is grounded, fittingly enough, in the transformation of 1877–1920. The basic liberal-capitalist belief system essentially split in two under the pressure from the substantive democratic claims of the era. One part moved toward acceptance of the new role of government; the other held strongly to the classic version of liberalism (see the following discussion of "true conservatism"). The *new* liberalism agreed with the democrats that government had an obligation to soften the hardships from which people were suffering. And it held that the new large corporations should be limited in order to protect the well-being of all. Though adopting some of democracy's goals, this new belief system retained the liberalism label throughout the Progressive Era. Later versions are variously known as "corporate liberalism" or "welfare liberalism." The *old* liberalism became known as "conservatism," even though it stands for exactly what all liberals stood for before the period of transformation. And substantive democracy faded away into the new liberalism's definitions and procedures.

For the American political spectrum, of course, the result has been a vigorous debate between one form of liberalism and another. To Americans, it appears as if great issues are at stake. To some other observers, it looks like the proverbial tempest in a teapot. This suggests that the American political spectrum, as discussed in the text, is a specially narrow version of the range of possibility. Neither the character nor the evolution of American political thinking can be understood without recognizing how naturally Americans have come to cluster around the capitalist-liberal middle. Radical substantive democracy has been made to seem far more threatening than its genuine roots in a continuing tradition actually justify. Other possibilities, both right and left, must be fully understood in order to gain perspective on the American liberal myopia. If our spectrum widens in the present era of transformation, one or more of these challenges may powerfully affect our futures.

HISTORICAL AND PROSPECTIVE CHALLENGERS

Some of the classic isms to be defined and developed briefly in this section do not fit comfortably on a left-right political spectrum. And any American version would have specially American features appropriate to our times and circumstances. True, or organic, conservatives posed the greatest challenge to liberalism historically. They were, after all, replaced by it. In the United States, organic conservatives have often been misunderstood as either irrelevant or as adaptive liberalism, but their critique is worth exploring. After looking at organic conservatism, we turn to the more likely challengers — socialism, communism, Marxism, anarchism, corporatism, fascism, and totalitarianism.

Conservatism

Perhaps the greatest contrast between ordinary American usage and classic definitions lies in the understanding of conservatism. To Americans, "conservative" usually means a highly individualistic and strict laissez-faire doctrine. This is essentially a very pure version of a late nineteenth-century form of liberalism. Sometimes known as "Manchester liberalism," it was never confused elsewhere with conservatism.

The essense of classical conservatism was articulated in the eighteenth century by the British leader Edmund Burke. He held an organic image of society as an independent entity with a life and needs apart from the individuals who happen to make it up at any given time. Conservatives strive to achieve the preservation and improvement of the civilization represented by this society. They believe, in contrast to liberals, that most people are not in fact reasonable or able to decide what is best for themselves. And certainly ordinary people are not capable of deciding what is best for the society by means of some majority vote. Instead, conservatives believe in the necessity of government by the relatively few people who have the talent and wisdom to discharge such functions.

The conservative principle of government by the talented few means opposition not only to majority rule but also to any special role for business corporations or economic elites. Conservatives have a profound respect for property, but for different reasons than liberals. Property is needed to give people a sense of being rooted, of having a stake in the society's future. Moreover, property allows some people the necessary time to study the history of the society so as to make the correct decisions regarding its future. Profit is not the end of property ownership; wisdom and stability are. The mere achievement of wealth or corporate position does not entitle any one to claim the right to govern. Too often business people, capitalists, have a short-term attitude, an orientation toward current gratification and profits. They over-look the real long-term needs of the society. In particular, this common capi-talist attitude leads to an avoidance of the sacrifices necessary to benefit the society as a whole in the long run.

Conservatism is not at all a status quo doctrine. History never stops; societies must adapt in order to survive. But changes must be made consist-ent with the traditions and experience of the society. They must be changes for which the society is ready. Conservatives imagine a long line extending from the past through the present into the future, a kind of partnership of generations past, present, and yet unborn. Today's members are only tran-sitory, in a sense irrelevant. They will be replaced tomorrow, as a new com-bination will reflect all births and deaths. As temporary beneficiaries, individuals have an obligation to further their *society's* needs so that the quality of the civilization will steadily improve.

Nor is conservatism unwilling to make use of governmental powers for appropriate ends. Purposeful use of government to shape and direct the society is a major conservative tenet. Obviously there are many fundamental differences between "true" or organic conservatism and what Americans mean by "conservatism." Some early New England Puritans and even a few of the framers of the Constitution had significant conservative principles. And it was the vestiges of American organic conservatism that spoke out against the appalling working conditions, squalid tenements, and general destructiveness of early industrialism. But later experience was so exclusively liberal and capitalist that conservative ideas began to disappear. When or-ganic conservatives look back to see what long-lived traditions should be conserved, all they find are liberal-capitalist practices.

Though organic conservatives can mount a critique of liberal capi-talism, they have been and are few in number in the United States. With the exception of literary versions of "a plague on all your houses," organic con-servatives are probably irrelevant to the present era of transformation. More likely possibilities arise from the remaining isms to be discussed.

Socialism, communism, and *Marxism* share a similar foundation while differing in some important facets. We first consider the commonalities and then discuss each separately, describing some of their differences. There are two commonalities in particular. First, all three focus on the "mode of produc-tion." The way in which a social order produces its material means of survival is a crucial factor influencing the social and political and cultural worlds. Spheres of activity are not, cannot be, separated. Like a prism, these spheres are reflections of each other around a fundamental core, the economic system. Therefore, prescriptions and political activity of these isms focus on a change in the ownership of at least the major means of productive activity.

Second, all three are based on a notion of a *social* world. This is not society as the unit of analysis, with needs and demands of its own, above and beyond the individuals that compose it at any one time. Similarly it is not the self-serving, isolated individual as the primary unit. The individual is assumed to be a social animal whose full development as a human being requires positive interaction with other human beings. For each of these three isms, an individual does not and cannot exist alone, in isolation. A human being only fully develops in concert with others. This does not mean, however, that the community or social world takes precedence over the individual. It means that the community and the individual should fit together. When it comes to the specific mix of community/individual and the relationship of that community/individual mix to the social/economic/political order, differences emerge among the three isms.

Socialism

Socialism derives its name from an underlying assumption that human beings are social beings. Full personal development can only take place within a healthy community. A primary prerequisite is material security and well-being for each member of the social order. In American terms, substantive equality in the economic conditions of life precedes the possibility of individual freedom and development. This does not mean that everyone is the same, or even that everyone is entitled to the same. But it does mean that everyone is entitled to the basic means of survival and to a healthy life situation. The material well-being of each citizen is not only a proper object of government concern but should be actively promoted.

In order to accomplish widespread material security and to remove economic coercion of individuals, at least the major units of the economy should be publicly owned. Private ownership of the means of production, for the purpose of private profit, can only lead to an unhealthy environment, useless production, and degradation of working people. Socialism would leave small units of production in private hands. Private property, especially in the sense of personal possessions, is accepted. However, large and overwhelming economic concentrations are not permissible. Social ownership of the major means of production, for the public good and social welfare, is a fundamental tenent of socialism.

Communism

Pre-Marxist and pre-Soviet-bloc communism has roots reaching at least as far back as early Christian communities. Many groups of people throughout the centuries have lived "communally." In that time, classic communism has changed very little. Though each community or utopian experiment devised its own adaptations, certain fundamentals remained.

Communism implies the common ownership of property or material goods. Substantive equality is much more widespread; material goods are equally distributed. The slogan "from each according to ability, to each according to need" summarizes communist aspirations. In this view, private property is the source of all exploitation and conflict between human beings and the state itself functions to maintain this coercive situation. Should private ownership and profit seeking be abolished, all other unnatural distinctions among human beings would disappear. Peace on earth would prevail.

Marxism

Socialism and communism preceded Karl Marx as political visions. However, Marx authored the systematic analysis and prescription that forever afterward underlay in some way most versions of socialism and communism. He devoted his life to development of the philosophical base and analytical method appropriate to these isms. Americans tend to lump them all together: anything anticapitalist is Marxist. In one sense, this is true; in another, it is completely false.

Marx begins with a notion of "species being," of human beings as social, productive, creative beings. For humans to reach their full development as a species, they need a healthy social world in which their productive and creative capacities can be freely used. What makes human beings distinctive is their ability to creatively produce. Capitalism deprives human beings of this capacity. When humans sell their labor, they turn their productive activity into a commodity. This alienates them from one of the most basic facets of their personalities. Equally important, liberal individualism alienates humans from each other. Therefore, individualistic capitalism prevents human beings from reaching their true nature as species beings.

Second, private ownership of the means of production for private profit, besides alienating workers from their true being, creates a class society. Class is a crucial analytic unit in Marxist thought. Some own the means of production — the bourgeois. Some do not — the proletariat. History is the story of the change in the underlying mode of production and thus in class relationships. Capitalism will be overthrown by the proletariat, the working (nonowning) class, once it becomes conscious of itself as a class, a class-for-itself. Following the proletariat revolution, the proletariat will run the state for the benefit of the working class. Once all have reached the same class level, or communism, the state will wither away.

More important than Marx's conclusions, perhaps, is the method he developed to arrive at them. "Scientific materialism" analyzes a social order through study of the means and relationships of production. Furthermore, "dialectics" enables one to see the world in motion. It assumes "contradictions" inherent in all things or processes, contradictions that will be overcome and transcended. Scientific materialism encompasses the empirical, tangible processes of the world. Dialectics encourages exploration of the multiple potentialities in that world, the many possible futures, even while recognizing the dominant tendencies.

Marxism is not really an ism in the same way the term has previously been used. Colloquially, "Marxism" is used to cover any ism that is anticapitalist, antiindividualist, proworking class, or revolutionary, or proclaims itself to be Marxist, or is claimed to be so by the United States. When used in this way, it has lost all meaning. But when specifically connected to one author, Marxism is a respected philosophical system. As a rigorous analysis and alternative vision to liberal capitalism, it is unmatched.

Thus socialism and communism could be said to be variants of Marxism, whether they give Marx credit or not. Or Marxism could be said to be the philosophical base of most versions of socialism and communism, in spite of their vast variety. And sometimes they are only very distantly related. However, anarchism stands alone.

Anarchism

Anarchism focuses on domination, whether it be by capitalists, the state, bureaucrats, or socialists, communists, or Marxists. People are assumed to be naturally good, cooperative, even harmonious. The imposition of social institutions destroys this natural order and creates the very problems supposedly solved. Domination of any sort, not only in productive terms, alienates individuals from their free, unfettered creative self.

Anarchism can be either individualist or community based, depending on the specific emphasis given to the characteristics of human nature. Both versions believe all institutional barriers to individual development need to be removed. But they differ on whether or not individuals will then spontaneously be communal or individualistic. In any event, spontaneous creativity is the answer to institutional domination.

This is one of the European isms with a peculiar force and history in the United States. In the early 1900s, a unique blend of communal solidarity and rugged individualism developed and found expression in the anarcho-syndicalism of the International Workers of the World. This was especially true among the frontier workers in the mines and logging camps of the Far West. More generally, the individualist version of anarchism naturally appeals to a country in which individualism is taken for granted. Liberal individualism, pushed to its limit, can lead to a version of anarchy where the only free individual is the totally undominated one. And the totally free individual always lurks beneath the surface as the American ideal.

Socialism, communism, Marxism, and anarchism view the world from the bottom up, so to speak. They begin with the working class or the oppressed and alienated individual. Capitalism — and the bureaucratic and social institutions necessary to sustain it — is the enemy. *Corporatism, fascism,* and *totalitarianism* come at it the other way around, from the top down. Among these three isms, too, there are some basic commonalities, with variance in degree. Each of these three isms is based on the notion of a partnership among the major social, economic, and political units of the system. Large economic units and a centralized and powerful state apparatus are accepted, even encouraged. The majority of the population maintains private activity. If not working directly for the major economic units, they are almost irrelevant, as long as they do not threaten the large and powerful economic base in any way. In general, the state's purpose is to maintain the profitability and growth of the economic sector, regardless of the social cost. Differences between corporatism, fascism, and totalitarianism arise out of the terms of the partnership and the degree of rigor imposed on the underlying population.

Corporatism

Corporatism appears to be a "true" partnership between big government and big business. Other major corporate bodies, such as labor or even consumers' organizations, are encouraged. Bigness is a fact of life that must be accepted. Each individual should be a member of some corporate body. Corporatism is almost feudal in that identity and power are connected with a larger corporate unit. Bigness is assumed to be efficient, as is private ownership and private profit. Threfore, bigness is accepted, even applauded and encouraged in the belief that eventually everyone will benefit with a generally stable and affluent system.

Fascism

Fascism carries a more negative connotation. Though usually assumed by Americans to apply solely to Nazi Germany and Mussolini's Italy, and the horrors associated with them, its application is in fact more general. Though sometimes equated with demagogic democracy, that is not the core of classic fascism. Again, the base is the partnership between the major economic units of the system and a centralized state apparatus whose business is to protect and maintain those units. Other major units, however, such as labor or the church, are discouraged. The state takes on the job of managing the population, usually in troubled economic times, in order to maintain the private profit structure. Managing the population includes rousing patriotic and nationalistic appeals, calls to sacrifice for the good of the nation. It implies an adept use of symbols in order to manipulate a gullible, sheeplike citizenry. Though the population may be engaged in the beginning, skillful manipulation of crises, economic and political, gradually leads to almost religious patriotic fervor. Suppression of any dissent becomes increasingly oppressive, though still within procedural, legal limits. Eventually, all necessary roads are taken to maintain the governing partnership.

Totalitarianism

This is, as its name implies, total state control. It can be of either the "right" or "left." In other words, the major economic units may remain in private hands, although they will be closely tied to members of the state. Or the state and the economy may be one and the same. The defining characteristic of totalitarianism is the total lack of private space for the individual. The state has complete control of all facets of people's lives — religious, educational, social, cultural, familial, not to mention economic livelihood. It is obviously a heavy police state. In order to manage an entire population, the state must also be skilled in terror. There is a strong and large secret police with very little pretence to any legal procedural forms. Only fear prevails: the bottom fears the top while the top fears the bottom.

Index

About the Authors

Linda Medcalf holds a B.A. in political science from Western Washington University and a Ph.D. in political science from the University of Washington. She has taught at the University of Massachusetts (Amherst) and Olympia (Washington) Technical Community College. She is the author of *Law and Identity: Native Americans, Lawyers, and the Legal Process* and several book chapters and professional papers. Her fields are American politics and public law.

Kenneth M. Dolbeare holds a B.A. in English from Haverford College, and L.L.B. from Brooklyn Law School, and a Ph.D. in political science from Columbia University. He has taught at Hofstra University, the Universities of Wisconsin (Madison), Washington (Seattle), and Massachusetts (Amherst), and now is director of the graduate program in public administration at the Evergreen State College. He is the author of *American Ideologies: The Competing Political Beliefs of the 1970s*, and *Democracy At Risk: The Politics of Economic Renewal*. His fields are American political economy, public policy, and political thought.